The Gospel of God

The Gospel of God

Romans as Paul's *Aeneid*

David R. Wallace

☞PICKWICK *Publications* • Eugene, Oregon

THE GOSPEL OF GOD
Romans as Paul's Aeneid

Copyright © 2008 David R. Wallace. All rights reserved. Except for brief quotations in critical publications or reviews, no part of this book may be reproduced in any manner without prior written permission from the publisher. Write: Permissions, Wipf & Stock, 199 W. 8th Ave., Suite 3, Eugene, OR 97401.

Pickwick Publications
A Division of Wipf and Stock Publishers
199 W. 8th Ave., Suite 3
Eugene, OR 97401

www.wipfandstock.com

ISBN 13: 978-1-55635-437-3

Cataloging-in-Publication data:

Wallace, David R.
The gospel of God : Romans as Paul's Aeneid / David R. Wallace.

xx + 224 p.; 23 cm. Includes bibliographical references.

ISBN 13: 978-1-55635-437-3

1. Paul, the Apostle, Saint. 2. Bible. N. T. Romans—Criticism, interpretation, etc. 3. Virgil. Aeneis—Criticism, textual. I. Title.

BS2665.52 W35 2008

Manufactured in the U.S.A.

To my Father and Mother,
Norman and Betty Rae Wallace,
who continually demonstrate
ὑπακοὴν πίστεως

Contents

Abbreviations viii
Preface xi
Introduction xiii

PART 1 • The Gospel of Augustus in the *Aeneid*

   1 The Gospel of Caesar Augustus   3

   2 The *Aeneid* as Epic History   38

   3 The Salvific Message of the *Aeneid*   71

PART 2 • The Gospel of God in Romans

   4 Paul's Gospel of Salvation to Rome   121

   5 God's Faithfulness to Save His People   164

Conclusion   193
Bibliography   199

Abbreviations

Ancient Works

Aen.	*Aeneid*
App. *Civ.*	Appian, *Civil War*
Clem.	*On Clemency*
De. Or.	*De Oratore*
Dio *Rom. Hist.*	Cassius Dio, *Roman History*
Diss.	*Dissertationes*
Hist. Rom.	*History of Rome*
Il.	*Iliad*
Jos. *Ant.*	Josephus, *Antiquities*
LXX	Septuagint
Metaph.	*Metaphysics*
MT	Masoretic Text
Nic. *Aug.*	Nicolaus of Damascus, *Life of Augustus*
Nic. *Eth.*	*Nicomachean Ethics*
Od.	*Odyssey*
Phil.	*Philippics*
Plut. *Caes.*	Plutarch, *Caesar*
Plut. *Ant.*	Plutarch, *Antony*
Poet.	*Poetics*
Pol.	*Politics*
RG	*Res Gestae*
Rhet.	*Rhetoric*
Servius *ad.*	Servius, 4th Century *Aeneid* Commentary
Suet. *Aug.*	Suetonius, *Life of Augustus*
Suet. *Vita Verg.*	Suetonius, *De Vita Vergili*
Tac. *Ann.*	Tacitus, *Annals*
Tac. *Hist.*	Tacitus, *Histories*
Tac. *Dial.*	Tacitus, *Dialogues*

Modern Works

AB	Anchor Bible
AJP	American Journal of Philology
ANRW	Aufstieg und Niedergang der römischen Welt
BDAG	Greek-English Lexicon of the New Testament and Other Early Christian Literature, 3rd ed.
CJ	Classical Journal
CP	Classical Philology
CQ	Classical Quarterly
HSCP	Harvard Studies in Classical Philology
Int	Interpretation
JRS	Journal of Roman Studies
JSNT	Journal for the Study of the New Testament
JSNTSup	Journal for the Study of the New Testament Supplements
JSOT	Journal for the Study of the Old Testament
LCL	Loeb Classical Library
NovT	Novum Testamentum
NovTSup	Novum Testamentum Supplements
NTS	New Testament Studies
SBLDS	Society of Biblical Literature Dissertation Series
TAPA	Transactions and Proceedings of the American Philological Association
TynBul	Tyndale Bulletin
WUNT	Wissenschaftliche Untersuchungen zum Neuen Testament

Preface

I HAVE APPROACHED WITH REVERENCE THE TASK OF COMPARING IMAGery in the *Aeneid* and Romans, and at the same time, have felt a sense of honor to be given the opportunity to interact with the ideas of the finest of scholars in both the Classical and New Testament fields of study. I trust that the result of this work will stimulate critical discussion, but I also hope in some way that it will encourage scholars from these related disciplines to work more closely together.

I wish first to thank my mentors—Professors Bruce Corley, Siegfried Schatzmann, and the late Paul Hunsinger—for their investment in my life and support of my work. It was Bruce Corley years ago who, after I had quoted the *Aeneid* in a discussion, planted the seed for this volume. I am also grateful for his encouragement along the way. I wish that everyone could have a friend such as the distinguished Siegfried Schatzmann whose editorial insight and proofing have proved invaluable. I should not forget Paul Hunsinger, who engendered in me a love for the Humanities early in my academic work and who instilled in me a respect for the creative power of story and poetry. It would be appropriate to show gratitude to many other persons who were generous with their time but will remain unnamed in order to keep this preface brief. Most significantly, I want to express appreciation to my wife, Hillary, for her patience in listening to my ideas and comparisons and for her willingness to allow countless hours of research and writing.

David R. Wallace
May 6, 2008

Introduction

DESPITE THE TREMENDOUS AMOUNT OF SECULAR STUDY ON THE literary style, symbolism, and influence of the *Aeneid* and an even greater amount of New Testament research on Paul's letter to the Romans, no significant attempt has been made to investigate Paul's political and religious response concerning the salvation of Israel as it might counter the symbolism and message of the *Aeneid* and its salvific promise for Rome. Virgil's Roman epic and Paul's letter to the Roman church were both written for the purpose of sending a universal message to a people of divine election with a promised, victorious future accomplished through the prophetic fulfillment of a divine son. This work employs socio-historical methods to discern Paul's discourse concerning Israel's salvation in Romans in response to an imperial gospel.[1]

Challenge

New Testament scholarship has not adequately attempted to integrate the history of the Roman Empire with New Testament interpretation, even though New Testament scholars have called for this socio-historical

---

1. J. R. Harrison proposes a similar perspective concerning "two cultural fronts" (distinctively Jewish and distinctively Greco-Roman) in Rom 5:12–21 and 8:18–39; "Paul, Eschatology, and the Augustan Age," 79–91. Harrison contends that the echoes of Augustan benefaction propaganda in Romans represents a rhetorical strategy of Paul rather than "an unconscious appropriation of familiar texts" and sees Virgil's eschatological emphasis of Augustus as persuasive; ibid., 79, 87. Harrison also makes a strong case for Paul's use of Roman political terms in 1 Thess 4:13—5:11; Paul transforms Roman ideological content to his "theological and social advantage" and overturns imperial eschatological beliefs; "Paul and the Imperial Gospel," 71–96. Also see Stowers, *Rereading of Romans*, 42–82.

effort.² In the age of Augustus, unlike modern times, politics, power and economy were inseparable from religion.³ Viewed as a system of communication, religion is a subset of multiple systems that make up the culture and subcultures of a society.⁴ It makes sense then that in order to discern the meaning of a New Testament text, interpreters should take great care to analyze the communication process by researching the frame of reference of the initial readers—their environment, traditions, and thought—to determine the possible constructs that the author drew upon when writing Scripture. Especially true for the occasional letters of Paul, understanding the recipients' context contributes directly to the interpretation of Paul's meaning. Yet literary, theological, and historical descriptions have not given a clear sense of what it was like to be an ordinary Christian in a believing community in Paul's day.⁵

Scholars have, at best, made only an attempt to formulate appropriate questions and research strategies in response to the challenge of learning the Roman imperial context of Paul's mission and his relations to it.⁶ In a recent anthology of essays by social historians on the Roman empire and Pauline Christianity, Richard Horsley arranges reprinted articles in a sequence that leads the reader to the conclusion that the apostle Paul counters the "gospel of Caesar" in a time when a Roman imperial savior had established peace throughout the empire.⁷ In one such example, Dieter Georgi discusses Paul's central terms in Romans—εὐαγγέλιον, πίστις, δικαιοσύνη, and εἰρήνη—arguing that Paul evokes the reader's associations to Roman political theology and that "every page of the letter to the Romans contains indications that

---

2. Meeks, *First Urban Christians*, 2. Meeks cites F. F. Bruce, "New Testament," 229–42, and Malherbe, *Social Aspects*, 1–4.

3. "Surely it is in that life [of the Roman family] that the famous word '*pius*' must have originated, which throughout Roman history meant the sense of duty towards family, State, and gods, as every reader of the *Aeneid* knows . . . the whole life of the Roman seems to me so inextricably bound up with his religion," Fowler, *Religious Experience*, 63.

4. Meeks, *First Urban Christians*, 6.

5. The answer to this question receives only "vague and stammering" replies; ibid., 2.

6. Horsley, "Introduction," 3.

7. Ibid.

Paul has very concrete and critical objections to the dominant political theology of the Roman Empire under the principate."[8]

In Rome, Octavian Augustus was the driving force for the ambition of the Roman rule that displayed its ideology and propaganda in the middle of the first-century A.D. in all kinds of ways—architecture, art, celebrations, religious festivals, rituals, etc.[9] Every visual communication, every theme, and every slogan reflected the new order,[10] an imperial gospel. It is not surprising that the literature of Rome promulgated an eschatological promise of the Golden Age of Augustus—revealing a close but not authoritarian relationship between poetry and empire.[11] Considered to be theologian/prophets, great Roman poets such as Horace and Virgil significantly contributed to the Augustan cultural renaissance.[12] To prove this point, Georgi singles out an official text composed by Horace, *Carmen saeculare* (relatively contemporary with the New Testament), which was commissioned for the official celebration of the secular games, an official jubilee proclaiming the miracle of the salvation of the republic.[13] Prophetically, the poet employs eschatological language and upholds the ideal of the return of the Golden Age and promises a savior in line with the heroes of old. The glorification of the *Princeps* is the "immediate fulfillment of heavenly order and as the execution of divine inspiration."[14]

The most well-known prophetic source in first-century Rome, which strengthened Roman ideology and assured Roman salvation, was Virgil's *Aeneid*.[15] Practically speaking, the influence of the great

---

8. Georgi, "God," 148. Georgi makes the point that the noun εὐαγγέλιον does not have a parallel in the Septuagint in the manner in which Paul uses it—meaning the act and the content of proclamation.

9. Tellbe, *Paul*, 144–47.

10. Zanker, *Power of Images*, 101.

11. Horsley, "Introduction," 13.

12. Georgi, "Who Is the True Prophet?" 36–46. Georgi describes the poet as belonging to the "sphere of the miraculous," one who has "turned into a heavenly bird," "an immortal," "an educator," one "effective in prayer," and one whose word is "powerful among the gods," ibid., 39.

13. Ibid., 41.

14. Ibid., 39.

15. Gavin Townend believes that the influence of the great Roman poets beyond Rome is questionable; Townend, "Literature and Society," 929. He asserts that shortly after the *Aeneid* appeared, the claim can be made that Virgil produced the bible of

writers outside of the educated elite was probably small, but this was not the case for the *Aeneid*—the opening words of the first two books of the *Aeneid* have been found written on some of the walls in Pompeii; and from places as remote as Masada and Vindolanda, a variety of odd lines from different parts of the same poem have been discovered which were probably used for writing exercises.[16] It is likely that the *Aeneid* served as a basic reading text for Roman education in the classical period, much like Homer's works did for the Greek classroom.[17] Even though literature remained the property of the upper class, public readings were a common form of entertainment, especially the *recitatio* of poetry or prose.[18] According to the Letter of Augustus, Tacitus writes that Virgil's poetry was popular among Roman citizens to the point that upon hearing a Virgilian line in the theater performance, they all stood in unison to show their adoration to Virgil, who was present, as if he were Augustus.[19] But to suggest that the believing community in Rome knew of the general theme and plot of the *Aeneid* would require a more direct connection between Virgil and Augustus, that their messages accorded the promise of a divine savior who brings about an eschatological fulfillment of peace for all Rome.

Rome, but most likely, the occasions of hearing the poem read could not have been frequent, which means his influence on Roman life might not have been widespread. On the other hand, Marianne Bonz argues that the theme of Roman dominion in literature during Augustus's reign was widespread, and "in no other work is it expressed with such artistic power, clarity, and religious overtones as it is in the *Aeneid*"; Bonz, *Past as Legacy*, 57. Furthermore, Bonz cites a letter from Seneca to the imperial slave Polybius (Seneca *Consolatio ad Polybium* 11.5) in which is noted the importance of Polybius's translation of Virgil's poetry into Greek and Homer's works into Latin; thus, Bonz reasons that the *Aeneid* was probably published in Greek in the mid-first century and read and admired throughout the major cities in Greece "at least by the time of Paul," ibid., 55. This study does not assume that Paul read the *Aeneid*, but it presupposes that Paul in his travels listened to the basic plot and episodes from those who retold Virgil's epic story, such as Roman citizens, soldiers, or philosophers.

16. Townend, "Literature and Society," 928.

17. The Greeks in the East rarely knew Latin. A comparison of Greek vocabularies or translations of the *Aeneid* found in Egypt from the end of the fourth century points to its use in the classroom; Moore, "Latin Exercises," 475–85.

18. Townend, "Literature and Society," 926.

19. Tac. *Dial.* 13.2.

Maecenas, minister to Augustus and Virgil's patron, encouraged a close circle of poets to write laudatory praise to Caesar.[20] In 29 B.C., Virgil began writing the *Aeneid* with a complicated theme that employed common Latin and Greek personages based on both of Homer's works (the *Iliad* and the *Odyssey*) for the purpose of giving an account of the origin of Rome and Augustus.[21] The reputation of the *Aeneid* became so great during the early phases of Virgil's writing that Augustus entreated him to send a rough draft or any section.[22] In its final years of composition,[23] Virgil planned to travel to Greece and Asia to complete his work, but met with Augustus in Athens only to decide to return with the emperor. During that time, Virgil became deathly ill, and before he died (19 B.C.) requested that the *Aeneid* not be published since it needed final touches. Augustus soon had the *Aeneid* published posthumously, after selecting experienced poets to make very slight corrections. In a short time, Virgil's heroic epic and its themes—divine election, providence, Rome's salvation through a promised son, and a new order and identity for the Roman people—promoted the aim of the *Princeps*.

Social historians, such as Richard Horsley and Dieter Georgi, reiterate that a close relationship existed between Augustan propaganda and Virgil's final work, the *Aeneid*, yet no significant attempt has been made to investigate the relationship of the religious and political message of the *Aeneid* and Paul's possible religious and political response to it. The recipients of the letter to Rome were familiar with Augustan propaganda and were probably familiar with Virgil's religious and patriotic

---

20. Dihle describes Virgil's relationship to Augustus as "involved" and "distant"—distant from the bloodshed and depressing events during the political revolution and involved because "his poetry gave a dimension of historical and moral profundity to the Emperor's declared aim of a renewal of Rome, and to his reign over the civilized world"; Dihle, *Greek and Latin Literature*, 31.

21. Suet. *Vita Verg.* 21. Virgil used Homeric narrative techniques which allowed Augustan Rome to be viewed from a distance; hence, the *Aeneid* is full of prophetic messages; Conte, *Latin Literature*, 278. Deryck Williams distinguishes two voices of Virgil: the public, patriotic voice which is intended primarily to celebrate the public aspect of optimism, power, and organized government, while Virgil's private voice becomes preoccupied with the suffering of those who fall by the way; Williams, "The *Aeneid*," 368. Virgil and the Augustan poets expressed values that contrasted "a dreary past and recent glorious future begun"; Dihle, *Greek and Latin Literature*, 47.

22. Suet. *Vita Verg.* 32.

23. Virgil worked on the *Aeneid* for eleven years.

message.²⁴ In addition, since Paul composes his distinctive letter with a formal literary style, and since he maintains his practice of selecting written symbols within his listeners' frame of reference, it seems reasonable to investigate whether Paul counters Virgil's eschatological message with the true gospel for "Israel."

Methodology

I am concerned here with two genres of literature—letter and epic—and apply a socio-historical approach to understand Paul's use of imagery and theme concerning Israel's salvation as it contests the ideology and symbolism of the *Aeneid*. Aristotle established guidelines for writing epic poetry that were still used in the first century,²⁵ to which Callimachus made some improvements.²⁶ The imagery, symbolism, and message of the *Aeneid*, particularly books 5–8,²⁷ establishes the focus from which Paul's gospel in Romans will be analyzed. Paul's arguments concerning God's election and plan for Israel share similar themes with the *Aeneid*—divine election, a divine son, the fathers, divine providence, prophetic fulfillment, and salvation.²⁸ Relevant form, style, and content in Romans will be addressed when the information contributes to a better understanding of parallel themes.²⁹

---

24. Bonz suggests that the historical situation of the composition of Luke-Acts is analogous to the *Aeneid* in key aspects—divine mission, divine son, prophecy, epic reversal, and some structural similarities; *Past as Legacy*, vii, 129–93. Furthermore, Paul's address to "Greeks and Barbarians, the wise and the ignorant" (Rom 1:14) should be understood in the bilingual context of Rome; "Greek" meant "Greco-Roman" and "Barbarian" refers to alien tribes who do not speak Greek or Latin; Jewett, "Response," 62–63.

25. Aristotle *Poetics* 24–26.

26. Callimachus *Aetia* 1.1–30.

27. Book 6 is a turning point for Aeneas. After visiting the underworld, he has renewed hope for Italy and its future. The story changes from its symbolical message to a more prophetic-historical perspective; his father shows him the future, a parade of great Romans. A new identity is promised through a divine son. In Book 8, Aeneas chooses a more difficult route, and victories for Augustus and Rome are foretold.

28. Other themes and imagery to be considered in Romans will include race (2:28 and 9:3–4), sacrificial imagery (3:21–26, 12:1–8, and 15:19), victory (8:36–37), reversals (9:11, 25), universal significance (9:18, 16:9–12, and 15:28), olive tree metaphor (11:17–24), stone (9:29), and descent into the abyss (10:7).

29. I accept the challenge of working with two distinct literary genres which have their own recurring characteristics and discourse coherence. The terms "imagery" and

Concerning a socio-historical model, Wayne Meek's eclectic approach serves a practical purpose for this study.[30] Society is viewed as a complex process, and no one particular theory of social history is used. In other words, religion plays many roles within a culture, and because of its integral and complex relationship between social structure and symbolism, it is "not necessary nor wise to decide in advance just what role religion plays."[31]

Organization

Part I (chapters 1–3) of this study analyzes the gospel of Augustus in the *Aeneid*. Chapter 1 explains the gospel of Augustus Caesar as propagandized through religious and political symbols of the first century. Based on the accounts of ancient historians and the interpretations of modern historians, the lucid elements of Augustus's persuasive campaign are canvassed. Thus, images in art, on coins, and in ritual that parallel the *Aeneid* prove important in understanding Paul's choice of imagery in Romans to countervail popular Roman ideals. The relationship between poetic literature and Augustus, particularly with Virgil, is also elaborated in order to help discern the degree to which the emperor may have influenced the most sacred, patriotic literary work in Rome.

Chapters 2 and 3 examine the *Aeneid*. Chapter 2 discusses the *Aeneid* as history and prophecy. Aristotle gives literary guidance with a set of rules for epic poetry, which Virgil generally follows. Virgil borrows extensively from Homer's *Iliad* and *Odyssey*, which simplifies and complicates the meaning of the *Aeneid*; therefore, Virgil's artistic choices are reviewed. The nature of prophecy in Virgil's Roman epic is also explained because of its significant contrast to prophecy in Paul's letter. Chapter 3 analyzes the salvific message of the *Aeneid*, with particular

---

"themes" have purposely been chosen for this study so as to allow for the discussion of a variety of literary devices (e.g., topology, allegory, analogy, metaphor, etc.) without meandering into a structuralist quandary. Whether discerning Paul's use of typology in Romans or deciphering imitated allegory in the *Aeneid*, a comparison of diachronic texts involves two levels of meaning, in which the complexity intensifies with intertextual possibilities and outside historical information. James Voelz provides a clear discussion and definition of terms for this complicated process; Voelz, "Multiple Signs," 149–64.

30. Meeks, *First Urban Christians*, 5–6.
31. Ibid.

emphasis on Books 5–8. An overall view of the structure and style of the *Aeneid* is given, followed by an examination of relevant imagery and themes.

Part II (chapters 4–5) reviews relevant research concerning key imagery and themes in the gospel of Romans that will be compared with the key imagery and imperial message in the *Aeneid*. Attention is given to each major section of Romans. Chapter 4 evaluates Paul's message of salvation in Romans 1–8, and chapter 5 discusses God's faithfulness to save his people in Romans 9–11 and the devotion required of his recipients in Romans 12–16. The conclusion summarizes the findings of this study and makes clear the relevance of these findings to New Testament study.

PART 1

✶

The Gospel of Augustus in the *Aeneid*

The Gospel of Caesar Augustus

This man, this is the one whom you hear so often promised to you,
Caesar Augustus, the descendant of God, who again will establish a
Golden Age in Latium, in lands formerly governed by Saturn,
Who will extend his empire beyond the Garymantian and
Indian peoples Whose land lies beyond the stars . . .

Oh Rome, remember to rule the nations by your authority;
These will be the arts for you: to establish the order of peace,
To spare the humble and war against the proud![1]

IN 49 B.C., AFTER THREE BLOODY YEARS OF CIVIL WAR, JULIUS CAESAR established himself as the first Caesar to rule alone. Masking his motives behind false diplomacy, Caesar said that "he was prepared to go to any length and endure any suffering for the cause of the republic . . . let everyone in Italy lay down their arms, let all fears be removed from the city, let *there be* free elections, and the whole republic be handed over to the Senate and the Roman people."[2] Four years later, a group

---

1. *Aen.* 6.791–95, 851–54. All translations are my own unless otherwise stated.
2. *Civil War* 1.9.5.

of assassins murdered Caesar as members of the Senate watched with jealous cooperation.

Caesar's adopted son Octavian was pronounced his heir.[3] Octavian's military victories over the next two decades demonstrated his ability to lead, but it was his victory at Actium in 27 B.C. which established him as the sole ruler of the Roman empire ushering in more than a century of peace. As an administrator and diplomat, Octavian Augustus restored and reorganized Roman rule in an unprecedented manner. He appointed governors under his authority who enforced Roman law to unify provincial communities. Cities had running water, open-air theaters, public baths, and central heating systems (for the wealthy),[4] and Roman roads brought Greek and Roman culture to the far ends of the empire. As Augustus methodically eliminated elements that hindered the organizational stability of the state, he also restored a new order of traditional Roman virtue—*fides, pietas, religio, disciplina, constantia, gravitas*—by directly and indirectly influencing the official messages of the empire in literature, art, architecture, coins, inscriptions, etc. Such imperial endorsement is prominently found in Virgil's epic, the *Aeneid*, which promotes the imitation of Roman virtue and pronounces a prophetic gospel of salvation inaugurated through a divine son.

It was this foundation of government and Augustus's political coordination which brought lasting peace, as the Caesars following the reign of Augustus maintained the legal, administrative, and communication processes initiated by him. Before an imperial gospel can be understood—for the purpose of interpreting the meaning of the *Aeneid* (chapters 2–3) and its possible contextual significance to the recipients of Paul's letter to the Romans (chapters 4–5)—it is important first to examine Augustus's background, character, and patterns of control, and then compare this information to the official imagery of the empire and his relationship to Latin poets, particularly Virgil.[5]

---

3. According to the will of Julius Caesar in 44 B.C., Octavian became Gaius Julius Caesar Octavian. In 27 B.C., he was honored by the Senate with the surname Augustus.

4. All of these advancements and architectural improvements do not necessarily mean that the common man enjoyed them; however, the remains from the empire suggest this image; see Branigan, "Images," 103–4.

5. In this rare age, poets were "intimately and affectionately" connected to those holding political power; see Woodman and West, *Poetry and Politics*, 195. This is not to suggest that there was a coordinated, written gospel; rather, the restrictions implemented through indirect means of Augustan patronage and the resulting imitation

Background of Caesar Augustus

Raised by his grandmother (sister to Julius Caesar) and protected by his mother, Octavian dutifully observed Roman tradition and learned the practice of associating with the right people. Despite his boyish appearance, frequent illnesses, and limited military experience, he gained favor with Caesar who commended him for his persistence, precision, and discernment.

Gaius Octavian

Before sunrise on a September morning in 63 B.C., a son who would soon be heralded as the "savior of the world" was born.[6] At the age of four, Octavian lost his father, a man who had achieved senatorial rank.[7] Octavian's grandmother took care of him until she died; Octavian was twelve. At her funeral, he delivered an oration that brought him recognition and appreciation from those present. His mother Atia, the niece of Julius Caesar, raised her son until he was nineteen with the help of his stepfather, a descendent of Macedonian royalty.

His mother protected him. Atia and Octavian's stepfather involved themselves in making sure Octavian spent his time learning, achieving, and interacting with people in power. When civil war broke out in Italy, they safeguarded him by sending him to one of his father's country estates. At age fourteen, Octavian fulfilled the sacrificial rites to become

---

affected Greco-Roman society on a grand scale, a complex social matrix.

6. The need to support the belief of a divine son occasioned a variety of stories. For example, Suetonius cites the *Theologamena* which describes Octavian's mother, Atia, falling asleep during a service to Apollo. A serpent slithers to her and slips away. Later, after purification, she noticed a body mark like a serpent which would not wash away. Ten months later, Augustus was born, the son of Apollo; see Suet. *Aug.* 94.4. Cassius Dio records signs which point to the birth of one who will attain universal kingship: Atia dreamed that her vitals were brought up to the stars and spread over the whole world, and later Octavian dreamed that the sun rose from his mother's womb. Also, based on the timing of his birth and the ordering of the stars, a senator prophesied that Octavian would be the "king of the world," and another senator, Cicero, dreamed that the boy Octavian came down from the heavens by golden chains to the Roman Capitol and was given a whip by Jupiter. Supposedly, Cicero met Octavian the next day having not known him before; see Dio *Rom. Hist.* 45.1.3–5; 45.2.2–3.

7. Octavian came from an old and wealthy equestrian order. Gaius, his father, used money to gain political leverage and had the ability to obtain high positions. As a provincial governor, Gaius gained a reputation for his diplomacy, just nature, and courage; see Suet. *Aug.* 2–4; for upbringing and lineage, see Nic. *Aug.* 2–4.

a man, yet his mother insisted that he remain at home. Encouraged to fulfill his religious duties, Octavian took the opportunity to sit on the tribunal in the forum, which gained him an honorable reputation.[8] Despite his ability, Atia dismissed Octavian's desire to serve under Caesar in the Libya campaign due to the fact that the change of lifestyle might increase Octavian's chance of illness.[9]

As a member of an esteemed family, Octavian demonstrated his loyalty to them and to his friends, but he did so by taking calculated risks, only ones worthy of their outcome. When the brother of his school friend Agrippa was captured, he courageously requested his pardon from Caesar. Having not asked Caesar for a favor before, his intercession was granted. His intelligent and keen ability to petition at the right moment in a fitting manner gained him considerable respect. For example, when Julius Caesar met with those in Carthago Nova, the *Saguntini* asked Octavian to represent them for charges that had been brought against them. With Octavian as their spokesman, Caesar dropped the charges resulting in a reputation of "savior." Consequently, others sought his patronage.[10]

Octavian had gained favor with his great uncle. At age sixteen, Caesar honored him with military awards even though Octavian did not go to war. After recovering from a severe illness at age seventeen, he decided to reach Julius Caesar in battle. Surviving a shipwreck, Octavian journeyed behind enemy lines to reach his goal, accompanied by only a few men. The relieved Imperator treated him as a son, keeping him near. He complimented the young Octavian for his enthusiasm, precision, and wisdom in choosing observant and excellent associates. From there, Octavian spent two years in study until it was made known to him that Caesar had been assassinated and that he was Caesar's heir.[11]

---

8. Suet. *Aug.* 5.1. His good standing is not without blemish. Seneca describes him in his youth as one who had a temper, regretting the outbursts and actions in his early years; see *Clem.* 1.9.1 and 1.11.1; also see Suet. *Aug.* 68.1.

9. Octavian suffered from several severe illnesses; see Suet. *Aug.* 80–81; Nic. *Aug.* 9. As an adult he had liver problems and experienced disorders which recurred at particular times during the year, such as a swollen diaphragm in early spring. He limped at times and suffered from kidney stones. Because of his poor health, he could not handle extreme weather. But in some cases, his ailments gave him the opportunity to demonstrate his persistence and determination.

10. Nic. *Aug.* 7–8, 12.

11. As a youth, Octavian only personally carried out a war in Dalmatia, where he

Caesar Octavian

Roman historians mostly underscore Octavian Augustus's virtue. At times, however, they depict a more human side. Enough information can be gathered to warrant basic claims to his artful, measured methods of achievement as evidenced in his rise to power from age nineteen in 44 B.C. to his conquest at Actium in 31 B.C.[12]

CAESAR'S AVENGER

In 44 B.C., six months into his war training at Apollonia (for the purpose of accompanying Caesar on his expeditions), Octavian received the news that Caesar was murdered by those closest to him.[13] With an apparent deep resolve to avenge his father's death, Octavian ignored his family's warning to renounce the will; he set out from Brundisium with appropriate caution to galvanize Caesar's veteran soldiers. They yielded their support to him because of Caesar's name and Caesar's wealth.

Opposition actuated Octavian's ability to use shrewd accounting practices. Marc Antony, seeking his own rise to power, ignored Octavian and attempted to obstruct Octavian's claim to adoption and have him barred from office. For the purpose of gaining favor with the people, Antony introduced new measurements for land settlement,

---

injured his knee; he seemed more interested in athletics and playing dice than military exercise; see Suet. *Aug.* 20.1; 83.1; for military awards, see Suet. *Aug.* 8.1; for Octavian's determined journey to Caesar, see Suet. *Aug.* 8.2; Nic. *Aug.* 11; for details of adoption and inheritance, see Suet. *Aug.* 8.3; Nic. *Aug.* 12.

12. The following chronology relies upon Cassius Dio's *Roman History* and Appian's *Roman History*. Dio's account provides invaluable material for Augustus. He expresses caution in using popular sources as well as official sources under the principate (53.19.4–6), and he succinctly presents both Greek and Roman perspectives. What he lacks in detail, Appian offers with specific factual information from both pro-Augustan and anti-Augustan sources. His chronology is not as accurate as Dio's nor does he reconcile major themes, but this shows a healthy distance from the political struggles involved. See Gowing, *The Triumviral Narratives*, 5; Grant, *Readings*, 567–624; Hannak, *Appianus*, 29; Millar, *A Study of Cassius Dio*, 118; and Cassius Dio, *The Augustan Settlement*, 1–20. Concerning Antony, Plutarch's *Antony* highlights more significant aspects than Dio does, but Plutarch's treatment is not as historical. Livy's history is not utilized as often in this study because his information is not reliable. He does not write in a traditional manner, and he often relies on one main source; see Miles, *Livy*, 13–14. In the *Annals*, Tacitus's distrust of Octavian provides helpful insight, although his sources are not easily identifiable; see Mellor, *Tacitus*, 24.

13. The Senate hated Julius Caesar for his sole power and tyrannical acts; see Dio *Rom. Hist.* 45.24.2–3; 45.37.2.

granted pardons, and replaced high positions. Yet, Octavian was more generous. Taking into consideration the many claims, investigations, and lawsuits made for the rights to Caesar's property, Octavian won the hearts of the people by auctioning properties at the lowest possible price and distributing the money to the head tribesmen in the name of Caesar. This resulted in praise from the people and offense at Antony's treatment of him.[14]

Octavian engaged others by following a simple, economic pattern. First he made clear his resolve to avenge his father's death. Then he promised reward, and followed this with an immediate offer of a considerable amount of money to prove his trust. At Campania, before Antony arrived, Octavian gave two thousand *sesterces* to each soldier for their service. Antony's soldiers in Brundisium were offered only four hundred *sesterces* each, and at the same time Antony threatened violent harm to the centurions for any subversive attitudes. He showed some hesitation in eliminating those who murdered Caesar which caused restlessness among his soldiers, but Octavian won the military's loyalty by exhibiting zeal for vengeance.[15]

When several high ranking officers made complaints against Octavian, he carefully explained how the Senate was motivated by fear of Antony and his legions: "and that will be the case until we sacrifice Antony and the friends of the murderers, those in the Senate and their relatives, who gather a military force for them. Knowing this, I act as though I am serving them. Let us not be the first to reveal this hypocrisy. If we take the office, they will call us arrogant and violent, but if we show respect, perhaps they themselves will give it, lest I receive it from you."[16] Thus, by pretending to side with two opposing forces—the

---

14. For Octavian's response to his inheritance, see App. *Civ.* 3.9; Dio *Rom. Hist.* 45.3.1–4.1; for growing conflict between Antony and Octavian, see App. *Civ.* 3.7–12; for Octavian's clever response to attract the people in contrast to Antony's methods, see App. *Civ.* 3.22–23; Dio *Rom. Hist.* 45.9.1–4. In contrast to the inexperienced and boyish Octavian, Marc Antony had a proven record of bravery accompanied by an appropriate masculine, noble appearance (with a beard resembling that of Hercules), good humor, and the ability to give and take criticism (he blatantly accused Octavian of being effeminate); see Plutarch, *Ant.* 3–4. Antony gained favor through his generosity with those in power while Octavian gained favor through his generosity among soldiers and the people.

15. For payment to soldiers, see App. *Civ.* 3.43–44; Dio *Rom. Hist.* 45.12–13.

16. App. *Civ.* 3.48.

Senate and Antony—Octavian gained by not pressing his fortune too quickly. Soon two of Antony's legions defected to Octavian's side; he distributed income and promised them more for victory.[17] Furthermore, since Antony did not help him attain a tribunal position reserved for senators, Octavian secretly hired slaves to assassinate Antony, but the plot was discovered.

Cicero led the Senate in declaring Antony a public enemy, siding with Octavian. Yet, the Senate appointed Brutus as commander rather than Octavian. They even neglected to give Octavian appropriate lands as reward. He expected to at least be granted consulship, but with the Senate uncertain about the outcome of the battles, they abolished all privileges that would lead to supreme power (e.g., restricting office holders to one year and limiting the power over the grain supply) and planned to blame the defeated party. Enraged that the Senate called him "boy," Octavian secretly arranged a truce with Antony, and with the support of Antony and his soldiers, Octavian marched on Rome in 44 B.C. and by show of force was elected consul.[18]

One evening in Italy in 43 B.C., the sun's light dimmed and three circles appeared with a fiery crown of sheaves foretelling a reign of three. Octavian, Antony, and Lepidus formed a triumvirate for five years (43–38 B.C.) dividing the provinces—Octavian over the West, Antony over the East (including Gaul), and Lepidus over Africa. They purged Rome of Caesar's enemies with massacres taking place throughout the empire; properties were confiscated, and communities experienced terror (three-hundred senators and two-thousand knights were sentenced to death). In 42 B.C., Antony, with Octavian, defeated Cassius and Brutus

---

17. Tacitus describes Augustus as seducing the army with gifts and the public with grain, especially those of obsequious deportment, and since the provinces did not trust the Senate nor the legal system, they accepted his rule; see *Ann.* 1.2.

18. For the significant aspects of the conflict between Antony and Octavian, see App. *Civ.* 3.49–73; Dio *Rom. Hist.* 45.12–46.38; Plut. *Ant.* 6–86; for Antony, as an enemy of all, see Dio *Rom. Hist.* 45.18–47; Cicero, *Phil.* 2.22, 25. Needing an official office, Octavian pressed Cicero to return to Rome and support him. To outsmart Antony, Cicero did not find it shameful that Octavian just emerged from "boyhood" and honored the young man for spending his own money for the preservation of the state; see Dio *Rom. Hist.* 45.38–41. For the assassination plot of Antony, see Suet. *Aug.* 10.3. Dio describes Antony playing on the feelings of the people toward Caesar as a pretext (πρόσχημα) for war only to take control of Gaul for his own advantage; see *Rom. Hist.* 46.35.2–3. For Octavian's political and military approach on Rome, see App. *Civ.* 3.74–9; Dio *Rom. Hist.* 46.45–46; Suet. *Aug.* 26.1.

at Philippi; showing no mercy, they killed all those who had participated in Julius Caesar's death. Octavian had Brutus's head displayed at the feet of Caesar's statue in Rome. Shielding his brutality, Octavian masked his intentions by using legal means to exact punishment of the murderers and awarding more than forty thousand veterans with lands taken from landowners, causing considerable fear and resentment.[19]

In 40 B.C., Octavian marched his forces to face Antony at Brundisium. To avoid war, Antony abdicated his authority over Gaul to Octavian and married Octavia, Octavian's sister. Soon Antony formed a treaty with Pompeius Sextus, who had been appointed by the Senate as the head of Rome's navy. In 38 B.C., when Sextus did not receive his promised consulship from the triumvirs, he blockaded Italy. Octavian's ships were not successful against him, so Octavian made an agreement with Antony and exchanged soldiers for ships, renewing the triumvirate for an additional five years. Lepidus attacked Sicily from the south and defeated Sextus. Now with twenty legions, Lepidus turned against Octavian, but the legions deserted him. Rather than have Lepidus killed, Octavian mercifully banished him to Circei for life. In Rome, the Senate honored Octavian with Lepidus' office, *Pontifex Maximus*, but Octavian refused the position until after Lepidus died, maintaining Roman tradition. Among many other honors voted to Octavian, the Senate had a golden image made of Octavian with an inscription—"Peace, defied for a long time, he re-established on land and sea." To fulfill the hopes symbolically that civil war had ended for Italy and her provinces, Octavian ordered that all of the war records be burned.[20]

In the East, Antony rebelled. Having had two children with Cleopatra (after 36 B.C.), he pronounced Cleopatra the "Queen of Kings" and Caesarion (Caesar's son by Cleopatra) "King of Kings" at a celebration. In 32 B.C., he formed his own senate in Alexandria. Consequently, Octavian secured Antony's will illegally from the Vestal Virgins and

---

19. For a list of omens, see Dio *Rom. Hist.* 45.17.1–5; for agreements of the triumvirate, see App. *Civ.* 4.2–7; Dio *Rom. Hist.* 46.55–56. The violence of the proscriptions are conveniently attributed to Antony. In summary terms, Ronald Syme writes, "*Pietas* prevailed and out of the blood of Caesar the monarchy was born," *Roman Revolution*, 201; also see App. *Civ.* 4.5–51; Dio *Rom. Hist.* 46.48–49; 47.9–13; Suet. *Aug.* 27.1; for land settlement and resentment, see App. *Civ.* 4.3; Dio *Rom. Hist.* 47.14.4–5.

20. For Sextus, see App. *Civ.* 4.83–85; Dio *Rom. Hist.* 49.1–18; for Lepidus, see App. *Civ.* 5.97–144; Dio *Rom. Hist.* 48.16–20; for honors to Octavian, see App. *Civ.* 5.130–2; Dio *Rom. Hist.* 49.15.3; also, see Suet. *Aug.* 31.

read it aloud in the Senate, exposing Antony's loyalties to Egypt. In 31 B.C., Octavian's fleet defeated the forces of Antony at the battle of Actium, causing a massive defection of soldiers from the East. Antony and Cleopatra committed suicide, and Octavian had Caesarion and Antony's eldest son (Antyllus) executed. Thus, Octavian effectively used Caesar's image, shrewdly distributed Caesar's wealth, and patiently, even brutally, regained the sole rulership of the empire.[21]

Virtuous Caesar

Octavian, like most Romans, placed his faith in spiritual forces which he believed determined the destiny of life.[22] With fearful reverence and acceptance of Fate's reversals and revelations, Octavian regularly sought interpretations of omens and dreams to discern the future or the best course of action to take in order to maintain an appropriate relationship with heavenly powers, resulting in his advancement (*auctoritas*). For example, he accepted that certain auspices were infallible, such as the bad omen of putting a shoe on the wrong foot or a drizzle of rain signaling a swift and successful journey. He went out of his way to associate with those who were fortunate, and perceived the less fortunate (e.g., those disfigured and crippled) as a bad omen. He interpreted rare phenomena as favor, such as a palm tree growing between the pavement leading to his house or withered branches from an old oak coming back to life. Even certain days were unlucky to him. Due to his fear of thunder and lightning (associated with the god Jupiter), he often brought a seal-skin for protection when traveling and took refuge underground during a violent storm.[23]

Octavian also seemed to enjoy the risk in discerning Fate's will. Before the outcome of wars, Octavian looked for divine signs reveal-

---

21. For the reading of Antony's will to the Senate, see Dio *Rom. Hist.* 50.3.3–4, Plut. *Ant.* 58.2–4; for the battle of Actium, see Dio *Rom. Hist.* 51.1–17; Plut. *Ant.* 68.4–86. Octavian planned to take Cleopatra alive for the purpose of displaying her in triumph. He even had persons attempt to siphon the asp venom from her.

22. This section relies on the accounts of Suetonius, whose writings offer the reader a rich source for socio-historical analysis. As a "professor-grammarian," he observes how Augustus behaved and does not focus on military matters or crisis but on how Augustus's patterns affected public life; see Wallace-Hadrill, *Suetonius*, 22–24, 129–30, 508. This attention to important personal detail (the kind that historians often disregard) and his impartial approach provide insight into Augustus's character.

23. Suet. *Aug.* 83.1; 90–92.

ing the final result, and he often paid attention to dreams—his own and that of others. At the battle of Philippi, even though he was ill, he heeded the dream of a friend and did not sleep in his tent. This spared his life since the enemy soon advanced upon his quarters. Even in fun, Octavian pressed Fate's outcome. At an evening dinner party, Octavian auctioned off lottery tickets for items of varying value just so the bidding guests would participate in the caprice of fortune, to be disappointed or fulfilled in their expectations. Not surprisingly, he enjoyed the aspect of chance, as summarized in the derogatory epigram circulated about him during the Sicilian war: "After two defeats at sea and the loss of his ships, he constantly plays dice in hopes of winning a victory."[24]

Caesar Octavian won wars not because of his military experience nor simply through Fortune,[25] but because of his determination, discernment, and keen administrative ability. He defeated Pompeius in the Sicilian war after the loss of ships, enduring difficult winters, surviving famine, and narrowly escaping death in battle. Although Octavian probably did not give directional tactics in battle, it seems that he controlled the general strategy of military campaigns, motivating and utilizing the abilities of his generals. He practiced the wise principle of pursuing victory when the hope of gain was clearly greater than the fear of loss. He describes the one who presses forward for small gain with no real risk as one who fishes with a golden hook; if the line breaks, there is no way to make up for the loss. Some of his favorite sayings reveal this prudence: "Make haste slowly"; "Better a safe general than a bold"; and "That *which* is done quickly enough is *that* which is done well enough."[26]

---

24. Suet. *Aug.* 70.2; 75.1; 83; 91.1–2; 96.1. Some of the omens signaling victory included eagles striking two ravens at Bononia, a Thessalian portending victory at Philippi, a fish springing out of water before Augustus's feet at the sea battle near Sicily, and encountering a man named Eutychus riding a mule named Nicon on the way to Actium; see Suet. *Aug.* 96.2.

25. Greeks and Romans believed in destiny (*fortuna*, τύχη). Livy, in his Roman history, expresses this common attitude when he places Fortune alongside military courage and the general's ingenuity as great powers over human destiny, especially in war (*fortuna per omnia humana, maxime in res bellicas potens*, 9.17.3).

26. For Octavian's determination, see Suet. *Aug.* 16. For principles of war, see Suet. *Aug.* 25.3–4. Paul Zanker explains that victories occupy a special place in Augustan ideology, for they are proof of the unique and godlike nature of the ruler in a similar manner as Hellenistic kings, but with Octavian, they demonstrate the moral and religious rebirth of the Republic in winning back the gods—such justification of war unites

The strict obedience of confidential orders without question by Octavian's military leaders and by his soldiers demonstrates the Roman virtue of *disciplina*. For example, he reluctantly allowed the generals to visit their wives, and only in the winter. He discharged an entire legion for insubordination without granting the rewards due them, he decimated a cohort for dereliction of duty and limited their rations, and he enforced death for any soldier who abandoned his post. He motivated through shame for other responsibilities, such as having a soldier stand the entire day in the general's tent for an infraction. Also, he avoided flattery, as seen in his calling all military personnel "soldiers," even his relatives who held military commands.[27]

Octavian's loyalty to his cause can also be seen in his cruelty. In 40 B.C., Augustus responded to all petitions for pardon by the defeated Perusians with the reply, "You must die." In another victory, one of his captors begged that his son live, and after having the father and son cast lots, Augustus executed the father and watched the son commit suicide. It is said by some that Augustus caused the deaths of certain consuls, ordered a soldier to be tortured and killed, and tricked persons by allowing them to show loyalty to Lucius Antonius, only to appropriate their estates to his veterans. It is not surprising then that he chose to drive Roman landowners from their lands for the purpose of rewarding his veterans.[28]

In addition to fear and possessions as a means of gaining power, Octavian knew that loyalty among associates strengthened his position. Octavian chose his friends carefully, showing great devotion to them by overlooking their mistakes and rewarding them for their virtue. Octavian often watched the Circus games with his friends in their box rooms and was always throwing formal dinner parties, especially to celebrate holidays and festivals. In return, he expected their affection, so much so that upon their deathbeds, he was more interested in their perception of him than any possessions they might have willed him. Whether they praised him or spoke negatively, he avoided displaying

---

pietas and victory; Zanker, *Power of Images*, 185.

27. The definition of *disciplina* is taken from Tac. *Hist.* 1.83. For examples of Octavian's disciplined nature, see Suet. *Aug.* 24; 25.1–2. For a review of the Roman army under Augustus, see Jones, *Augustus*, 110–16.

28. Suet. *Aug.* 12–15. Most likely, Virgil's father lost his land due to Octavian's rewarding of the veterans.

emotion and consistently returned the inheritances left to him to the children of his deceased friends.[29]

Octavian Augustus displayed an image of duty (*pietas*) rather than self-glory. In what seems to be a theatrical performance after Actium (remembering the actions of Julius Caesar), Octavian begged the people not to make him dictator while he took off his toga and beat his breast. He made it clear that he did not like flattering titles such as "Lord" or phrases such as "Oh just and gracious Lord." He refused temples voted to him, even in the provinces, and melted down silver statues in his honor and dedicated the money toward things like golden tripods to Apollo. Without favoritism, he selectively honored soldiers with gold and silver medals and made ineligible for awards those military leaders who celebrated triumphs on their own.[30]

Octavian Augustus effectively eliminated rebellion and conspiracies at their incipient stage, showing no mercy to those operating in secret. When addressing an assembly of soldiers and civilians, he noticed a Roman knight taking notes, and thinking that he was a spy, he ordered him stabbed on the spot. This type of leadership engendered fear. A consul-elect committed suicide after speaking against some of Augustus's acts in spiteful terms. In another example, Augustus, thinking that Quintus Gallius, a praetor, had a sword under his robe commanded him to be searched and found only folded tablets. Later, soldiers took Gallius to be tortured and executed—by first tearing out his eyes.[31]

It seems, however, that Octavian Augustus permitted others to disagree with him respectfully. When Tiberius wrote to Augustus about someone voicing a bad opinion of Augustus, the *Princeps* enjoined Tiberius not to take too seriously the one who spoke evil against him, but that Tiberius should be satisfied with the fact that evil action had been stopped. In the Senate, he honored freedom of speech, emphasizing that no one should suffer for their opinion: "Yet when slanderous libels were made against him and disseminated in the senate-house, he did not become anxious, but took great care to disprove them. He did not even ask who produced the libels, but proposed that from now on

---

29. Suet. *Aug.* 45.1; 74; 66.1–4.

30. Suet. *Aug.* 52–53. Octavian learned from his great uncle. When Julius Caesar abnegated the golden crown, the crowd rejoiced at first but then responded with hatred, see App. *Civ.* 2.109; Dio *Rom. Hist.* 44.11–12; and Plut. *Caes.* 61–62.

31. Suet. *Aug.* 19.1–2; 27.3–4.

defamatory notes or verses published by anyone under a false name should be called to account."[32]

In addition to emulating traditional Roman virtues such as *disciplina, pietas, fides, constantia,* and *gravitas,* Caesar Octavian's comportment and lifestyle exhibited simplicity. His villas lacked statues, pictures, and rare objects, and he chose furniture that reflected the lifestyle of a private citizen, as he disliked large country palaces. When at home, he slept on a low, plainly furnished bed (in the same bedroom in winter and summer for more than forty years). He often wore a common toga with a traditional purple stripe; he wore high-soled shoes for the purpose of portraying a taller image, and he was always prepared with the appropriate clothing for various public occasions. He ate regular food and drank wine sparingly. A handsome, graceful man, he maintained a direct calm expression, although he enjoyed it when others believed him to have divine powers.[33]

Religious Father

In 2 B.C., the whole body of citizens offered Augustus the title *Pater Patriae*. At first he declined, but upon his return to Rome, the people in full theater insisted. They crowned him with laurel, and the Senate commissioned him "Father of His Country."[34] To understand the significance of this honor and the means by which it was attained requires a better understanding of Roman religion in the home and a better understanding of the role of the father (*paterfamilias*), and his relationship to city and state. In most Roman houses the family altar was adorned with non-Greek paintings (which probably related to early religious conceptions of Italy) and an arched niche in the wall to protect the sacrificial fire.[35] On the altar or wall were paintings depicting the rites performed in honor of the Genius of the *paterfamilias* and of the Lares and Penates (the Lares are outdoor gods, the Penates are inside gods). The father

---

32. Suet. *Aug.* 55; he greeted the senators in their seats by name. For written communication from Tiberius, see Suet. *Aug.* 51.3.

33. For Octavian's simple lifestyle, see Suet. *Aug.* 72–73; 76–79.

34. Suet. *Aug.* 58.1–2. Augustus had already acquired the power to convene the Senate in 23 B.C., the power to oversee Rome's grain supply in 22 B.C., censorial power in 19 B.C., and religious authority through the office of *Pontifex Maximus* in 12 B.C.

35. Grenier describes what is found at a discovery at Delos which agrees with the archeological findings at Pompeii. Grenier, *Roman Spirit,* 367.

with a toga drawn over his head poured out a libation before the altar, accompanied by a prayer and flute. Other deities associated with family worship included Fortune, Mercury, Hercules, Hermes, Apollo, and Poseidon. Roman worship exalted the home, the fields, and the gods of family, agriculture, and skill who protected daily life and work.[36] The beliefs of the Romans were conservative and their actions cautious.

In a similar manner to the home, the Roman city served first as a religious center (something like a judicial center).[37] The *pomerium*, a sacred territory around a city which was protected by its own divinities and rites, defined the sacred land of the city, which was consecrated to the gods. Legal authority extended from the *pomerium*. For example, every year before taking office, the consuls had to climb to the capitol where they swore an oath to Jupiter (the ruling god of the city). Without this oath, they held no authority. Furthermore, inside the city, consular power was absolute, while outside the city their power was limited by exact constitutional rules.[38] Thus, just as the temples of Rome were sacred, so also the administration of Rome was sacred, which meant that temples functioned for the purpose of government.

Roman people perceived their world in terms of "family" which means that the Roman city and the Roman state modeled the family; consequently, the gods of the state were the gods of a family and were worshiped in like manner.[39] A parallel can be made between the *paterfamilias* and the *filiusfamilias* to the *pontifex maximus* and the Vestal virgins; the *paterfamilias* and the *pontifex maximus* had the power of discipline but not of property. This distinction has significance: the *imperium* and the power of the *patria potestas* had far-reaching influence and only limited restraint from statutes and custom, and the consul had the same right to determine the will of the gods for the people as the *paterfamilias* did for his *familia*. Thus, the state needed a *paterfamilias*

---

36. Ibid., 368.

37. Grimal, *Roman Cities*, 4; for city and religious rituals, see 12–15.

38. Ibid., 5. Grimal gives another example of a victorious general who was forbidden to cross the *pomerium* as long as he remained an imperator; he waited for the Senate to vote him the honors of a triumph. If he even placed a foot inside the *pomerium*, he lost his rank.

39. Lacey, "Pater Potestas," 123–27. Lacey defines Vesta as the "living fire on the hearth of the home," the "god of place," and the "spirit of the innermost sanctuary of the *domus*" which could not be moved. See Ovid *Fasti* 6.267–8 (*Vesta eadem est et terra: subest vigil ignis utrique: significant sedem terra focusque suam*).

to rule with little restrained power, without the hindrance of excessive magistrates.[40]

Just as the *paterfamilias* exercised his power in consultation with his peers so also the magistrate formed his opinions with the advice of *consilium*. Neither the *paterfamilias* nor the magistrate was obliged to take the advice of his *consilium*. And for the member of the *consilium*, the weight his *sententia* carried determined the measure of his *dignitas*.[41] Thus, when Augustus became *Pontifex Maximus* (12 B.C.) and associated his family gods with the Roman state and when he associated his successes of the Julian house with those of the Roman state, he clearly had identified his roles as *paterfamilias* and as *pater patriae*.[42] This was a natural development for the Romans, for the *paterfamilias's* power of governing his family through *patria potestas* was reflected in the patron's management of his independent clients based on *potestas* (but later on *fides*).[43]

Not only did Augustus's role as the *Pontifex Maximus* parallel the religious role of the *paterfamilias* to his family, but the Roman integration of the Greek practice of honoring their ruler as god magnified Augustus's benevolence. S. F. R. Price examines thousands of texts inscribed on stone during the imperial period, with particular interest in (1) inscriptions which commemorate offices and activities of local nobles and (2) official regulations and order of ceremonies of Greek and Roman cults.[44] Ruler cults established by Hellenistic cities are simply honors in appreciation for political benefactions—they were not a uniform institution. The divine cult was offered to Alexander, and the cities of the Greek empire "established cults as an attempt to come to terms with a new type

40. Lacey, "Pater Potestas," 137–38.

41. Ibid., 138.

42. See Livy *Hist. Rom.* 1.26.

43. Augustus lavished particular care on the cult of Vesta. As *Pontifex Maximus*, he built a sanctuary of the goddess in his own house on the Palatine; thus when Augustus, the descendant of Aeneas, conducted a sacrifice in front of the Temple of Vesta, where the Palladium was displayed, it was as if the myth of the Penates and Palladium being rescued were recreated. "Augustus had in fact rescued the images of the gods—from neglect and oblivion"; see Zanker, *Power of Images* 207. Furthermore, Augustus did not create new *nobiles* but secured their recognition. Matthew Gelzer notes how the *Princeps* belonged to the *nobiles* and, for political reasons, was careful not to give the impression that he was above them; *Roman Nobility*, 141–61.

44. Price, *Rituals and Power*, 1–60.

of power."[45] The cults of the gods were the one model available for accommodation,[46] but with Augustus came a decisive change. In 29 B.C., eastern provinces honored Caesar Augustus as "a savior who put an end to war and established all things," and they announced him as "son of god."[47] Augustus existed among the deities as a benefactor who brought peace, unity, and prosperity to the whole world.

As "Father" of the Roman class with absolute power, Augustus proved that provision and *dignitas* came from his hand, making steady conquest through passive-aggressive means. He circuitously showed mercy to those in authority and even his enemies by acting as a "father" to their sons, minimizing vengeance upon himself. He permitted senators' sons: (1) to become acquainted with the affairs of administration at a young age, (2) to assume also the distinction of the senatorial robe, and (3) to be present at the debates in the senate-house. He gave senators' sons (4) the rank of military tribunes in the legions, and (5) an opportunity of acquiring military experience (he commonly gave joint command to two sons of senators for each troop of horses). Concerning his enemies, after Antony and Cleopatra committed suicide, he had three of Cleopatra's sons (two by Antony and one by Caesar) killed, but he allowed the remaining children from Antony and Cleopatra to live, treating them as his own children. Furthermore, he showed similar kindness to rulers from other kingdoms by bringing up many of their children and educating them with his own. In this way he treated possessed lands as integral parts of the empire.[48]

With his authority, Augustus universally sought to revive and regulate morality. When he became *Pontifex Maximus* in 12 B.C., he burned all prophetic writings except the Sibylline books and revived

---

45. Ibid., 29.

46. Ibid., 30–31.

47. Ibid., 54–55. Priests of Augustus were found in thirty-four different cities in Asia Minor, and the vitality of the imperial cult remained strong during the first two centuries A.D. For information on the imperial cult, see Taylor, *Divinity*; and Fishwick, *The Imperial Cult*. After 20 B.C., virtually all monuments erected in Augustus's honor had a votive or religious character; see Zanker, *Power of Images*, 160.

48. For Augustus's favor to sons, see Suet. *Aug.* 17.5; 38.2, 48. Octavian dominated with moderation and efficiency. Rather than overextend his forces, he forced the barbarian leaders to swear in the temple of Mars that they would keep peace, and rather than kill those who rebelled, he sold them into slavery to serve in a country near their own for thirty years; see Suet. *Aug.* 21.2–3.

the priesthood and its ancient rites. Sacrificial practice permeated the highest levels of society under Augustus; for instance, he required each senator to offer incense and wine on the altar to the god in the temple where they met. Throughout the empire, travelers now viewed the Lares of the Crossroads crowned with spring and summer flowers. As a means of motivation, next to the immortal gods he honored Romans who came from humble means and had advanced to contribute greatly to the state. Augustus made it clear that he did such things to motivate citizens to strive to live by traditional Roman standards in the present and in the future.[49]

In an unprecedented manner, Augustus also tried to regulate marriage and procreation throughout the empire in order to maintain the domination of the ruling class by enacting legislation based on morality and virtue.[50] A father could kill an adulterer having relations with his daughter, and severe penalties awaited the guilty wives and promiscuous daughters.[51] In this way, the aristocracy preserved power and maintained the traditions of Rome. The laws of marriage and adultery were intended to subject through fear and reward those who obeyed: "He [Augustus] found the people utterly averse to submit to it, unless the penalties were abolished or mitigated, besides allowing an interval of three years after a wife's death, and increasing the premiums on marriage . . . the equestrian order clamored loudly, at a spectacle in the theater, for its total repeal . . . but finding the force of the law was eluded, by marrying girls under the age of puberty, and by frequent changes of wives, he [Augustus] limited the time for consummation after espousals, and imposed restrictions on divorce."[52] Despite the grievances, freedmen were motivated to adopt this style of life as part of their status as citizens.[53]

---

49. Suet. *Aug.* 31.1–5; 35.3.

50. Augustus enacted the *Lex Iulia de maritandis ordinibus* in 18 B.C. and the *Lex Papia Poppaea* and the *Lex Iulia de adulteriis* in A.D. 9. For marriage laws, see Mette-Dittmann, *Die Ehegesetze des Augustus*, 131–98.

51. Augustus's daughter committed adultery, for which he blames Fortune for failing him; Augustus also committed adultery, see Suet. *Aug.* 65.1–4; 69.1–2.

52. Suet. *Aug.* 34.1–2. This quotation is translated by J. C. Rolfe.

53. In addition, Augustus allowed the nobility (with the exception of the senators) to marry freedwomen, acknowledging the legitimacy of their children; see Dio *Rom. Hist.* 54.16.

Augustus restricted citizenship requirements and set limits on manumission. When Tiberius requested citizenship for a Grecian dependent of his, Augustus wrote in reply that he would not grant it unless the man appeared in person and convinced him that he had reasonable grounds for the request. When Livia requested citizenship for a Gaul from a tributary province, he refused and declared that he would more willingly suffer a loss to his privy purse than the prostitution of the honor of Roman citizenship, adding that no one who had ever been put in irons or tortured should acquire citizenship by any grade of freedom.[54]

His sweeping reforms eliminated opportunities for corruption. He revived traditional election privileges by assessing penalties for bribery, had soldiers stationed to regularly inspect workhouses, disbanded all illegitimate guilds, and burned the records of old debts to the treasury which were often a source of blackmail. In order to hold knights accountable, he employed ten assistants from the Senate to compel each knight to render an account of his life, punishing, censuring, or reprimanding the scandalous. As a judge, he administered justice regularly, sometimes up to nightfall.[55]

So when Augustus made his donations to the people—sometimes 400, sometimes 300, or 250 *sesterces*—or when grain was scarce and he would frequently let them have it inexpensively or for free, he provided as a benevolent father would to his *dominion*. This is also true when he boasted of his generosity in spending large sums of money to entertain the people with a great spectacle of a naval battle. When he provided for the military colonies by paying for land, purchasing Italian estates, and buying provincial fields, he established himself as the one in whom authority rests and from whose hand property is transferred. When Augustus permitted the senators' sons to become acquainted with the affairs of administration at a young age and to assume the distinction of the senatorial robe or to be present at the debates in the senate-house,

---

54. Suet. *Aug.* 40.3–4. Augustus's restrictions were put in place to restore Roman tradition and to set an example for following generations; *RG* 8. See also, K. R. Bradley, *Slaves and Masters in the Roman Empire: A Study in Social Control* (New York: Oxford University Press, 1987), 84–95.

55. Suet. *Aug.* 32.2; 39. He even desired to revive the ancient fashion of dress (40.5); once when he saw an assembly of men in dark cloaks, he cried out a verse from the *Aeneid* in an indignant tone, "Behold those Romans, masters of the world, the nation clad in the toga" (1.282).

he acted as their father from whom *dignitas* is given. When Augustus administered justice while reclining on his couch at home, he acted as a father whose power it is to judge his household. When Augustus built the temple of Mars Ultor, and constructed the theater at the temple of Apollo, and consecrated gifts from war-spoils in the Capitol and in the temple of divine Julius, in the temple of Apollo, and in the temple of Vesta, he served as priest and father of Rome. And when Augustus conquered the whole world waging civil and foreign war on land and sea, he was the savior of all those who sought pardon.[56]

Great Administrator

Augustus sought to make a change in 27 B.C. which would allow him to retain his position as the head of the Roman state and, at the same time, hold together the old forms of the constitution. Since he transferred his authority only temporarily, it is probable that Augustus wanted to make the Roman people realize the great need of his directing hand by having them experience the possibility of his withdrawal from public life, and to have them perceive his tremendous powers as their free gift to him.[57] He wisely avoided the perception of a monarchical position by accepting a new position which did not conflict with Republican tradition, bringing him great gain. An example of this strategic pattern is evidenced in the right of coinage.

When Augustus handed back the *res publica* in 27 B.C., he clearly handed back the right of coinage, a mark of sovereignty.[58] Augustus resumed this right in 19 B.C. as part of the constitutional settlement of that year when he became a source of law, acquiring the right to sit between the two consuls of the year.[59] But Augustus did more than take ultimate responsibility for minting in the empire—he reorganized the bronze coinage. Since no bronze coinage was produced between Sulla and Julius Caesar, it can be concluded that Augustus not only reformed

---

56. For donations to the people, see Suet. *Aug.* 41.1–2; for naval battle, see *RG* 23; for military benevolence, see *RG* 16; for Augustus as judge, see Suet. *Aug.* 33.1–3; for consecration of temples, see *RG* 21; and for gracious savior, see *RG* 3.

57. Abbott, *History*, 268–69; for temporary transfer of authority, see Dio *Rom. Hist.* 53.3–11.

58. Crawford, *Coinage and Money*, 257–61. The right of coinage was usurped by Augustus in 43 B.C. and retained for seventeen revolutionary years.

59. Ibid. For constitutional settlement, see Dio *Rom. Hist.* 54.10.5–6.

the fixed standard but utilized a two-monetary-metals system. This not only minimized loss through forgery (bronze forgeries were lighter in weight and were produced outside Italy), but allowed money to be saved in minting.[60]

Augustus made conquests over time through precise administrative changes—in the Senate, in the provinces, and for the military. His changes came through different sources of law: (1) legislation, (2) enactments of the plebeians, (3) resolutions of the senate, (4) constitutions of the emperor, and (5) the edicts of those who have the right to issue edicts, and the answers of the jurisprudents.[61] The Senate's jurisdiction was established before the death of Augustus, and one of the steps in this change of power can be traced back to the fifth edict from Cyrene, which covers a *senatus consultum* passed in 4 B.C. This was upon the recommendation of the Emperor's *consilium*, laying down a new procedure to be adopted, limiting prosecutors' claims for monetary damages.[62] The preliminary hearing for this case took place in the Senate, and a commission of four consulars, three praetorians and two other senators was set up, giving a verdict within thirty days.

This type of reversion of procedure is representative of the trend of constitutional development which Augustus undertook. The "royal authority" of the Senate was removed. Peace, war, treaties, etc., became powers of the principate. Over time, Augustus aligned the needs of his absolute position with the needs of the Republican institutions. He gave specific attention to molding the procedure of the Senate while also delegating formal duties. For example, he increased the fines for nonattendance in the senate and reduced the quorum of the four hundred necessary for the passing of a valid *senatus consultum* (11 B.C.).[63] Tacitus describes how this changed the political environment: "Augustus won over the soldiers with gifts, the populace with cheap corn, and all men

---

60. Ibid., 261. For a clear presentation of numismatic and literary evidence during Augustan rule, see Sutherland, *Roman History*, 3–53; also see Wallace-Hadrill, "Image and Authority," 66–87.

61. Crook, *Law and Life*, 18–23; categories are taken from Cicero *Topica* 28. Two hundred years later these sources of law did not change much; see Gaius *Institutes* 1.2. Under Augustus, imperial edicts, letters, and decrees were displayed publicly, see Harris, *Ancient Literacy*, 206–7.

62. Jones, "Senatus Populusque Romanus," 170–74.

63. Ibid., 180.

with the sweets of repose, and so grew greater by degrees, while he concentrated in himself the functions of the Senate, the magistrates, and the laws . . . the remaining nobles . . . were raised the higher by wealth and promotion, so that, aggrandized by revolution, they preferred the safety of the present to the dangerous past. Nor did the provinces dislike that condition of affairs, for they distrusted the government of the Senate and the people."[64] The senate was under the control of the *Princeps*.[65]

Concerning the provinces, Augustus appointed governors outside of Rome; they had sole independent jurisdictional authority.[66] All suits involving a Roman citizen in principle came to the governor. He was not bound by the list of statutory offenses or penalties, but he could try and punish in any form anything he thought contrary to the good order of his province.[67] Governors had always been entitled to delegate non-capital jurisdiction to their *legati*. But governors of "provinces of Caesar" were already delegates and could not delegate further (they had no *legati*).[68] This reveals the absolute control of the emperor and the huge burden of litigation on the governor. The emperor's gubernatorial appointments had a direct, expedient result on the practice of law as the governors had to publish an edict when they entered their province, to provide the special rules of law applicable to their territory.[69]

Concerning the military, Augustus made efficient, practical decisions. Over time, Augustus reduced the number of legions from sev-

---

64. Tac. *Ann.* 1.2. This quotation is translated by A. Church and W. Brodribb.

65. Augustus created new positions for the Senate and for the Equites with longer terms; this innovation served to keep power with the *Princeps* and give the impression that tradition was not altered. Augustus probably did not appear as a controller; for example, A. H. M. Jones challenges the accepted doctrine that Augustus systematically gerrymandered the elections for higher office; "Elections Under Augustus," 112–19. Even though the liberty of the elections was limited by the predominant influence of the *Princeps*, Jones strongly suggests, based on the evidence, that genuine electoral contests continued for lower offices, for the praetorship, and even for the consulate.

66. Augustus directly governed the greater provinces himself; to the others he assigned proconsular governors selected by lot; see Suet. *Aug.* 47.

67. Crook, *Law and Life*, 70–72.

68. Ibid.

69. Ibid., 24. The implication is that Augustus's *imperium* overrode that of the governor (23 B.C.). He could intervene in the affairs of any province in the empire. Unlike other governors, he was also given dispensation to retain his power within the city limits of Rome (the *pomerium*). For an overview of provincial administration, see Bleicken, *Augustus*, 391–438.

enty-five to twenty-eight.⁷⁰ He assimilated the peoples of the lands of his conquest through colonization, and in his *RG* celebrates that he founded colonies of soldiers in Africa, Sicily, Macedonia, Spain, Greece, Asia, Syria, Narbonian Gaul, and Pisidia, and had twenty-eight populated colonies founded in Italy under his authority.⁷¹ His promise of land and retirement pay motivated his soldiers, and their presence in hostile territories served as a stark reminder of his mighty power.⁷²

From a socio-historical perspective, Caesar Augustus consistently demonstrated the ability to gain power gradually and effectively lead others, in times of war and in times of peace. During military crisis, he played a passive-aggressive role by waiting patiently for other parties to reveal their intentions first, and took risks only when the outcome seemed certain. In victory, he carefully shielded his intentions behind traditional and legal means, as when he had the war records burned, a decision he claimed was symbolic for the purpose of fulfilling the hopes of no more war.

During peace time, Augustus's patterns of manipulation continued, and his lust for power increased. Learning from the mistakes of his adopted father, he chose to give the impression of offering up his imperial rights, but unlike Julius Caesar, Augustus gradually had them offered back to him. Instead of the war-time pretense of revenge against Caesar's enemies or exacting justice to those disloyal to Rome (e.g., Antony), Augustus championed the cause of Rome's rebirth and renewal. Instead of promising greater reward to an army of veteran soldiers, he now promised recognition for wealthy patrons for their imitation of his noble example. In this same way, he persisted in effectively eliminating those who competed with his power; he "out-supported" them by offering greater rewards to their sons. To those who were loyal and shared his values, he permitted freedom of opinion; to those who did not share his goals, he motivated through fear and the withdrawal

---

70. Adcock, *Roman Political Ideas*, 71–88.

71. *RG* 28.

72. Goodman and Sherwood, *Roman World*, 121. The religious nature of military service to Caesar should not be understated. Soldiers took an oath invoking the vengeance of Jupiter on themselves in the event of perjury (see also *Aen.* 7.614; 8.1). It is interesting that at the end of his life, Augustus recommended against the resettling of territories due to the difficulty of guarding an extended frontier; see Shuchburgh, *Augustus*, 171–93; for colonizing under Augustus as a continuation of Julius Caesar's work, see Salmon, *Roman Colonization*, 126–44.

of provision and status. As a pious benefactor, Augustus received glory and only from him was glory bestowed.

In addition to his need for increased *auctoritas*, it is very possible that Augustus believed in providence and divine destiny. His superstitions and the stories surrounding his rise to power give credibility to the idea that he believed he was born as a result of the divine fulfillment of a promise through royal lineage. He placed faith in revelation and in maintaining a right relationship with the gods, showing a developed curiosity in the outcome of chance. Even though his success can be attributed to his determination, wisdom, and leadership, it seems that his survival (overcoming illnesses and opposition) reaffirmed to him that providence was at work. But regardless of whether it can be shown that he believed in divine destiny or whether he used religious ideas to control, it is highly likely that Augustus chose to restrict the official messages of the empire to accomplish or fulfill a specific purpose.

Images and Power of the Augustan Age

When Octavian had all of the "illegal" acts of the triumvirate annulled,[73] in a sense he erased the moral debt from the state's ledger, and after Actium, the process of transferring the republic from "my power" to the "dominion of the senate and people of Rome" began.[74] Yet more and more, the symbolism of power centered on Augustus and the imperial family.[75] He wanted nothing less than sole reign which became more clear during peace time. Following the defeat of Antony and Cleopatra, he visited the tomb of Alexander the Great. After placing a golden crown on Alexander's sarcophagus, he was asked if he wanted to see the Ptolemies. He replied that he wanted to see a king, not corpses. Not surprisingly, the image on his seal for passports, formal communication, and personal letters was first a sphinx, later an image of Alexander the Great, and eventually an image of himself.[76]

In 27 B.C., the Senate and the people honored Augustus with traditional Roman symbols—a sacred laurel tree representing religion,

---

73. Dio *Rom. Hist.* 53.2.6.

74. *RG* 34.

75. Augustus achieved absolute power; see Dio *Rom. Hist.* 51.20.4–5; 51.19–21; *RG* 34. Particularly helpful is Salmon, "Evolution of Augustus's Principate," 456–78.

76. Suet. *Aug.* 18.1–2; 50.1.

the oak wreath *corona civica* representing victory, and the Greek shield *clipeus virtutis* representing virtuous rule.[77] But in the Augustan age, these and other salvific symbols communicated a new message, one that said, "The victor at Actium brings restoration."[78] Eventually, this new salvific imagery assimilated itself into the private sphere. For example, the Victory on a *clipeus virtutis* appears on terracotta lamps which show loyalty to Augustus. These early lamps have the legend *ob cives servatos* on the shield (reflections of the honorary shield in the Curia) which in time changed to a material greeting *Annum novum felicem mihi et tibi* ("Happy New Year to you and me") so that the goddess of victory and the emperor's honorary shield bear personal greetings.[79] Also, the *corona civica* and the laurel wreath carry identical meanings, "the salvation of the citizens and the State," which came to be a popular expression for praise to the emperor, "applicable to every object in any context."[80]

Just as Augustus's motivation is evidenced in his censoring of the historical accounts of his moral liabilities before Actium, so also his motivation can be seen in his indirect influence over official imagery in the skillful portrayals of the past sculpted in memorials, statues, and decorative detail. The available narrative imagery and symbolic representations from which artists could choose were apparently restricted for the purpose of promoting repetitive, didactic messages.[81] Throughout the empire, with some innovation, the political and religious architecture preserved traditional Roman values through a classical Greek style. For example, after Actium battle scenes were rarely depicted and the glorification of the emperor was not part of populated narrative scenes.[82] "Given such a system, all change and innovation in pictorial imagery

---

77. The year 27 B.C. marks the significant change where Rome exalted its ruler; see Wardman, *Religion and Statecraft*, 63–79.

78. Zanker, *Power of Images*, 93.

79. Ibid., 275.

80. Ibid., 276. Zanker explains this change by discussing a small cameo in Vienne where a noble victor rides the waves in a cart drawn by sea centaurs (helpers in the naval battle) holding symbols that refer to the restoration of the Republic. In another example, on globes are symbolic images of imperial rule: on one side of Victoria is the *corona civica* and on the other side is *clipeus virtutis* framed by oak wreaths; ibid., 97.

81. Augustus introduced a system of conservative innovation over time which then remained unchanged for two centuries; ibid., 338. See also Dio *Rom. Hist.* 53.27; 56.30.3; Suet. *Aug.* 28.3.

82. Zanker, *Power of Images*, 111.

had to originate at the top and could as a rule be managed only from Rome . . . [but] nothing was explicitly prescribed, nothing supervised, and there were no advertising campaigns."[83]

The chief common feature of all Augustan empire imagery is its "high recognition factor."[84] Although size is a commonality, the architects maintained a simplicity of essential forms (e.g., "a prismatic block, a grand arch, an unobstructed vaulted space") in such a way that these elements remained in view regardless of the applied decor.[85] The traditional constructions reinforce familiarity and meaning. Bridges, aqueducts, and other structures keep their order and stable geometry, with their overlays of traditional classicism recognized everywhere.[86] Imperial archaistic forms stood out against Greek architecture, and with the societal system of patronage, Roman architecture became firmly established.[87] For example, the Roman arch distinctly represents the development of Roman fashion. After Octavian returned from his triumphs and receptions in the East, Italian cities began to establish their own branch of sophisticated archways to Octavian Augustus as "the Savior of the Empire."[88] Much in the same way that Roman coins of Thrace present the city-gate as a triumphal arch, many early Augustan stone arches were built into existing gateways, expressing gravity and stability, with slender sophistication and not without experimentation.[89]

Augustus's revival of religion, virtue, and tradition involved the restoration of temples and monuments. Cities throughout the empire now imitated Augustus's program by building and renovating temples associated with Augustus—Apollo on the Palatine, Mars Ultor in the new Forum of Augustus, and Jupiter cult on the Capitol. Augustus called on wealthy patrons to imitate his example by erecting new monu-

---

83. Ibid., 338.

84. MacDonald, *Architecture*, 182–83.

85. Ibid.

86. Anderson and Spiers, *Architecture of Greece & Rome*, 234–39.

87. Garnsey and Saller, *Roman Empire*, 107–25. After the civil war, Augustus advanced his cause through patronage. The wealthy became his "soldiers" on the "image" fronts in the empire. MacMullen describes this contribution of the wealthy patrons in a pointed question—"The regime remade the capital, the State expressed itself in stone?"; *Romanization*, 69.

88. Smith, *Architectural Symbolism*, 24.

89. Ibid. Also, see Sear, *Roman Architecture*, 62–63, 146.

ments and restoring old ones.[90] For example, the hooded Augustus as sacrificer soon became a standard type of statue for leaders in provincial cities. In the Capitoline Museum, an Augustan votive altar depicts Augustus handing over a statue of Minerva to the *ministri* of the cult of the woodworkers' guild.[91] The *Princeps* contributes the cult statue, and the *ministri* respond with the dedication of a votive altar or god statue (one of political significance) which is combined with the epithet *Augustus* or *Augusta* to honor the *Princeps*. In addition, throughout the empire, pious portraits of the imperial family evidenced the renewed religious reverence connected to those in power.[92] Rarely was there a single monument or building that did not include in its decorative scheme "the skulls of sacrificial animals, offering bowls, priestly tokens, or garlands wound with fillets, even when the structure itself is purely secular . . . even slaves contributed to *pietas* of new age in service to the gods."[93]

Augustan monuments repeatedly employ similar mythological cycles with few images, mainly those of Aeneas and Romulus whose imagery emphasizes the virtues of *pietas* and *virtus*.[94] The actions of the heroes are displayed and whenever possible linked with the living exemplum of the *Princeps*, creating an emotional and spiritual association between the present and the mythological past. For example, the mythical account in Virgil's *Aeneid* is visually expressed most prominently in the Forum of Augustus, celebrating Augustus's victories over Julius Caesar's murderers. No legends are created; rather, the innovation is seen in the reinterpretation of the two legends of Troy and Romulus, linking Augustus and the Romans as descendants of Venus and Mars.

In the Temple of Mars Ultor in the Forum of Augustus, the gods Mars, Venus, Fortuna, and Roma are honored along with Julius

90. *RG* 20; Suet. *Aug.* 29.1–5.

91. Zanker, *Power of Images*, 129.

92. Ibid., 292.

93. Ibid., 116, 131. Imperial messages through visual imagery reached the entire empire, including Palestine; see Jos. *Ant.* 15.339. Nearly every motif was borrowed directly from the new pictorial vocabulary created in Rome, seen in nearly every Roman city (e.g., vine friezes, motifs of the sacred, laurel or oak leaves, and arms and armor); see Zanker, *Power of Images*, 311. For building projects, see *RG* 19–21, 24; Augustan encouragement, Suet. *Aug.* 28.2–29.5; also see Ward-Perkins, *Roman Imperial Architecture*, 21–44.

94. Zanker, *Power of Images*, 207. For the origins of Rome and the mythological tale of Aeneas, see Dionysius, *Roman Antiquities* 1.8–88.3.

Caesar and Romulus. One scene depicts Aeneas fleeing from Troy with his father, son, and the Penates, with representations of the kings of Alba Longa and members of the Julian house. Another scene depicts Romulus, the son of Mars, as a victor with a parade of military heroes from Rome's early history.[95]

In the Forum of Augustus, the reliefs along the marble walls of the *Ara Pacis* communicate allegorical and ceremonial meaning through repetitive symbolism. The *Ara Pacis,* the most representative work of Augustan art, presents the idea that Augustus is the guarantor (*auctor*) of peace, and it links the concept of peace with his military victories which secured the Roman *imperium*.[96] The monument focuses on Augustus, his arrival, and the rite of sacrifice (represented by Aeneas sacrificing the sow to the Penates). On one wall, Augustus, religious officials, and the imperial family move in a procession, and on the opposite wall, senators, dignitaries, and their families also move in procession (possibly to give the impression of a circular procession).[97] Another relief presents the *Terra Mater* with two babies and fertility symbols during the *Pax Romana*.

The *Ara Pacis* also celebrates divine providence rather than exalting individual heroes. Based on the scene prophesied in the *Aeneid* (3.390, 8.84), the altar depicts the traditional infant scene of Romulus and tells of Aeneas's arrival in Latium. Much like a vision illuminating the daily rituals of Rome, one observes the details of the stone altar, wreathed attendants, plate of fruit, and the veiled Aeneas pouring the libation and holding a spear (*pietas*).[98] On the one hand, the multiplicity of meanings can be experienced on different levels due to the rich artistic mythological traditions (like reading the *Aeneid*), and on the other hand, the artists communicate a unifying message based on the Augustan value system, "Peace and prosperity depend on Roman mores."[99]

Just as represented in the Forum of Augustus, this repetitive mythological imagery of Aeneas is found in artwork and coins. Aeneas symbolizes the virtue of *pietas* demonstrated before the gods. Before

---

95. Also, see *Aen.* 6.756–885.
96. Galinsky, *Augustan Culture,* 141–42. See *RG* 12.2.
97. Billows, "The Religious Procession," 80–92.
98. Zanker, *Power of Images,* 194–95.
99. Galinsky, *Augustan Culture,* 148–51.

Actium, Venus was portrayed holding the arms of Mars, but in the pediment of the Temple of Mars Ultor, she reflects a new role—wearing a long garment and holding a scepter, standing beside the war god.[100] As in the statue group in the Forum of Augustus and as on the coin, the dramatic story is not what is most important, rather the specific references and specific places in the overall design.[101] In other words, the imagery of the *Ara Pacis* encourages participation with other symbolism of the artistic program of the Augustan age. The denarius of Octavian (32–29 B.C.) with the goddess of Pax holding an olive branch in the right hand and a cornucopia in her left, is another straightforward representation which yields "to the multiplicity of historizing and mythologizing images . . . that can be combined and recombined in a variety of ways."[102]

The mythological symbolism of Aeneas and his family served as a token of loyalty. These images have been found on finger rings, lamps, and terracotta statuettes. Wall paintings in a house from Pompeii reflect the imagery of Aeneas and Romulus depicted in the Forum of Augustus.[103] Furthermore, sculptors and patrons use the scene of Aeneas and his family on grave monuments as a symbol of personal piety and devotion.[104] The "subliminal absorption over time even if unconscious was not inconsiderable."[105]

Poetic Literature under Imperial Patronage

Augustus influenced Roman poets, but it is not certain as to what degree he influenced them. On one end of the spectrum, Ronald Syme argues that the aristocracy guided literature through individual patronage with poets taking their tone and tastes from those above.[106] In this

---

100. Zanker, *Power of Images*, 197–200.

101. Ibid., 209.

102. Galinsky, *Augustan Culture*, 148–49.

103. Zanker, *Power of Images*, 200.

104. Ibid., 278.

105. Ibid., 274; Political symbolism such as this was found on every imaginable object—jewelry, utensils, furniture, textiles, walls, ceilings, clay facings, roof tiles, tombs, and ash urns; ibid., 266. Even objects as common as milestones declared the name of Augustus (his name was inscribed above the name of the *legatus* and the legion that made the road); see Rushforth, *Latin Historical Inscriptions*, xv.

106. Syme, *Roman Revolution*, 459–75.

age, propaganda outweighed arms, as Augustus imitated the traditional leadership that preceded him. This view evolved in the 1930s and 40s when critics teased out from Augustan poetry dark, subversive aspects, interpreting the poets as reacting to an "authoritarian" regime. On the other end of the spectrum, Peter White disagrees with Syme's analysis and argues that Augustan poets enjoyed an amicable relationship with Augustus and other aristocrats.[107] Poets participated in ongoing conversations, working things out among friends with intimate, sustained contact.[108] White places emphasis on reader interpretation more than he does political history. Both the political nature of Augustus and the creative literary environment need to be taken into account when assessing his influence.[109]

To argue that Augustus indirectly exerted a reasonable amount of control over select poets through tacit restrictions and positive manipulation, a relationship between the poets and Augustus or a relationship between the poets and their patrons would need to exhibit some form of loyalty, patriotism, and shared value system for the purpose of achieving power. The argument for Augustan persuasion would also be strengthened if Augustus showed an interest in literature, and if a positive relationship with Virgil existed.

Augustus did show significant interest in literary compositions, his own and others. Augustus studied and wrote literature. He supported gifted writers and expressed his critical standards openly. As a youth, he devoted himself to studies and oratory skill, especially during his late teenage years. Even though he did not speak Greek fluently, he enjoyed Greek poetry, and whether Latin or Greek writings, he often looked for didactic principles and examples for the public or individuals. He would send quotations from the works of well-known authors to family members, generals, and governors for admonition, and was known for citing Homer for particular life situations. He encouraged talented men by listening to their readings of poetry, history, and speeches. Augustus himself wrote prose, philosophy, and an autobiography (not further

---

107. White, *Promised Verse*.

108. Ibid., 33–34. White believes that the grand themes and ideas of Greek and Roman culture were simply transferred to Augustus; not much had changed; ibid., 167–69. In contrast is the celebration of Augustus as a new phenomenon; see Millar, "State and Subject," 60.

109. Galinsky, "Empirical and Theoretical Approaches," 104–23.

than the Cantabrian war), and his two poetical essays entitled "Sicily" and "Epigrams" were written in hexameter verse (he started composing a tragedy but was not satisfied with it).

Augustus showed careful precision in his communication. He did not appreciate extreme innovation and was particular about certain themes and slogans. Instructing his grandsons in reading and other aspects of education, he made certain they imitated his handwriting, and when speaking to the people, the army, or the senate, he carefully prepared written addresses, even though he possessed effective impromptu skills. He always gave the exact hour in his letters to show when they were written, and he did not carry superfluous letters from the end of one line to the beginning of the next, but wrote them just below the rest of the word.[110]

Literature, like all other avenues of influence in Augustus's life, served as a means for advancing dominion. After the assassination of Julius Caesar, Virgil and Horace both suffered loss as sons of Italian landowners.[111] During this era of great fear, from Caesar to Actium, Augustan literature is praised for its tranquility, poetic symmetry, and diminished contrasts, except in the contexts of civil war.[112] But just as Julius Caesar sought sole power, so also did Augustus, only through different agencies. He applied indirect strategies for conquest, strategies which did not produce jealousy, an emotion resulting in vengeance. Augustus's trusted friend and adviser, Maecenas, financially supported Virgil and Horace (beginning in 39 or 38 B.C.), and these poets developed alongside Augustus's rise to power. In the same way that Roman art, architecture, and culture subsumed Greek style to advance and renew Roman tradition during Augustus's reign, Latin writers such as Virgil and Horace participated in the *Princeps's* aim to surpass Greek literature, taking Latin literature to its highest level.

In some instances, poets were given a particular subject for composition; some pressure could have been applied in the interests of Augustus and the state, such as Horace's *Carmen Seculare* which was

---

110. App. *Civ.* 3.13; Suet. *Aug.* 54, 65, 85–87. He even read important conversations from manuscript to persons, such as his wife Livia, fearing that his message might be inappropriate in length.

111. Syme, 464–65; Suet. *Vita Verg.* 20. Wendell Clausen does not think Virgil suffers personally; "Theocritus and Virgil," 304.

112. Conte, *Latin Literature,* 250.

written for a specific festival. But for the most part, the term "propaganda" fits awkwardly, as Townsend points out that poets like Virgil may only have been "aware" of Augustus's ambition to recast the image of *Princeps* in a re-born Rome with moral renewal as a basis for the new age and an extended empire.[113] Yet, this modern view does not take into account Augustus's shrewd, calculated, and steady gains of imperial rights over the empire—his complete power over the army, the Senate, provinces, grain supply, coinage—in addition to the monopoly of political imagery celebrating his cause of peace. It seems to be more in line with Augustus's character to harness and guide the potential powers of nationalistic literature through passive-aggressive means. Conte makes an insightful point when he writes that the gap of Augustan propaganda can be measured between the Augustan poets and the *RG*—where Augustus is honored for his just wars against those who assassinated his adopted father and against those who threatened peace.[114]

Just as Agrippa served in an important administrative capacity for Augustus, so too did Maecenas serve Augustus concerning internal affairs. Augustus sought Maecenas's approval for plans, commissioned him for diplomatic visits, and asked him to act on his behalf to the populace in Rome.[115] A long-time close friend, Augustus would jokingly imitate Maecenas's way of saying certain phrases and often received comfort when he was ill by staying at Maecenas's home.[116] Augustus listened carefully to him, even when Maecenas advised to have his sister Octavia marry Antony. Until the end of Virgil's career, Maecenas remained an effective, committed servant of the emperor.[117]

It is not incidental that *pietas, religio, disciplina, fides,* and other Roman virtues are expressed through the mythological legend of Aeneas and Romulus for the purpose of advancing the state and foretelling the Golden Age of the future, an election to "faithful struggle."[118] Virgil's *Georgics* makes it clear that the past is still kept present in the minds of Romans (Book 1), showing support for Octavian's aims; not surpris-

113. Townsend, "Literature and Society," 910. Galinsky prefers the phrase "a complex mixture of tradition" rather than "propaganda"; *Augustan Culture*, 225.

114. Conte, *Latin Literature*, 251.

115. App. *Civ.* 5.99; Dio *Rom. Hist.* 51.1.5–6; and Nic. *Aug.* 30.

116. Suet. *Aug.* 66.3; 86.2–3.

117. Williams, "Maecenas," 258–75.

118. Galinsky, *Augustan Culture*, 118–19.

ing then is the horrific battle between the Trojans and Latins in Virgil's *Aeneid*.[119] Augustus discerned that the selection of interpretive lenses in which history was remembered greatly affected his sovereignty and the Roman establishment. In this case, understanding the "indirect" nature of Augustus is more important than debating the semantic difference between "influence" and "control." For poets like Virgil who supported his cause, Augustus motivated through positive means.

Virgil's Relationship to Augustus

Born in 55 B.C. in a small village near Mantua in the countryside of Italy, Publius Vergilius Maro first took an interest in poetry as a boy. Apparently, Virgil was raised in Cremona and after age fifteen moved to Mediolanum and then to Rome. Unfortunately, his parents and one of his brothers died in his early years. With a reticent personality, he did little to attract attention. Because of generous gifts from friends, he afforded a house in Rome near the gardens of Maecenas, though he often stayed in Campania and Sicily. He studied math, medicine, and law (but pleaded only one case).[120]

Before writing the *Aeneid*, he first wrote the *Bucolics* to sing the praises of the men who saved him from the veteran settlements of the *triumvirs* after the victory at Phillipi. He then wrote the *Georgics* in honor of Maecenas because of his assistance during Virgil's dispute with a violent veteran over Virgil's farm. Finally, he wrote the *Aeneid*, which mirrored Homer's poems, the *Iliad* and the *Odyssey*, for the purpose of giving an account of the origin of Rome and Augustus, using both Greek and Latin personages.[121]

After returning from Actium, Virgil read the *Georgics* to Augustus in his resonant, mellifluous voice for four days in succession. It was Maecenas who took turns with Virgil in reading whenever Virgil's voice became tired. At the beginning of Virgil's composing of the *Aeneid*, Sextus Propertius said, "Yield Oh Roman writers! Yield Oh Greeks! Something greater than the *Iliad* is born." When Augustus was away on

---

119. Conte, *Latin Literature*, 251.

120. Suet. *Vita Verg.* 1–2; 6–17.

121. Suet. *Vita Verg.* 19–21. The *Bucolics* (or *Eclogues*) is comprised of ten poems in hexameter (written between 42 and 39 B.C.); *Georgics* is comprised of four books in hexameter (29 B.C.); the epic poem *Aeneid* is comprised of twelve books in hexameter.

his Cantabrian campaign, he insisted that Virgil send him something from the *Aeneid*, the first draft or any section. When the poem had taken shape, Virgil read three of the books to him (the second, fourth, and sixth) whose inspiration greatly affected even Octavia.[122]

At age fifty-two, in 19 B.C., Virgil resolved to spend three years in Greece and Asia to complete the rest of the *Aeneid*, and then would dedicate his life to philosophy. But early on his journey after arriving in Athens, he met with Augustus who was returning to Rome from the East. Virgil did not wish to be away from the emperor and decided to return to Rome with him. But Virgil became deathly ill. During this time, he continuously requested that the books of the *Aeneid* be brought to him so that he could have them burned. Being a perfectionist, he did not want something published that was not in finished form. Virgil died before reaching Rome, and Augustus had Virgil's friends Varius and Tucca publish the *Aeneid* with only a few slight corrections.[123]

Augustus's relationship to Virgil epitomizes Augustus's relationship to the rest of his friends. He did not make friends hastily, but chose friends and associates who were fortunate and who aligned with the cause of the state. Virgil's relationship to Augustus might be described as "distant" and "involved"—distant from the bloodshed and depressing events during the political revolution and involved because his poetry gave a dimension of historical and moral profundity to the Emperor's aim of renewal and dominion.[124] The support of Virgil through Maecenas resulted in themes of laudatory praise offered unto Caesar Augustus. Virgil, like other poets, creatively and independently participated in the ideals and values of his time, conversing with elite artists over nationalistic and traditional issues, but Augustus set the tone, and it is certain that Virgil contributed to his cause.

---

122. Suet. *Vita Verg.* 27–32.

123. Suet. *Vita Verg.* 35, 37, 39–41. Virgil bequeathed half of his estate to his brother, one-fourth to Augustus, one-twelfth to Maecenas, and the rest to his friends, Varius and Tucca.

124. Dihle, *Greek and Latin* Literature, 31.

Summary

A socio-historical analysis of Caesar Augustus reveals three relevant conclusions which contribute to a better understanding of Augustus's relationship to Roman poets, particularly Virgil:

1. Caesar Augustus achieved and managed power at a level unprecedented in history;
2. his indirect methods of governing during peace time permeated all areas of the empire—political, religious, and social—including literature; and
3. he showed considerable faithfulness to his friends, one of whom was Virgil.

Just as the *paterfamilias* presided over all aspects of the home, so also Augustus ruled his empire. He harnessed all potential powers of government. The patterns of leadership exhibited by the young Octavian during political and military conflict readily transferred to similar patterns of control while serving as emperor during peace time. Augustus held everyone accountable—financially, morally, and politically. In this way, he detected rebellion or anti-sentiments early and eliminated them quickly if they posed a threat to his power. His ability to withdraw favor, resources, and to execute violence sent a dual message to all levels of society, "Nothing remains hidden," and at the same time, "No one receives glory except by the hand of Augustus" (leaving only Augustus to be heralded). Under Caesar Augustus's reign, virtue and nationalism became the political and social currencies. He limited the value of "self-glory" (behaviors that threatened his power) and consistently reinstated Roman virtue, such as the spiritual responsibility of duty (*pietas*). In this way, order was maintained. "Peace" meant "no war," but it also meant "submission." Through the complex web of patron-client relationships, exalting the emperor and making contributions to the state symbolically (and ceremonially) placed a person in right relationship with the gods. Another way to look at this social reality is to measure the degree of obsequious praise that a citizen or inhabitant generated and interpret it as an indication of his or her level of fear or their desire to gain approval. Augustus did not hide the fact that he championed a traditional cause that increased his *auctoritas*; rather, he effectively removed the appearance of domination and used positive manipulation to motivate, a method that far exceeded what had been offered in the past.

Virgil understood Augustus's needs. Not immune to the power of the *Princeps*, Virgil produced poetry which pleased the ruler. They both came from traditional backgrounds, and both lost parents and family members at a young age. In time, Augustus became more and more acquainted with Virgil and honored his talents. When Augustus encouraged Virgil to write a nationalistic epic which transcended Homer's great works, the challenge was both appropriate and a natural fit. Roman people enjoyed conquest and they interpreted their world in terms of their nationalism, their past in relation to their future. For Virgil to employ the limited, repetitive symbolism within the tacit guidelines of Augustus made sense, and Virgil's eleven years of literary work on the *Aeneid* demonstrated the significance of his task—to model Roman virtue for the empire, exceeding the Greeks, and to proclaim restoration, salvation, and peace through a promised, divine son.

2

The *Aeneid* as Epic History

> *Virgil can sing of Actium's shores that Apollo protects,*
> *and Caesar's valiant powerful fleet,*
> *who now brings to life the arms of Aeneas of Troy*
> *and the walls built on Lavinium's shores;*
> *Yield Oh Roman writers! Yield Oh Greeks!*
> *Something greater than the Iliad is born.*[1]

EPIC POETRY RETELLS THE PAST THROUGH MYTHOLOGICAL STORY. The poet reinforces a central theme by employing symbolic tools, such as repetition of action, and tells of a future connected to the past by including omens in the story, such as prophecies, dreams, and visions. This type of poem weaves a narrative tapestry which lauds a central hero and affirms the religious and political ideals of the ancient Greeks. Homer's epic poems, the *Iliad* and the *Odyssey*, established "heroic myth" as the epic subject matter for the centuries that followed.[2] The interrelationships and interactions between the gods and men became

---

1. Propertius Sextus 2.34.62–66.
2. H. L. Lorimer dates the composition of the *Iliad* in the eighth century B.C. with the composition of the *Odyssey* following sometime later; see Lorimer, *Homer*, 452–53.

a symbolic method of recording history.[3] At the time of the *Aeneid*, Homer's epics were considered the definitive source of cultural values for the Hellenistic world,[4] reinforcing the national identity of the Greeks.[5] So when Virgil decided to write his Roman epic, he not only imitated Homer's works, he aspired to surpass them.

This monumental challenge also involved assimilating the different elements of Homeric tradition.[6] In the centuries immediately following the *Iliad* and the *Odyssey*, feelings and ideas continued to find expression through heroic myth in the Cyclic Epics (e.g., *Thebais*, *Cypria*, *Aithiopis*, *Telogonia*, *Nostoi*), but this inspiration dwindled before 450 B.C.[7] Some time after the founding of Lyceum in Athens (335 B.C.), Aristotle attempted to save the epic genre from decline by discovering a "single core of significance" in Greek tragedy by identifying six basic components.[8] In the mid-third century B.C., the Alexandrian poets (most notably, Callimachus) maintained the subject matter of Homeric poetry but modified the standards of Greek poetry for the "serious" poets that followed.[9] Callimachus shortened the narrative portions of his epic, the *Aitia*, and introduced a more realistic, subjective approach, since he believed that imitation of the real Homer was impossible.[10] But Callimachus's rejection of the continuous epic did not hinder others from imitating lengthy episodes from Homer, such as the *Argonautica*, written by Callimachus's pupil, Apollonius Rhodius. About this same time, Naevius wrote the first Roman epic, *Bellum Punicum*, an unsophisticated historical epic, and more significantly, in the second century

---

3. Aristotle claims that ποίησις is more philosophical and profound than written history. Since the historian records what actually happens, which is in the realm of the particular, and the poet writes with regard to what might occur, which concerns the universal, the poet seeks a more noble aim; *Poet.* 1451b5–7.

4. Nagy, *Pindar's Homer*, 215.

5. Kirk, *Homer*, 3.

6. Virgil writes to Augustus, "... the subject on which I have embarked [the *Aeneid*] is so vast that I think I must have been almost out of my mind to have started it at all"; Macrobius, *Saturnalia* 1.24., trans. C. J. Emlyn-Jones. In Chisholm, *Rome*, F5.

7. Otis, *Virgil*, 9.

8. Halliwell, "Introduction," 12. For evidence supporting the date of the *Poetics*, see Appendix 1; ibid.

9. Otis defines "serious" as "intrinsically worthwhile" or "an available model for any later original poet"; *Virgil*, 8.

10. Ibid., 38.

B.C., Ennius sought to rival Homer with his retelling of the early legends of Rome.

At the time Virgil wrote his prophetic epic, which exalted Roman ideals and the emperor Augustus, the whole body of Greek myth had evolved into a "web" of endless characters and events.[11] Virgil, as well as other writers, evoked particular meanings by alluding to specific aspects of plots from other established epics. This meant that poets did not have to retell sections of the story but could employ an "economy of contexts" in which listeners could enjoy discerning the similarities and differences among stories and interpret the poet's message (much like interpreting the echoes of meaning within New Testament texts based on Old Testament contexts).[12] This philological challenge has created significant interest in the intertextual meanings of the *Aeneid*.[13] But making sense of the intricate web of possible word meanings behind the *Aeneid* does not serve as effective a purpose as does understanding the ideas and events that Virgil creatively intended based on his imita-

---

11. Lloyd-Jones, "Curses and Divine Anger," 14.

12. G. N. Knauer extends this analogy to show that Virgil has written an historical epic (not an aesthetic or literary interpretation) much nearer to Homer than the traditional Latin epic attempts concerning the rising of the new Troy (Rome): "It seems to me as if Vergil had understood the relation of his poem to Homer's epics in a way which can be compared to that of Christian exegesis in understanding the relation between the Old and the New Testament, namely by 'typology.' The Old Testament was understood as an account of real historic events which represent in an earlier stage the expectations of salvation which are fulfilled in the New Testament. The same event is repeated in the New Testament, only on another level, even by way of reversal . . . Of course eschatology for a Roman of this period could not mean the same thing as for a Christian; but it could mean the hope that now, at this very moment, in Augustus's and Vergil's lifetime, the Golden Age of Saturnus might return. Here, too, history is understood as a repetition of things past." "Vergil's *Aeneid*," 78–79. "Virgil" is the more common spelling for Publius Vergilius Maro, and it will be used in this study. The traditional spelling, "Vergil," is used in direct quotations from authors and when authors use this spelling in their books and article titles.

13. The list of articles and chapters written on the topic of intertextual and etymological wordplays in the *Aeneid* is extensive. Some of the more helpful works are listed below: Cairns, *Virgil's Augustan Epic*, 129–51; Cameron, *Callimachus*; Clausen, *Virgil's Aeneid*; George, *Aeneid 8*; Harrison, "Cleverness in Virgilian Imitation," 241–43. For less recognized similarities, see Hollis, "Hellenistic Colouring," 269–85; Hügi, *Vergils Aeneis*; Jocelyn, "Ancient Scholarship," 280–95; Maltby, *Lexicon*; Nelis, *Vergil's Aeneid*; O'Hara, *True Names*; Paschalis, *Virgil's Aeneid*; Thomas, "Callimachus," 1:197–225; and Wigodsky, *Vergil*.

tion of Homer's *Iliad* and *Odyssey*.[14] Furthermore, it is essential to keep in mind that Virgil incorporated a subjective purpose—to proclaim the Augustan gospel—which navigated the course of his unique poem.[15] Therefore, before an analysis of the structure, themes, and imagery of the *Aeneid* is undertaken (chapter 3), the general rules and concepts associated with the epic genre are explained, as well as the significant aspects of Virgil's technique in imitating Homer's *Iliad* and *Odyssey*, with specific attention given to Virgil's use of prophecy.

Aristotelian Rules of the Epic

For several reasons, Aristotle's collection of lectures on poetry, the *Poetics*, provides the modern interpreter with a systematic view of epic poetry. First, the *Poetics* is the earliest surviving work which exclusively discusses poetry as an art. Second, Aristotle places considerable importance on poetry as a means for influencing society. Third, his impact on Greek education and culture is universally recognized, and most relevant to this discussion, Aristotle avows that Homer demonstrates supreme poetic ability of *mimesis* in the tragedies, the *Iliad* and the *Odyssey*, and supports his claims with examples from these epics.[16]

---

14. "For the modern reader, to try and make sense of the *Aeneid* without continual recourse to Homer is like trying to read a code whose secret is lost"; Gransden, *Virgil's Iliad*, 4. The *Aeneid* is "first and foremost an *imitatio* of Homer's epics" which means that "the *Argonautica* cannot be taken seriously as essential anterior text" to the *Aeneid*; ibid.

15. For the significant works which advocate this view, Cairns, *Virgil's Augustan Epic*; and Hardie, *Virgil's Aeneid*. In contrast, scholars associated with Harvard take a more pessimistic view; see Clausen, "An Interpretation," 139–47; Lyne, *Words and the Poet*; Lyne writes, "The *Aeneid* probes, questions, and occasionally subverts the simple Augustanism that it may appear to project"; *Further Voices*, 212; and Putnam, *Poetry of the Aeneid*.

16. For the significance of Aristotle's work, see Halliwell, *Poetics*, 1–26; for Homer's superiority, see *Poet.* 1448b34–36; 1451a23; 1459a30–31; and 1459b13–17. For the influence of Aristotle on Virgil, see Stadler, *Vergils Aeneis*, 63–64; also see Heinze, *Virgil's Epic Technique*, 261, 348–49. Heinze's work has prompted other detailed studies; see Albrecht, "Zur Tragik von Vergils Turnusgestalt," 1–5; and Wlosok, "The Dido Tragedy," 4:158–81. For criticism of Heinze's use of the Aristotelian model, see Hardie, "Virgil's Epic Techniques," 269–71.

Mimetic Influence

Aristotle defines epic poetry as a type of *mimesis* (μίμησις) which imitates noble or ignoble action.[17] The poet focuses his artistic ability on three aspects of imitation: what is past or present, things said and thought, and things that are moral. This *"mimesis* of actions" is accomplished through plot structure with a didactic purpose. Aristotle taught that from early childhood people have an instinctive desire to learn, and they engage in *mimesis* (imitative behavior or "image-making") for the purpose of understanding. The learning process does not only involve the acquiring of scientific knowledge and art from universals but the gaining of knowledge through the experience of particulars. This means that the scripted actions of epic tragedy are ripe opportunities for influencing listeners. Aristotle describes this process as memories of the same thing which achieve the effect of one experience, and many experiences result in the acquiring of scientific knowledge and art. Thus, epic as art is created out of many impressions of experience (many episodes replete with action) which brings about one universal judgment.[18] In this manner, Virgil imitates Homeric poetry to actuate his listeners.

---

17. For μίμησις of noble and ignoble actions, see *Poet.* 1448b24–28. There is little doubt that Aristotle took the concept of μίμησις as the common character of ποίηκή from Plato; Else, *Aristotle's Poetics*, 12. However, Plato speaks against μίμησις for its potential to betray reality, affecting both the individual and the state; *Republic* 394d–398b, 605c–608b. He describes three modes of reality for an object: (1) the "idea" that is essential to nature, (2) the actual object made by the artist, (3) and the imitation or model of the object; *Republic* 597a–598d. For Plato, the idea is the higher form of reality, more so than the actual object, which means that the image (μίμησις) represents a distant reality. Where Aristotle encourages the evocation of intense feelings, such as pity and fear, through a constructed plot, Plato finds the emotional process to conflict with rationality. Consequently, Plato discourages participation in Homer's mimetic poetry because of the impairment of reason that suffering and pleasure could cause; *Republic* 602c–605c. It is not surprising that Plato promotes imitation that reinforces intellectual, moral behavior (see *Laws* 817), an aim that Aristotle achieves through different means.

18. Aristotle does not give a general orientation showing how the field of Poetics relates to other kinds and levels of knowledge, which means his other works (e.g., *De Anima*, *Metaphysics*, *Nicomachean Ethics*, and *Rhetoric*) provide helpful background; one must surmise the "forest" before settling "down in one corner to study the trees"; Else, *Aristotle's Poetics*, 2. For the three elements of μίμησις, see *Poet.* 1460b7–10; for μίμησις used for the purpose of understanding, see *Poet.* 1448b4–19. For Aristotle's view on the universal desire to learn, see *Metaph.* 981a1–8; for experience as means

The Aeneid *as Epic History* 43

Epic poetry has the same forms as tragedy does (such as simple plot, complex plot, characterization, pathos, thought, and diction), even though tragedy is not necessarily classified as epic material. Whereas tragedy is *mimesis* written in a variety of meter for theater performance with specific time limitations, epic poetry comprises several tragedies without time limitation, except for the fact that epic poetry should be written in fixed hexameter and able to be heard in one sitting. The benefit of writing different sections (epic poetry) gives the poet the opportunity to present more action, but also creates a challenge for the poet to achieve coherence from beginning to end. In other words, the length of the epic narrative and its capacity for simultaneous action generates greater significance than a tragedy performed on stage. Epic has merit for magnificence as long as the poet varies the content for his hearers and provides variety in the episodes.[19] Virgil imitates Homer's epics by writing several tragedies, coherently structured, without time limitation and in hexameter verse.

Yet, even though epic tragedies, such as the *Iliad* and the *Odyssey*, have many parts, they are structured as closely as possible to *mimesis* of a single action so that no event is missing and the whole is not disturbed or dislocated. For example, Aristotle describes the story of the *Odyssey* in a few sentences: "Guarded by Poseidon, a man travels for many years, and while away from home, his property is seized and his son is plotted against. After being shipwrecked, he returns home with some understanding and brings about his own deliverance by destroying his enemies." Aristotle says that the rest of the narrative is made up of episodes."[20]

In the *Odyssey*, Homer does not include all aspects of the hero's life but only those actions which might occur—actions with probable

---

of achieving scientific knowledge and wisdom, *Metaph*. 981a1–14; even so, Aristotle stresses that the wise person, the master of his art, is the one who knows the reason or cause for things.

19. For similarities and differences between epic poetry and tragedy, see *Poet*. 1449b8–20; 1459b28–30. Since many of the elements of tragedy apply to the epic genre, the term "epic tragedy" is used interchangeably with "epic" and "epic poetry" in this study.

20. For μίμησις of a single action, see *Poet*. 1455b12–23; 1459a16–1459b7; and 1462b1–15. Epic poetry is not concerned with individuation of actions; the "one action" excludes a sequence of unrelated events and the intertwining of layered subplots; Barnes, "Rhetoric and Poetics," 282.

and necessary connections. This method of retelling history involves the universal—what a certain type of person might say or do, rather than the particular—what a character did or experienced. Names are attributed to characters, and events are constructed to make the possible believable, which means that producing real events is not the objective. In essence, the rule of the poet is *mimesis* of actions accomplished through plot.[21] So also, Virgil first lays out the overall structure for the *Aeneid*, followed by the development of integral episodes.

Epic poets follow principles of coherency, size, and perceptibility. Aristotle defines size as beauty, order, and unity which is exhibited in the sequence of events. He reasons that a beautiful animal (or other object) has a structure of parts, but must also have beauty (magnitude, unity). Something small and imperceptible is not beautiful, and neither is something gigantic and out of proportion. This means that Virgil, like Homer, carefully selected the length of his epic, arranging multiple episodes with artistic balance, without dislocation, so that he might effectively influence his audience by a single transformational action.[22]

Literary Rules

In order to interpret the significant action in the *Aeneid*, certain literary terms and concepts related to plot composition deserve explanation. After relevant terms—the use of reversal and recognition, the emotional affectation of fear and pity, and the application of probability and necessity—are defined, an example of Virgil's plot construction is demonstrated in the story of Aeneas and Dido. This information leads to an understanding of Virgil's persuasive purpose.

---

21. For "probable" and "necessary," see *Poet*. 1451a36–1451b32; it might be helpful to understand "necessary" as that which ensues from preceding events, that which comes out of structure; see *Poet*. 1452a15–20. Aristotle does not suggest a hard fast rule of using familiar names, nor does he suggest always seeking traditional plots; see *Poet*. 1451b20–24; for *mimesis* of actions accomplished through plot, see *Poet*. 1450a–1451a32.

22. For coherency, proportion, and length, see *Poet*. 1450b38–40 and 1451a5–15, 33–35; for relationship between structure and sequence, see *Poet*. 1455a33–1455b2. In addition, epic tragedies have a complication which runs from the beginning until the part of the plot where there is a change to good fortune or bad fortune, and a denouement which runs from the change to the end; see *Poet*. 1455b1 and 1455b23–28. An "end" is needed in a tragedy, and the plot must not be unified around one individual; *Poet*. 1451a15–35.

Reversal and Recognition

Plot is the primary element of epic tragedy; character is a secondary element. Aristotle differentiates between two types of plot—simple and complex—based on the use of the literary technique of reversal and recognition. A "reversal" refers to an unexpected, opposite change of action in accordance with "probability" and "necessity" (these two terms are discussed in more detail below). For example, in the *Odyssey*, Agamemnon tests the commitment of his warriors and then decides to return home. Or in the *Aeneid*, Dido tragically falls in love with Aeneas, but later curses him and takes her own life. A "reversal" often involves another kind of change called "recognition," where a person comes to a new realization (moving from ignorance to knowledge). This awareness leads to either friendship or enmity, or to good fortune or bad fortune. For example, in the *Odyssey*, the Phaeacians remembered Odysseus (recognition); or in the *Aeneid*, Aeneas sees (recognition) the belt of a fallen comrade, Pallas, around the waist of his enemy, Turnus, and is moved to rage. Simply stated, actions based on good intentions and actions based on human blindness are more tragic.[23]

Recognition and reversal determine the type of action in an epic. Simple action is unified and does not include reversal or recognition (e.g., the *Iliad*). Complex action involves a major transformation, as well as reversal, recognition, or both (e.g., the *Odyssey*). Therefore, it makes a difference "when" the events occur (what happens before, on account of, or after their antecedents; τὸ γίγνεσθαι τάδε διὰ τάδε ἢ μετὰ τάδε). Aristotle estimates that the highest quality of recognition occurs when

---

23. For major elements and types of plot, see *Poet.* 1450a38–39; 1451a15–35; and 1452a10–1452b13. John Jones makes the distinction that "action" cannot mean "plot," since "action" is a "form" that the tragedian contemplates, preceding the composition; rather, "plot" comes to life during the process of composition as a type of *mimesis* of action; *On Aristotle*, 24–25.

Concerning Aristotle's literary design, William Greene contends that fate is not the dominating motive in tragedy; fate is in character. Thus, Aristotle compensates with the use of περιπέτεια (a reversal of fortune or situation)—"it is the outcome of an action which is the opposite of what was intended"; *Moira*, 92. With regard to "recognition," the aspect of intentionality is worth noting. Lock explains how recognition that is unintentional and contrary to expectation is more exemplary, as is the recognition in the *Odyssey* between Odysseus and Eurycleia (Book 19) in comparison to that of Odysseus and the swineherd (Book 14). He also emphasizes the close association of recognition with reversal where the turn of events causes an action and the consequences of that action completely overturn the agent's intentions; Lock, "The Use of Peripeteia," 251–53.

it happens simultaneously with reversal.[24] Since Virgil seeks to surpass Homer, the *Aeneid* integrates simple action and the complex action of recognition and reversal, a distinct feature of *mimesis*.

An epic with a complex plot, however, is not necessarily more tragic than an epic with a simple plot. The *Iliad* employs simple plot structure based on suffering, with limited recognition and reversal, and it involves the best tragic action. In the *Iliad*, tragic actions are carried out knowingly, and they are carried out in ignorance. In some cases a character may decide to do a terrible deed but, instead, comes to a realization of relationship (recognition) before acting it out. Aristotle finds the least tragic situation (no suffering) to be the one where the actor knows what he is about to do and does not carry it out. The next least tragic situation would be an actor who knows what he is doing and carries it out. However, the best kind of action involves an act done in ignorance followed by recognition, which produces amazement.[25]

From an overall perspective, the *Aeneid* itself is a type of reversal of Homer's epics. In the *Iliad*, the gods elect the Greeks as world rulers, evidenced in the destruction of Troy. In the *Aeneid*, the gods elect Trojan Aeneas (a minor character in the *Iliad*) and his descendants to establish a Latin nation. It is the Romans, not the Greeks, who will rule the world. In addition, Aeneas becomes aware of his divine destiny through various prophecies, conquests, and different events throughout his journey (types of recognition).

---

24. For reversal and recognition, see *Poet.* 1452a10–1452b9. Aristotle discusses several different kinds of recognition employed in epic tragedy and delineates which ones demonstrate artistic skill (a means of prioritizing tragic significance). The first three types of recognition show lack of skill and inventiveness: (1) recognition through signs which are often intrinsic, such as spears, stars, scars, or necklaces; (2) recognition that poets construct; and (3) recognition as proof (πίστις). Other types of recognition demonstrate greater skill: (a) recognition through memory (for example, a character hears a singer, remembers, and then weeps); (b) recognition which comes through reasoning (drawing conclusions based on correct premises) or deception (drawing conclusions based on false premises); and (c) the best recognition comes from the actions themselves which bring about amazement through probable sequence (a contrast to worked signs); see *Poet.* 1454b18—1455a20.

25. The second best structure recommended is the double structure, as in the *Odyssey*, with an opposite outcome for the best characters and the worst characters; *Poet.* 1453a30-33. For elements of suffering and tragic action, see *Poet.* 1452b10-13 and 1453b10-39.

FEAR AND COMPASSION

Epic action must also arouse the emotions. Suffering concerns destructive or painful actions, such as public deaths, excessive hurt, and woundings (these are replete in the *Iliad* and the *Aeneid*). Such undeserving situations arouse fear and compassion. The best method for affecting fear and compassion comes through the structure of actions (*mimesis* made evident in the events). Most importantly, epic tragedy concerns suffering among friends or between family members (e.g., brother and brother, son and father, mother and son, etc.), which usually involves killing or a similar action (an enemy fighting against an enemy does not arouse tender emotions except when there is suffering; neither is there compassion if the acts are between neutrals).[26]

The types of outcome which do not cause necessary fear or compassion in the listener are: (a) when a good person's circumstances change from fortunate to unfortunate; (b) when a bad person's circumstances change from unfortunate to fortunate; or (c) when an extreme fall from good fortune to bad fortune occurs. What is left from the above three situations is that which is in between (ὁ μεταξύ). This kind of person (similar to the mathematical term "mean") does not have character of great virtue or righteousness (δικαιοσύνη), nor is this person evil or

---

26. For Aristotle's discussion of fear and pity, see *Poet.* 1453b1–25; for definition of suffering, see *Poet.* 1452b8–13. For a summary of main presuppositions shared by most writers on the subject of "fear and pity," see Else, *Aristotle's Poetics*, 226–27. Aristotle does not provide a formal definition of κάθαρσις (the concept of a change of feeling within the listener which emotionally purifies) in the *Poetics*. He expresses himself more clearly in his *Politics*; see 1341b36–1342a16. For a more thorough discussion of κάθαρσις, see Golden, *Aristotle*, 5–39. For Aristotle, enjoyment is the primary purpose of epic poetry, even if the emotions are difficult to feel; *Poet.* 1448b8–19. Yet in the Augustan age, poetry was seen as an elementary philosophy which instructs—pleasurably—in regard to character emotion and action; Jebb, *Growth and Influence*, 257.

According to Aristotle, only those destructive relationships between family are appropriately tragic (γένος, *Poet.* 1453a11 and 1454a9; οἰκία, 1453a18 and 1454a12). Belfiore explains the important political connection of Aristotle's use of φιλία, a central concept in Greek tragedy. The term φιλία is associated with blood relationship or marriage, and since humans are political beings with a need to live in community, such relationships are essential. Consequently, φιλία equates to good fortune, and loss of φιλία is pitiable; Belfiore, *Tragic Pleasures*, 73. "Thus, tragedy, because it imitates actions within *philia* relationships, teaches us about our nature as human beings. An understanding of imitation and *philia* is fundamental to an analysis of Aristotle's view on plot structure and emotional arousal"; ibid., 82. For Aristotle's use of φιλία, also see Else, *Aristotle's Poetics*, 349–52, 378.

bad. Rather, the person's circumstances change to misfortune or change to good fortune (a single change) due to some kind of error or mistake in judgment (ἁμαρτία). For example, in the *Iliad*, Patroclus dies because he did not listen to Achilles' warning. In the *Aeneid*, the queen of Carthage lied to herself concerning her commitment to her deceased husband when falling in love with Aeneas.[27] Before analyzing Virgil's epic strategy in this account of Dido's tragic mistake, the terms "probability" and "necessity" need to be explained.

Probability and Necessity

Following the Alexandrian tradition, Virgil incorporates epic methods which are similar to Aristotle's theory on "probability" and "necessity." Even though Aristotle is ambiguous in his use of these terms, his definitions are useful to a discussion of Virgil's technique.[28] An important connection exists between the meaning of "necessity" in the *Poetics* and Aristotle's view of human nature in his other works. In *Metaphysics*, Aristotle defines "necessity" as that which is needed to live or that which is necessary for the good. In this sense, "necessary" means preservation (eating, sleeping, reproducing). "Necessity" also includes those activities that create and preserve "political" relationships, such as threats to family relationships, because they are necessary to life. Harm to a family member will, by necessity, lead to bad fortune once it is recognized. On the contrary, recognizing one's family responsibility will lead a person to avoid a terrible event (suffering) which then results in the enjoyment of good fortune.[29]

"Necessity," in other words, is that which comes about through force or by human nature. These actions contrast the freedom to choose.

---

27. For "mistake" (or "error") in tragedy, see *Poet.* 1452b30–1453a10; for moral speech, see *Poet.* 1454a15–27. Aristotle instructs against irrational elements in actions (events); *Poet.* 1454b6. In his *Nicomachean Ethics*, Aristotle reiterates this literary principle when he says that a person should aim for the "mean" which is a mark of virtue; 1106b5–23.

28. Only in the *Poetics* does Aristotle link "probability" with "necessity," and not without difficulties; see O'Sullivan, "Aristotle," 9–63.

29. For the universality of "probability" and "necessity," see *Poet.* 1451b8–10. A consequence of loyal family ties is preservation (σωτηρία); see *Pol.* 1253b1–2; 1276b28–29. For clarification on familial threats in tragedy, see Belfiore, *Tragic Pleasures*, 114–19. For definition of "necessity," see *Metaph.* 1015a20–33; also, for "necessity" as a fact of human nature, see *Rhet.* 1.10.7–18; *Pol.* 1252a26–30; and *Nic. Eth.* 1135b20–22.

For example, in the *Aeneid,* Rome's political destiny is determined by the gods (necessary action) dependent upon Aeneas's faithful service (creating literary tension between choice and necessity). This distinction raises the issue of whether acts done out of anger or other natural emotions are considered necessary to fulfill political purposes (such as Aeneas's rage against Turnus in the final passages of the *Aeneid*).

In addition to "necessity," all poetry must include "probability." The principle of probability belongs primarily to rhetoric. Its application in the *Poetics* is more similar to persuasion than instruction, which makes the subject philosophical.[30] For Aristotle, artificial proofs through the construction of enthymemes make the practitioner a master of the art. Enthymemes depend on probability. They are more than "forensic pleading"; they are an "indispensable instrument of the science of ethics."[31] This kind of reasoning does not depend on "necessary" types of facts, since most decisions come from alternative possibilities, and since actions have a contingent character. Tragedy shares the orator's reliability on probability, which distinguishes him from the historian.[32] In epic poetry, probability determines plot structure, controls character development and thought, and provides the best kind of recognition.

In essence, the truth of poetry is different than the truth of fact. "Things that are outside and beyond the range of our experience, that never have happened and never will happen, may be more true, poetically speaking—more profoundly true than those daily occurrences which we can predict with confidence."[33] In epic poetry, the poet skillfully tells stories of fantastic deeds and strange happenings while blending facts of real events. S. H. Butcher describes the essence of this persuasion in the phraseology of the Poetics, ". . . the ἄλογα (the impossible or what is improbable to the reason) are so disguised that they become εὐλόγα: the ἀδύνατα, things factually impossible in fact, become πιθανά, and therefore δυνατὰ κατὰ τὸ εἰκός ἢ τὸ ἀναγκαῖον."[34]

---

30. The theory of emotions seems to have been developed for rhetorical purposes where the scope is broader than it is in the *Poetics*; Hutton, "Introduction," 21.

31. Eden, *Poetic and Legal Fiction*, 18–19.

32. Ibid. For construction of enthymemes, see *Rhet.* 1.1.3–11; for probability of enthymemes as part of ethics, see *Rhet.* 1.2. All poetry must include "probability"; *Poet.* 1451a36–38.

33. Butcher, *Aristotle's Theory*, 171.

34. Ibid., 173. While it is commonplace from Aristotle onwards that the elements of

When interpreting epic poetry, the reader should not look for the tragedy that plays out the change of a virtuous man brought from prosperity to adversity (this is not tragedy) nor look for the downfall of the villain (this does not inspire pity or fear).[35] Rather, the reader should look for the potential of tragedy in a character who is between two extremes—a man who is not eminently good and just, yet whose misfortune is brought about by some error or frailty (ἁμαρτία), and not brought about by vice or depravity.[36] This is the artistic device in which action is brought to a crisis.

Tragic Dido

Virgil scripts the actions and words of Aeneas and Dido (Books 1–4) as part of his larger singular plot to influence his listeners toward a universal message of Rome's promised age of peace. Here the literary and historical past connect to the present as the noble and ignoble actions of the Carthaginian queen and the Trojan prince unfold. A discussion concerning the relationship between these two main characters serves the purpose of illustrating the epic techniques outlined above, and it provides important background for the main themes that follow (in Books 5–8), which include other key tragic characters (such as Turnus in Books 9–12).[37]

In his invocation to the muse (1.1–11), Virgil prophesies the destiny of Aeneas, that he would lead a remnant to found a Latin nation which would one day defeat Carthage. This African city stands at the mouth of the Tiber river, at the port of the future site of Rome. The goddess Juno favors Carthage above all other cities, and against the will of Jupiter, she desires that Carthage become the ruling city of the world (1.17–23).[38] Providence determines Aeneas's journey, as evidenced in

---

tragedy can be found in the *Iliad*, it is important to note that these elements are the "result of the natural instinct of the story-teller to tell his story . . . guided by an ill-defined awareness . . . of the pathos inherent in human suffering"; Quinn, *Virgil's Aeneid*, 325.

35. Greene, *Moira*, 93–94.

36. Ibid. Also see Lucas, *Tragedy*, 91–96.

37. It is important to clarify the nature of epic poetry so that an effective comparison can later be made to possible tragic aspects of Paul's message to the Romans. One should not dismiss too quickly the possible connections of Paul's literary style to tragic elements—undeserved suffering, fear, compassion, φιλία, etc.

38. Carthage and Rome were rivals (264–146 B.C.).

Jupiter's sending the god Mercury to ensure Aeneas's safe welcome at Carthage. Aeneas's mother, the goddess Venus, also prophesies a positive reception. In contrast to the Dido legend, but remaining consistent with epic tradition, Virgil does not portray Dido as unjust, nor is she depicted as an enemy (1.503–08):[39]

> *talis erat Dido, talem se laeta ferebat*
> *per medios, instans operi regnisque futuris.*
> *tum foribus divae, media testudine templi,*
> *saepta armis solioque alte subnixa resedit.*
> *iura dabat legesque viris, operumque laborem*
> *partibus aequabat iustis . . .*

> Such was Dido, who carried a joyous countenance
> among them, attending to the work of her future kingdom.
> Then at the door of the goddess, under the arch of the temple,
> surrounded by arms and upon a raised throne, she took her seat.
> She rendered justice and laws to men; she apportioned their work
> with equal justice . . .

To ensure their success, Venus sends Cupid in Aeneas's place to facilitate Aeneas's relationship with Dido. Consequently, Dido throws a banquet for Aeneas (and for the remnant from Troy) and asks him to tell her about their wanderings. Aeneas shares his story with her (the content of Books 2 and 3).

In Book 4, it becomes apparent that Dido has fallen in love with Aeneas, despite her sincere commitment as a widow not to remarry. With Juno and Venus supporting their union (*et conscius Aether conubiis*, 4.167–8), the Queen and the Trojan consummate their relationship during a thunderstorm. Dido interprets their relationship as marriage and falsely anticipates that the two will reign together (4.169–73):

> *ille dies primus leti primusque malorum*
> *causa fuit. neque enim specie famave movetur*
> *nec iam furtivum Dido meditatur amorem;*
> *coniugium vocat; hoc praetexit nomine culpam.*

---

39. Initially, Virgil describes Dido's background through the words of Venus, specifically about the circumstances surrounding the loss of Dido's husband and Dido's rise to power (1.340–41). More importantly, Virgil emphasizes Dido's royal status in Book 1 (303, 340, 389, 454, 496, 522, 563, 572, 594, 631, 637, 660, 674, 686, 697, 717, and 728); Cairns, *Virgil's Augustan Epic*, 2.

> That day—the first of death, the first of woes—
> was the cause. For she is neither moved by appearance or fame
> nor does she consider a secret love;
> she calls it marriage; with this name she covers her sin.

Dido had broken her vow to the gods not to remarry after her husband's death.

After hearing about this, Jupiter commands Aeneas to sail for Italy. Aeneas plans a clandestine departure, but the impassioned Queen finds out, and in her unreasonable rage (*saevit inops animi*, 4.300), she begins to accuse Aeneas for his wicked, cruel, and treacherous motives. For the grieving Aeneas, duty comes first (4.393–96):

> *At pius Aeneas, quamquam lenire dolentem*
> *solando cupit et dictis avertere curas,*
> *multa gemens magnoque animum labefactus amore,*
> *iussa tamen divum exsequitur classemque revisit.*

> But pious Aeneas, though he desired to soothe her grief
> by consoling her and alleviating her anxiety,
> with much lamenting, his soul weakened by mighty love,
> he obeyed the divine command with great loyalty and returned
>   to the fleet.

Dido's sadness overwhelms her. She expresses her guilt, "I have not kept the faith promised to Sychaeus' ashes" (*non servata fides cineri promissa Sychaeo*, 4.552).[40] She interprets her fate as retribution for her sinful deeds (*facta impia*, 4.596), for violating her own honor (*pudor*, 4.27). After Aeneas sets sail at night, Dido curses him and threatens to respond in violence. Instead, she kills herself with a sword that Aeneas had given her.[41]

---

40. N. Rudd's survey of Roman literature from Virgil's era (70–20 B.C.) shows that the attitude of the Roman people was disapproval for a widow to remarry; "Dido's Culpa," 155–59. Dido violates her conscience.

41. Dido's betrayal and humiliation cause her death, which means that she dies before her time with a proud but rational heroic attitude; ibid., 162. In contrast, N. M. Horsfall argues that Dido's expressions of violence, greed, duplicity, and hatred are linked by Virgil to the old hatreds of the Punic wars; Horsfall, "Dido," 127–44. Similarly, Brooks Otis views Dido as realizing the "criminal folly" for her deed; *Virgil*, 84. Fowler notes that Dido's death as a consequence of abandonment diverges from the popular legend to introduce an artistic element of pathos (alluding to Julius' escape from Cleopatra). Jupiter, ruler of the Fates and the Roman destinies, and Venus, the reputed progenitor of the Julian family, rescue Aeneas, something Augustus wanted to

Unknown to Dido, the gods had actuated her falling in love.[42] At the human level, Dido made the mistake of not being honest with herself concerning marriage; she could have put *pietas* or *pudor* before infatuation and resisted more successfully.[43] Her situation unexpectedly changed from passionate love to doubt and enmity (reversal) with a simultaneous awareness (recognition) concerning her error in judgment (ἁμαρτία), part of a carefully structured complex plot.[44] In Book 4, her blindness intensifies the emotional effect, which means that the conclusions she draws about Aeneas are based on improbability (false premises). This single change from ignorance, followed by recognition, brings about fear, pity, and amazement among the listeners of the *Aeneid*, producing the best type of epic tragedy. Later, Virgil makes this clear when Aeneas, in the underworld, shows compassion for Dido because of fate's dealings (6.475-6):

> *nec minus Aeneas, casu percussus iniquo,*
> *prosequitur lacrimis longe et miseratur euntem.*

> Nonetheless, Aeneas, having been shaken by the injustice
>   rendered her,
> followed from a distance with tears and pitied her as she left.

For Dido, her violent act results from a broken relationship (φιλία). The literary tension exists because of the consequences caused by the decisions of the gods (Juno and Venus) and Dido's unmerited destiny and passion (*nam quia nec fato, merita necmorte peribat, sed misera*

---

be preserved in the tale; Fowler, *Religious Experience*, 414-17.

42. Tension exists in that Dido is unaware that her love is caused by Venus' substitution of Cupid for Ascanius (1.657-60).

43. Quinn, *Vergil's Aeneid*, 325. Based on Aristotelian and Hellenistic theoretical writings on the subject, A. Wlosok emphasizes the Dido story and its paradigmatic nature as a tragic episode within an epic; Wlosok, "The Dido Tragedy," 159. Wlosok makes four points concerning the development of Dido's character: (1) she deceives herself and clings to this illusion (4.316, 338f, and 496); (2) she shows no comprehension of Aeneas's mission and rejects his obligation to obey *fata*; (3) none of the speeches refer to Dido committing a fault (even though that *pudor* has been betrayed, this counts as a responsible sacrifice made for Aeneas); and (4) although death runs through the whole discussion, there is no mention of suicide (death is an external threat from her enemies); ibid., 169-70.

44. Wlosok divides Book 4 into five dramatic parts. Interestingly, he outlines an "outer reversal" (4.296-449), and with Dido's decision to die, an "inner reversal" (4.450-583); ibid., 176.

ante diem subitoque accensa furore, 4.696–97). For Aeneas, the temptation to remain in Carthage threatens his future. His political destiny is providentially determined (necessary action) but dependent upon his faithful service (tension between choice and necessity). Aeneas's fault is his delay of the mission (4.224–25), but at the end of Book 4 he makes the correct decision. In this sense, he is not a tragic figure but a "non-tragic" foil.[45]

Evidently, Virgil intends this episode of the *Aeneid* to challenge the audience's perceptions of what "faithful" and "unfaithful" mean. The Romans during Augustan times believed in innate ethnic characteristics, and historically the Carthaginians were known by the Romans for being unfaithful to their word, barbarously cruel, and disrespectfully sacrilegious.[46] Dido accuses Aeneas of several negative attributes which were Roman stereotypes for Carthaginians.[47] In Book 4, Dido stresses Aeneas's perfidious nature most as one who breaks his agreements. At this point in the story, sympathy increases for Dido. But by the end of Book 4, Virgil balances the characteristics of Dido and Aeneas (employing the "mean") which allows the audience to feel and question the meaning of faithfulness.

Books 1–4 express continuous action for Aeneas. In recounting to Dido the events surrounding the fall of Troy, Aeneas tells her of his desire to die rather than leave without his father Anchises (2.567f.), so as not to fail in his Roman duty (*pietas*).[48] For his mission would have no value if he were to desert his father. Thus, Virgil sets forth an intense familial conflict between what Aeneas and his father see as most important.[49] Aeneas perseveres, and while carrying his father on his shoulders (Anchises holds the sacred Penates), Aeneas leaves holding his son's right

---

45. Ibid., 180.

46. Starks, "*Fides Anneia*, 255. *Fides Punica* became synonymous for faithlessness; see Livy, *Hist. Rom.* 22.6 and 30.30.

47. Starks lists these: *perfidus* (4.305, 366, 373, and 421), *crudelis* (4.311, 661), *durus* (4.366, 428), *improbus* (4.386), *superbus* (4.424), *ferus* (4.466), *impius* (4.496, 596), *nefandus* (4.497), *periurus* (4.542), and *infandus* (4.613); ibid., 63. Starks also discusses the reversal (or transference) of stereotypes concerning Punic effeminacy (4.140–50) and the lack of religious and filial piety (4.598). Moreover, it is interesting that Antony accused the young Octavian of effeminacy early in Octavian's rise to power; see Plut. *Ant.* 3–4.

48. No family or gods exist without *patria*; Otis, *Virgil*, 244–45.

49. Ibid., 245.

hand.[50] Meanwhile, Creusa, Aeneas's wife, dies (2.766) which begs the question as to who his new wife will be. This bond between father and son (2.701-3) fulfills the *Iulius* dynasty that Jupiter prophesied about concerning a predestined kingdom (1.267-71) which is confirmed by Apollo's prophecy concerning the dominion of the House of Aeneas (3.97-98).[51] As Aeneas tells Dido his history, he also lets her know of his awarded title *pius* (3.393), and he recognizes the formal nature of the justice of the claim in his response to her (4.354-55).[52]

It is not surprising then that Virgil portrays Aeneas as the "good king."[53] Three of the ideal monarch virtues are ascribed to him—*iustior*, *pietas*, and courage (1.544-45):

> *rex erat Aeneas nobis, quo iustior alter*
> *nec pietate fuit, nec bello maior et armis*
>
> Our king was Aeneas, no one more just
> or devoted than he, nor greater in war and arms

Francis Cairns keenly observes the omission of two virtues, self-control and wisdom, which Aeneas's character lacks in Books 1-4, but attributes that he will eventually gain. Still, Aeneas is portrayed as the "salvation" of his people and the "noble father of the Roman people" (*sin absumpta salus, et te, pater optime Teucrum*, 1.555). His appearance is godlike, an inheritance from his mother Venus (1.588-93),[54] and he obeys the will of Jupiter, seeking royal destiny.

In contrast, Dido starts out as a "good king" but fails in the end.[55] Virgil does not make an implicit judgment about love; rather, he dis-

---

50. It is evident here that Virgil portrays Aeneas as the father of a nation and the personification of Rome.

51. Eidinow notes the legal context where the failure of Aeneas's mission is seen by the gods as reason for disinheritance; Eidinow, "Dido," 260-67. Mercury gives Jupiter's command to move on (4.272-76), and Mercury refers to Iulus as Aeneas's heir (a precise expression for kingdom succession in Italy and used only twice, 4.274 and 7.424); ibid.

52. Ibid.

53. Aeneas is *Teucrorum . . . regem* (1.38), he reigns over Latium (1.265), he is king of the Trojan remnant (1.544 and 575), and his gifts are *regia* (1.696); Cairns, *Virgil's Augustan Epic*, 4.

54. Possibly, this is a reference to Octavian; see Suet. *Aug.* 79.2.

55. Cairns uses the term "good king" synonymously with "good queen," *Virgil's Augustan Epic*, 54-55.

tinguishes between a good and bad kind of love (one which leads to self-control and the other to irrational, destructive behavior).[56] Dido seeks honor in her marital love for Sychaeus (1.343–52, 4.38–39), and at the same time she seeks honor in her relationship with Aeneas (4.18–19). Apparent to Virgil's audience, Dido's irrational love for Aeneas increases, an amour regarded by the ancients as "a spiritual disease, a form of madness akin to other passions such as greed and anger . . . a dangerous, anti-social and censurable affliction even in an ordinary citizen."[57] Virgil contrasts Dido's personality with Aeneas to persuade his audience to believe in the more excellent Roman ideals.[58] Furthermore, the character distinction between Dido and the "good king" Aeneas prepares Virgil's audience for another moral comparison of "kings" (Aeneas and Turnus in Books 9–12), imagery that reinforces Virgil's imperial message.

Homeric Borrowing in the *Aeneid*

Aeneas's actions provide a unique sequel to the story of the *Iliad* (the fall of Troy in the *Aeneid* was only revealed through prophecy in Homer's epic), and the *Aeneid* connects with the *Odyssey* in part (Aeneas encounters similar adventures of Odysseus). In this way, Virgil repeats the experience of the epic cycle, a chain of epic narratives that combine Homer's poetry into "a sort of continuum."[59] Not only does Virgil continue Homer's mythological story, he imitates, reduces, and transforms much of Homer's material for a nationalistic emphasis. Because the meaning of the *Aeneid* involves both general and specific semantic connections to Homer's epics, a brief discussion of Virgil's technique is needed. This will provide important background for the analysis of the *Aeneid*'s main themes and imagery (chapter 3).

---

56. Dido was not the only heroine in Hades who died from love; see 6.440–41.

57. Cairns, *Virgil's Augustan Epic*, 56. A decade before Virgil began writing the *Aeneid*, two rulers, like Dido, brought destruction through "love"—Antony and Cleopatra; ibid., 57.

58. Williams, "Purpose of the *Aeneid*," 36.

59. Conte, *Latin Literature*, 277.

Specific Homeric Context

Virgil transforms large Homeric passages by quoting one or more Homeric verses with exactness so that his listeners recognize the passage and its Homeric context. The similarity of the situation draws upon the Homeric constructs in the listener's mind. This means that an obvious quotation needs to be reviewed to determine whether it is a *Leitmotiv*, or whether detailed imitations are neglected.[60]

Virgil's catalogue of ships in Book 7 of the *Aeneid* is an example of his specific use of Homeric context from Book 2 of the *Iliad* which provides a clue to Virgil's structural transformation. Knauer discusses how Virgil chooses the Trojan War as a pattern from *Iliad* 2, "imitating the whole rather than just selecting the catalogue as an epic ingredient."[61] In Book 1 of the *Iliad*, Agamemnon realizes through a dream that Zeus restores Achilles's honor, a pattern that Virgil uses for the Allecto and Turnus's dream scene (the dreams result in military build up). In the *Iliad*, the army retreats to the ships for the purpose of sailing home. Hera intervenes by asking Athene about Helen, and Athene stops the army. The catalogue of ships follows. In a similar manner that Zeus is detoured by Hera through Athene, so also in the *Aeneid*, the Juno-Allecto scene (Book 7) parallels the Juno-Aeolus scene (Book 1).[62] Hera and Juno cannot alter fate. They both refer to the causes of war (Helen and Lavinia), they send their aides (Athene or Allecto), and in both epics, a military build-up follows.[63]

General Homeric Context

In response to the "intolerable situation" in Virgilian scholarship concerning the inconsistent parallels and comparisons between the *Aeneid* and Homer's epics, G. N. Knauer collects all available commentaries and monographs (from Servius to the twentieth century) to show how Virgil incorporates the whole *Iliad* and the whole *Odyssey* into the *Aeneid*.[64] Overall, Virgil transforms the Homeric epics by reducing,

---

60. Knauer, "Vergil's *Aeneid*," 67.

61. Ibid., 74.

62. Both stem from a scene from *Odyssey* 5 and both are similarly structured to the Hera-Athene scene in the *Iliad* (see 2.155–68); ibid.

63. Knauer, "Vergil's *Aeneid*," 75.

64. Ibid., 61–84. For helpful general works on this subject, see Schlunk, *The Homeric*

combining, and selecting passages from the *Iliad* and the *Odyssey* while incorporating various ancient interpretations of Homer (especially the allegorical explanation of the Stoics), to elevate the Romans over the Greeks.[65]

Virgil shortens the Homeric narratives.[66] For example, Virgil reduces four books of Odysseus's narrative (Books 9–12) to two books in the *Aeneid*, but he maintains the proportion to the whole poem. This means that the *Aeneid* is almost one-third the size of the *Iliad* and the *Odyssey* (approximately 9,900 verses compared to 27,800 verses). Common to the *Aeneid* are other combinations, such as the typical "god assemblies" in Homer (at the beginning of books 4, 8, and 20) which Virgil composes in only one scene in Book 10. In addition, while some passages retain Homeric length, such as the games for Anchises (*Aen.* 5) or Aeneas's *katabasis* (*Aen.* 6), Virgil often mingles or contaminates parallel passages, as he does when he combines Telemachus's visit to Nestor at Pylos (*Od.* 3) and Menelaus's visit at Sparta (*Od.* 4 and 15) into Aeneas's one visit to Evander's Pallanteum (*Aen.* 8).

Virgil also combines Homeric characters into one:[67] Odysseus, Telemachus, and Achilles are united to create Aeneas. Arete, Alcinous, Circe, Calypso, and Medea are combined to create Dido. Helen and Penelope are combined to create Lavinia; and Virgil's character Elpenor becomes three of Homer's characters—Palinurus, Misenus, and Caieta.

Conte notes that Virgil's complex arrangement of the Homeric models has no parallel; overall, he inverts the order of the Homeric content.[68] The first six books involve Aeneas's journey from Carthage to Latium while also telling the circumstances of Troy which led up to Carthage (an intended imitation of the *Odyssey* where "destroyers"

Scholia; Clausen, *Virgil's Aeneid*; Wigodsky, *Vergil and Early Latin Poetry*; and Barchiesi, *La Traccia del Modello*. The complexity in this area of intertextuality in the *Aeneid* is great, with scholars differing in their meaning of "reference," "intertext," "alusion," etc. For relevant discussions on this topic, see Conte, *Virgilio*; Conte and Segal, *The Rhetoric of Imitation*; Farrell, *Vergil's Georgics*; Preminger, ed., *The New Princeton Encyclopedia*, s.v. "allusion" and "intertextuality"; and Hinds, *Allusion and Intertext*.

65. Knauer, "Vergil's *Aeneid*," 81–82. Although the *Aeneid* is written in the tradition of the annalistic-historical epics of Naevius and Ennius, Virgil has made an epic much nearer to Homer than the traditional Latin epic attempts; ibid.

66. Ibid., 64–65.

67. Ibid., 67.

68. Conte, *Latin Literature*, 277.

return home). The last six books reflect points of reference in Homer's *Iliad*, where the city is razed as Virgil's account begins preparations of war with the Trojans at the Tiber (7.42) and ends with Turnus's death.[69] Generally speaking, Books 1–6 of the *Aeneid* are the "Virgilian Odyssey," because Virgil first analyzed the plan of the *Odyssey* and made it the base of his poem, but it is more difficult to make clear the correspondence of Books 7–12 to the *Iliad* and other parts of the *Odyssey*.[70]

It seems, however, that something more than Homer's "heroic myth" drives the plot of the *Aeneid*. R. D. Williams notes some of the basic distinctions between Virgil's two main sources—the Homeric poems and Augustan Rome.[71] In Book 1, Aeneas parallels Odysseus (based on the episodes and speeches from *Odyssey* 5–8), but the unique difference between the *Aeneid* and the *Odyssey* is that the *Aeneid* embraces the new while the *Odyssey* maintains the old. For example, the character Odysseus tries to return home, whereas Aeneas seeks to build a new life in a new home. The great individualist, Odysseus, achieves his goal only after losing the "lesser" men; however, Aeneas leads his men safely home to a life of responsible community.[72] Aeneas's character gradually develops from a valiant, impulsive Homeric hero to a leader who learns his mission (from his father, Book 3; from Mercury, Book 4, from Jupiter and Nautes, Book 5; and a vision in Book 6),[73] gaining the virtues of a Roman leader.[74]

Virgil's Nationalistic Context

Comparing the *Iliad* or the *Odyssey* with the *Aeneid* and noting the differences serves a fruitful task, but this kind of study has "the disadvantage of concentrating attention on what Virgil did to Homer rather than on the much more important matter of what Homer did to Virgil."[75] In other words, Homer is the necessary model, but his heroic epics come

69. Ibid.
70. Knauer, "Vergil's *Aeneid*," 396–410.
71. R. D. Williams, "Purpose of the *Aeneid*," 27.
72. The few parts in Book 1 of the *Aeneid* without Odyssean sources are those concerning the gods (Juno, Jupiter's prophecy, Venus, and Cupid); ibid.
73. Ibid.
74. Richard Heinze lists some of these: *clementia* (12.940), *virtus* (12.435), *fides* (12.311), *pietas* (10.516), and *iustitia* (11.126); *Virgil's Epic Technique*, 166.
75. Otis, *Virgil*, 221.

later in the genesis of the *Aeneid*. Virgil starts his epic composition with a system of Augustan symbols in mind which drives the organization of the plot. This "symbol complex" is the "'real' plot . . . the formation and victory of the Augustan hero [Aeneas] . . . the *theios aner* (the man who achieved divine status) of Roman tradition who actually belonged to the Homeric saga."[76] Aeneas represents the Stoic ideal, a model of *pietas* and sacrifice, more than he models the Homeric attitude.

Even before Virgil began to write the *Aeneid*, he disclosed his purpose of writing a nationalistic epic praising Augustus. In the *Georgics*, Virgil speaks of himself when he says that he will be the first to lead the Muses when he returns to his home to build a marble temple in honor of Caesar (*Georg.* 3.10–39). Virgil tells of his plans to place Caesar in the center with games, gifts, and honors to be given to him. Virgil does not promote an Augustan monarchy, for this would go against Augustus's policy, but he praises the emperor for delivering Italy from her troubled times toward universal peace—a nationalistic and patriotic emphasis.[77] The mood of the times and certain passages in the *Aeneid* point to the conclusion that the *Aeneid* is a Romantic national epic. As Norden articulates it, the idealized past forms a complete whole with the present—a grand sequence of prophecies, expectations, and fulfillment unfold according to plan, uniting beginning and end. The ancients held to this circular philosophy of life in which a new age repeats the events from an earlier age. During the Age of Augustus, heightened expectations arose out of the chaos of civil war. In the center of the old cycle stood Aeneas, and in the new stood his descendant Augustus, the spiritual focus of the story.[78]

76. Ibid., 222.

77. Georgi, *Die Politische Tendenz*, 31.

78. Norden, *Kleine Schriften*, 397: "in dem die Gegenwart mit den leuchtenden Farben einer idealisierten Vergangenheit umkleidet, die Vergangenheit selbst in die Gegenwart hineinprojiziert wird, so daß die römische Geschichte als ein großer, aus Verheißung, Erwartung, Vorbereitung und Erfüllung planmäßig sich zusammenschließender Kreislauf erscheint, in dem Anfang und Ende unterscheidungslos sich vereinigen. Diese Vorstellung, die uns vielleicht fremdartig berührt, war für antikes Denken unmittelbar gegeben. Denn daß der Gang der kosmischen und politischen Verhältnisse gewaltigen Kreisen von bestimmtem Umfang gleiche, und daß daher von Zeit zu Zeit ein neuer Weltlauf mit genauer Wiederholung des früheren eintrete, war eine seit Jahrhunderten bei Griechen und Römern feste Anschauungsform, von der gerade auch das Zeitalter des Augustus beherrscht wurde: denn die unnatürliche Störung der normalen Verhältnisse durch das Chaos der Bürgerkriege schien im

Such an aim sets Virgil apart. The fulfillment of the promise in Augustus, the descendent son of God, proves that the gods helped Rome survive and that Roman history repeats itself—Latium might experience again the Golden Age which had been known at the time of Saturn (*Augustus Caesar, Divi genus, aurea condet saecula qui rursus Latio regnata per arva Saturno quondam*, 6.792–94).

Virgilian Poetry as History and Prophecy

Virgil employs prophecy on different levels to communicate his message. On a literary level, the characters and gods in the *Aeneid* speak deceptively, often withholding information to achieve their purpose as part of the mythical story. On a historical level, Virgil weaves mythological and historical material through the prophecies of characters and gods concerning Aeneas's journey to Italy and the founding of the Italian nation. On a futuristic level, Virgil foretells the reign of Caesar Augustus and the dominance of imperial Rome by making a direct and present address to his audience as a *vates*.

The Poet-Prophet

After Aeneas leaves the underworld and sails for the shores of Italy, Virgil introduces himself into the epic as a *vates* (a poet-prophet). By doing so, the poet brings the mythological story to a new level (7.40–41, 44):

> *expediam, et primae revocabo exordia pugnae,*
> *tu vatem, tu, diva, mone. Dicam horrida bella . . .*
> *maius opus moveo.*
>
> I will explain, and I will recall the opening of the first battle.
> Instruct your poet, Oh goddess. I will sing of horrible wars . . .
> I will begin a greater work.

Concerning the destiny of Rome, Virgil's prophetic messages apply to an immediate audience, those listening to the reciting of his epic poem.

Vates refers to the poet's inspirational gifting as bearer of truth, but the term also carries the connotation of hiddenness, mysticism, or even

---

Verein mit furchtbaren Prodigien den Beweis zu liefern, daß der alte Kreislauf beendet sei und eine Periode der Regeneration beginne . . . Im Zentrum des alten Kreises hatte Aeneas gestanden, in dem des neuen stand sein Nachkomme Augustus. Seine Person bildet daher den geistigen Mittelpunkt des Gedichts auch da, wo er nicht unmittelbar genannt oder indirekt bezeichnet ist."

deceit. In the *Aeneid*, the use of *vates* refers, at times, to messengers or prophetic messages that often do not tell the whole truth (e.g., 4.65, 5.636, and 7.435–42). It is likely that an Augustan poet, such as Virgil, used the unreliability of the *vates* to influence society by expressing hope through less certain means, an attractive type of persuasion that resembles love poetry.[79]

Scenes of prophecy or omens have recurring features in the *Aeneid*. James O'Hara lists these (though not all of these occur in any one scene):

1. a description of setting and mood (usually discouragement) preceding the prophecy;
2. a claim of divine authority;
3. a qualification of the prophecy (which often adds an element of doubt);
4. a call to action (often with the omission or hidden reference of a death to one individual, or some other discouraging event);
5. a sign or partial fulfillment of the prophecy;
6. a prayer or sacrifice of acceptance by recipient;
7. the resulting mood of the recipient.[80]

While the prophecies that Aeneas hears seem encouraging at first, the messages tell him what he needs to know so that he continues on with his mission. However, the prophetic words are questionable. In fact, these deceptive prophecies cost him the lives of those closest to him (e.g., Orontes, Palinarus, Anchises, and Pallas). Repeatedly, Fate brings about success at the price of the death of an individual, and death is omitted from the optimistic prophecy.[81] For example, in a carefully structured speech, Venus tells Aeneas that he and his companions will land safely as the north winds turn (1.390–91), but she does not include the information about Juno's wrath and the death of Orontes and his men.

Achates recounts Venus's prophecy to Aeneas, reminding him that one ship was lost and not all safely landed (1.582–85). It seems that a fulfillment of "most" of the prophecy gives credence to Venus's "optimistic

---

79. O'Hara, *Optimistic Prophecy*, 177, 181.
80. Ibid., 14–15, 54–60.
81. Ibid., 9, 53.

view of the situation."[82] In other words, prophecy for the gods becomes a form of rhetorical discourse; they downplay the negative.[83] In this case, Venus tells Aeneas that he is not hated by the gods (1.387–88).[84]

This kind of deception parallels Roman aristocracy where religion was used to control the public in a way similar to the gods in the *Aeneid*. But it seems likely that in the Augustan age, the role of the *vates* changed some. The poet played a significant role in shaping the morals of society,[85] and the inspired poet was considered the mouthpiece of the Muses, the guarantor of truth.[86] In the *Aeneid*, Virgil was the "guarantor and spokesman" for Aeneas's mission which was willed by Fate for the foundation of Rome and its salvation by Augustus.[87]

Virgil's Historical Prophecy

In the *Iliad*, most of the prophecies center on Achilles, a hero whose tragic fate is determined. Likewise in the *Odyssey*, the prophecies tell of the victorious fate of the tested hero. But in the *Aeneid*, the poet employs prophecy for three distinct purposes: he must bring Aeneas to Italy (prophecies in Books 1–5), give him a secure foothold there (prophecies are interwoven with Books 1–5 and find their climax in Sibyl's words, 6.83–97), and foreshadow future Rome (prophecies in Books 1–12).[88] These Virgilian prophecies, particularly those which promote an Augustan gospel, provide insight into Virgil's specific aims.

Established Italian Remnant[89]

In Book 1, through what Juno has heard, the reader learns of a promised, victorious Trojan race. A race will descend from Trojan blood, a

---

82. Ibid., 12.

83. The speeches of the gods are seldom wholly accurate, with Venus appearing no less cunning and cruel than Juno; see Highet, *The Speeches*, 259–76.

84. Aeneas is also told falsehoods and half truths by Cruesa, 2.783; Helenus, 3.438–9; Apollo, 6.345–56; Tiberinus, 8.40–41, 60–61; Cymodocia, 10.244–45; his mother, 1.387, 390; 8.522–36; and by his father Anchises, 6.760–66; O'Hara, *Optimistic Prophecy*, 12.

85. Newman, *Concept of Vates*, 15–16.

86. Thomas, "The Place of the Poet," 114.

87. Conte, *Latin Literature*, 283.

88. Moore, "Prophecy," 99–175.

89. Few prophecies in the *Aeneid* speak to individuals. Moore lists these: Neptune

people ordained by Fate, who will rule as triumphant kings (1.19–22). After enduring considerable hardship and being driven by a storm to Carthage, Aeneas encourages the remnant from Troy. He tells them that Jupiter has a purpose for them to reach Latium, a place of rest (1.199–205), and that Troy's kingdom will rise again (*illic fas regna resurgere Troiae*, 1.206). With compassion for her son, Venus questions Jupiter concerning the disasters which Aeneas and the Trojans have faced and calls for Jupiter to be true to his promise (1.234–37):

> *certe hinc Romanos olim volventibus annis,*
> *hinc fore ductores, revocato a sanguine Teucri,*
> *qui mare, qui terras omnis dicione tenerent,*
> *pollicitus* . . .
>
> Surely, the Romans hereafter, as the seasons change,
> will rise as leaders, restored from the Trojan race,
> who have dominion over sea and over all of the land,
> as you have promised . . .

In disguise, Venus then tells Aeneas of Dido's past and questions him about his journey and direction. Calling himself "*pius* Aeneas," he informs his mother that he is known in the heavens (1.378–79), and that his Italian race descends from Jupiter (*Italiam quaero patriam et genus ab Iove summo*, 1.380).

During the banquet which Dido hosts for Aeneas and his people (Books 2 and 3), Aeneas tells her that Hector's spirit was the one who warned him to flee Troy with the Penates, and it was Hector who presaged that Aeneas would sail the ocean to establish a mighty city for holy purposes (2.289–97). Aeneas also shares with Dido the time that his wife's spirit alerted him to his future mission to Italy, where prosperity, kingship, and a royal wife will be provided for him (*illic res laetae regnumque et regia coniunx parta tibi*, 2.783-4). Another supernatural moment occurs when he seeks Apollo's wisdom concerning the place where he should lead his people to settle. Apollo tells him to search out his ancient mother (3.97–98; 102–5):

---

foretells the fate of Palinurus, 5.813–15; Latinus is warned of a great war, and he is told not to marry his daughter to a Latin but to look for a son-in-law from abroad, 7.64–80, 96–101, 253–58, and 268–73; the death of Turnus is foretold, 10.606–7; ibid., 138. Moore's outline is generally followed in this section.

The Aeneid as Epic History 65

'hic domus Aeneae cunctis dominabitur oris,
et nati natorum et qui nascentur ab illis' ...
tum genitor, veterum volvens monumenta virorum
'audite, o proceres,' ait, 'et spes discite vestra.
Creta Iovis magni medio iacet insula ponto,
mons Idaeus ubi et gentis cunabula nostrae.

Here the house of Aeneas will rule over all the earth,
and his children's children, who will be born from them ...
Then my father remembering the memorials of the old men, says:
"Listen Oh nobles and learn of your hopes.
Crete, an island of great Jupiter, lies in the middle of the sea,
the place of Mount Ida, and the cradle of our race."

Aeneas continues to narrate his travels in the presence of Dido, the queen of Carthage. He tells her about his voyage to Crete and the strong winds behind their sails. After enduring a drought, the images of the gods (the Penates from Troy) appeared to Aeneas in a dream to tell him that he must move to a new home, a place rich in soil and powerful in arms, a land called Italy (3.147–48).[90] Aeneas realizes that these prophetic words repeat an earlier prophetic message given to his father Anchises (3.182–91). Aeneas and his ships set sail, but after being hurled off course, they are forced to land on islands in the Ionian sea. Here the dreaded Calaeno prophesies that Aeneas will successfully reach Italy by sea, but that the walls of the promised city will not be built until violence and hunger cause them to "eat their tables."[91] As they continue their wanderings, they encounter a prince from Troy named Helenus, who is a prophet and interpreter for the god Apollo. Helenus forewarns of specific challenges and gives detailed directions for Aeneas's mythological journey, especially to visit Apollo's prophetess, Sibyl, who will grant them a prosperous voyage and reveal the wars to come and the future of the nation of Italy (3.374–462).[92]

The banquet ends and Dido has fallen in love. Aeneas's relationship with Dido delays his mission, but he remains faithful to the will of

---

90. A parallel prophecy occurs in Book 7. When the Trojans first seek alliance with King Latinus, he remembers this tale but adds that a heavenly appointed ruler, one from the Trojan race, will increase the altars of the gods (7.205–11).

91. After arriving in Italy, the food-cakes and bread that Aeneas and his men eat resemble those of tables. They rejoice at the fulfillment of this prophecy as Heaven's will and a sign that they are home (7.105–35).

92. In Book 6, Sibyl guides Aeneas in the underworld of Hades.

Jupiter and sails for Italy (Book 4). Acestes, a fellow Trojan, welcomes Aeneas and the remnant to Sicily, where athletic contests are held in honor and in memory of Anchises (Book 5). After the games, Aeneas finds out that some of his ships were set on fire, but he is comforted by the aged Nautes, "Whatever comes, fortune is to be overcome by endurance" (*quidquid erit, superanda omnis fortuna ferendo est*, 5.710).[93] Soon, Anchises's spirit from heaven visits Aeneas, encouraging him to follow the advice of Nautes. Anchises also informs Aeneas that he will encounter a hard and rugged people when he subdues Latium (*gens dura atque aspera cultu debellanda tibi Latio est*, 5.730) and that he must follow Sibyl to find him in the underworld (Anchises dwells in Elysium, a place of blessedness, 5.724–45).

Historical Imperial Rome

Virgil uses the device of prophecy, rather than narration, to retell the history of Rome in the *Aeneid*. At the beginning of the poem, the reader learns that Juno favors Carthage, an ancient city lying opposite of Italy (1.12–13). The goddess has heard about offspring from Trojan blood, a people proud in war and ordained by Fate, who would bring Libya to ruin (1:19–23). Again Virgil refers to the age-old rivalry of the Punic Wars when the disheartened Dido prays for endless hate between Carthaginians and the Italian race (4.628–29): "May shores come against shores, waters against waters, I pray, arms against arms; and may their descendants war in battle" (*litora litoribus contraria, fluctibus undas/ imprecor, arma armis; pugnent ipsique nepotesque*). (Later, Virgil scripts Jupiter, who had called a council of the gods, as prophesying the second Punic War,[94] where Carthage will unleash destruction on the Roman strongholds, resulting in immense hatred, 10.11–14).[95]

---

93. These words embody the two Roman virtues that will make Rome great—*pietas*, obedience to duty, and *constantia*, firmness of purpose; Moore, "Prophecy," 137.

94. This is most likely a reference to Hannibal's invasion of Italy in 218 B.C.

95. It is possible, too, that Octavian's founding of Nicopolis correlates to Aeneas's words about Epirus and Italy. They are "sister cities and allied peoples" (*cognatas urbes olim populosque propinquos*, 3.502) who have the same ancestors and share the same misfortune. Aeneas says, "we will make one Troy in spirit. May that charge await our children's children" (. . . *unam faciemus utramque Troiam animis; maneat nostros ea cura nepotes*, 3.504–5). In addition, Virgil uses the poetic pictures on Aeneas's shield to portend the soldiers of Gaul (the Gauls attacked the Roman capital in 390 B.C.) who laid siege, shielded by darkness, to the Roman city (8.655–62).

Also in the opening book of the poem, Venus, Aeneas's mother, petitions Jupiter on behalf of the Trojans, the future Romans. She questions Jupiter's plan of allowing them to endure hardship while being kept away from Italian shores (1.229–53). Jupiter declares that the Romans would be "rulers of the world, people of the toga" (*rerum dominos, gentemque togatam*, 1.282), and that the Trojan race would subdue and dominate Greece (*cum domus Assaraci Pthiam clarasque Mycenas servitio premet ac victis dominabitur Argis*, 1.283–85).[96] In this proclamation of universal rule, Jupiter also pronounces the reign of Augustus.

Emperor Augustus

Responding to Venus's concern for her son and the Trojans, Jupiter assures the goddess that he has not changed his mind. Jupiter foretells that Aeneas will be victorious in battle, crush the proud nations, establish laws, build city walls, and reign for three years (1.263–66). Then Julius will reign for thirty years and build the walls of Alba Longa, followed by three-hundred years of unbroken Trojan rule (1.267–73). At this time, a royal priestess will bear twin offsprings to Mars, one of whom, Romulus, will found a city called Mars, named after his father, and thereafter his descendants will be called the "Romans" (1.273–77). Jupiter then prophesies (1.286–96):

> *nascetur pulchra Troianus origine Caesar,*
> *imperium Oceano, famam qui terminet astris,*
> *Iulius, a magno demissum nomen Iulo.*
> *hunc to olim caelo, spoliis Orientis onustum,*
> *accipies secura; vocabitur hic quoque votis.*
> *aspera tum positis mitescent saecula bellis;*
> *cana Fides et Vesta, Remo cum fratre Quirinus*
> *iura dabunt; dirae ferro et compagibus artis*
> *claudentur Belli portae;*

> From this distinguished lineage will be born the Trojan Caesar,
> who will limit his imperium with ocean, his glory with the stars,
> called Julius, a name descending from the magnificent Iulus.
> Him to the heavens, bearing Eastern spoils;
> you will safely receive; he will also be invoked with vows.

---

96. Greece became a Roman province in 146 B.C. In the above Latin citation, *Assaracus* refers to the Trojan race and Roman descendants; *Phthiam*, *Mycenas*, and *Argis* refer to Greece.

> Then bitter ages will soften when wars have been put aside;
> venerable Faith and Vesta, Quirinus with his brother Remus,
> will give laws: with iron and tightly fitted bars, the dreadful
> gates of war will be shut....

The gospel of peace comes through the mouth of Jupiter.

The next explicit Augustan text occurs at the end of the first half of the *Aeneid*. In the underworld, Aeneas's father (Anchises) reveals to his son the Roman kings and heroes, especially Caesar Augustus (6.791–95, 850–54):

> *hic vir, hic est, tibi quem promitti saepius audis,*
> *Augustus Caesar, Divi genus, aurea condet*
> *saecula qui rursus Latio regnata per arva*
> *Saturno quondam, super et Garamantas et Indos*
> *proferet imperium....*
>
> *tu regere imperio populus, Romane, memento*
> *(hae tibi erunt artes) pacique imponere morem*
> *parcere subiectis et debellare superbos.*

> This man, this is the one whom you hear so often promised to you,
> Caesar Augustus, the descendant of God, who will establish again a Golden Age in Latium, in lands formerly governed by Saturn,
> who will extend his empire beyond the Garymantian and Indian peoples....
>
> Oh Rome, remember to rule the nations by your authority;
> These will be the arts for you: to establish the order of peace,
> to spare the humble and war against the proud!

The third and final prophecy which directly refers to Octavian Augustus is pictorial. The goddess Venus, Aeneas's mother, brings a gift from heaven, a shield fired by the god of fire, telling the prophetic story of Italy and the age to come (8.626–28). In the center of the shield are the brazen ships of the battle of Actium, with Augustus Caesar leading his people, bearing the great gods of the Penates, with flames coming from his joyous brow and the radiance of his father's star upon his head (8.675–77). The battle against Antony and Cleopatra is vividly depicted (8.678–713) with Octavian triumphant (8.714–23):

At Caesar triplici invectus Romana triumpho
moenia, dis Italis votum immortale sacrabat,
maxima ter centum totam delubra per urbem.
laetitia ludisque viae plausuque fremebant;
omnibus in templis matrum chorus, omnibus arae;
ante aras terram caesi stravere iuvenci.
ipse, sedens niveo candentis limine Phoebi
dona recognoscit populorum aptatque superbis
postibus; incedunt victae longo ordine gentes,
quam variae linguis, habitu tam vestis et armis.

But Caesar passed through the gates of Rome in triple triumph,
and offered to the Italian gods immortal sacrifices:
three hundred grand temples throughout the city.
The streets resound with noises of joy, games, and praise;
in all the temples was a chorus of matrons, in all were altars;
and slain bulls were strewn across the land before the altars.
Caesar himself, seated in the brilliant, snow white gate of
    Apollo,
accounts for the gifts of the nations and hangs them on the lofty
posts. The conquered peoples march on in long array,
as diverse in languages as is their customs of dress and arms.

In the final passages of the *Aeneid*, Juno cedes to Jupiter's will but petitions him to have the Trojan races keep "Latins" as their name (12.823–28). Jupiter grants Juno her request (12.838–40):

hinc genus Ausonio mixtum quod sanguine surget,
supra homines, supra ire deos pietate videbis
nec gens ulla tuos aeque celebrabit honores.

From hence you will see a mixed race arise from Italian blood,
which will surpass humankind, and surpass the faithfulness of
    the gods,
nor will there be any nation that will equal the celebration of
    your honors.

Summary

Before the main themes and relevant imagery of Virgil's epic tragedy can be extracted (for the purpose of a comparative analysis to Paul's formal letter to the *Romans*), several approaches must be taken into consideration when interpreting the message of the *Aeneid*. First, the nature and symbolism of the Homeric myth must be understood in light of its repetitious, singular action, lauding a religious, political hero. Second, important aspects of the epic genre—such as reversal, recognition, and emotional aim—clarify meaning, which warrants analysis. Third, through prophecy, Virgil uniquely links the epic past to the Augustan present and embeds key passages within his story to foretell Rome's future, an imperial proclamation of lasting significance.

Virgil writes to influence his audience toward a moral purpose. The actions of the characters in the *Aeneid* center around a single action so that the audience learns through imitation. The action of the *Aeneid* might be described as, "Aeneas leads a remnant from fallen Troy through different wanderings to reach Italian shores to establish a nation." An audience of epic poetry listens for single changes in the action that include aspects of probability (things that might occur) and necessity (circumstances of the characters in which there is no control). More importantly and in accordance with epic form, Virgil scripts his main characters (Aeneas, Dido, and Turnus) so that they move from adversity to prosperity or from prosperity to adversity (a single change) because of some mistake or error. The tragic action of the Carthaginian queen, Dido (Books 1 and 4) provides an example of how the epic produces an emotional learning event for the listener.

Aeneas's actions provide a unique sequel to the story of the *Iliad*, and the *Aeneid* links with the *Odyssey* in part. Thus, Virgil repeats the experience of the epic cycle (the chain of epic narratives that combine Homer's poetry) which means that relevant *leitmotifs* of Homer warrant explanation. But Virgil first bases the direction and shape of his moral epic around Augustan symbolism and themes for the Augustan hero—a θεός ἀνὴρ and sacrificial servant of *pietas*.

As a poet-prophet, Virgil introduces himself as both a truth-bearer and truth-withholder. As a voice of traditional poets, his inspiration involves a "mystical hiddenness" and uncertainty not unlike the political use of religion in Augustan Rome. As the voice of the Augustan gospel, his message speaks directly to his Roman audience, a guarantor of truth; he is the spokesman for Aeneas's mission—the foundation of Rome.

3

The Salvific Message of the *Aeneid*

From this distinguished lineage will be born the Trojan Caesar, who will limit his imperium with ocean, his glory with the stars . . .

Caesar himself, seated in the brilliant, snow white gate of Apollo, accounts for the gifts of the nations.[1]

DESCRIBING HIMSELF AS A POET-PROPHET (*VATES*), VIRGIL BEGINS his poem by seeking the muse of poetry for inspiration. Confirmed by the will of the gods and revealed through prophecy, the Romans will one day defeat Carthage, and Aeneas's descendant, Caesar Augustus, will fulfill the promise of establishing peace among the nations. In the first half of the *Aeneid* (Books 1–6), Virgil narrates Aeneas's past, which leads to a *katabasis* into the underworld, where Aeneas experiences rebirth and renews his commitment to his divine mission. In the second half of the *Aeneid* (Books 7–12), Aeneas and his fleet sail to Italy and establish a Latin nation, ensuring Rome's destined future. After reviewing key elements of the structure and style of the *Aeneid*, significant themes and imagery for the two main divisions of Virgil's poem will be discussed.

1. *Aen.* 1.286–87; 8.720–21.

Structure and Style of the *Aeneid*

Virgil composed his poem, an eleven-year task, with an intricate design of coordinated elements and aesthetic symmetry on a grand scale. The poet imitated Homer's epics, aiming to surpass them. This means that he incorporated the improvisational *oral* elements of Homer's poetry, but also increased the involvement of the listener through vibrant *written* language, enhancing participation through metaphor, description, imagery, and dialogue.[2]

General Overview

At a higher level in the *Aeneid*, the omnipotent god Jupiter acts with justice, order, and peace, a god whose words are always true. Venus petitions her father, Jupiter, on behalf of her son, Aeneas, and seeks to protect him. In contrast, the goddess Juno acts out of jealous wrath and destruction to hinder Aeneas's mission. This opposition is also played out on a smaller level between Neptune, the god of the sea, who shows favor to Aeneas, and Aeolus, the god of the winds, who works closely with Juno.[3]

The first half of the *Aeneid* (Books 1–6) narrates the wanderings of Aeneas from Troy to the Latin shores. In Book 1, Jupiter reassures Venus with prophecies concerning her son's trials, and he facilitates Aeneas's safe and welcomed arrival at Carthage. Dido, the majestic queen of Carthage, honors Aeneas and his people with a banquet. In Books 2 and 3, Aeneas recounts for Dido the Trojan war and his difficult travels, which evidence his election as the father of a nation.[4] In Book 4, Dido's love for Aeneas increases, and with Juno and Venus in agreement with

---

2. Out of the many different stylistic devices that Virgil employs, these aspects were chosen based on their possible relevance to a discussion on Paul's letter to the Romans.

3. See *Aen.* 1.52–53 and 1.124–25.

4. Hundreds of years before Virgil wrote the *Aeneid*, a legend tells of a Trojan ruler named Aeneas (see *Il.* 20.307–8). As evidenced in art and literature during the first century, the Romans trace their Italian origins from both Greek and Trojan war heroes. A common pictorial image has Aeneas fleeing burning Troy with his father Anchises on his back. Although the legend and the *Aeneid* reference the land of Latium, the Trojan Romulus was known as the founder of Rome, not Aeneas. When Virgil links Aeneas's son, Iulus (*gens Iulia* family), to Julius Caesar and his adopted son Augustus, a "sense of completion" occurs; Conte, *Latin Literature*, 279.

the relationship, Dido and Aeneas consummate their love. Jupiter hears about this and commands Aeneas to sail for Italy. He obeys. Distraught and hurt, Dido curses Aeneas and kills herself. The grief in the story intensifies as Aeneas's father Anchises dies also. In Book 5 (an interlude), Palinarus, the lead helmsman, advises Aeneas to land at Sicily because of a storm. Upon arrival, sacrifices are made, and games of celebration are begun in honor of the one-year anniversary of Anchises's death. Juno then stirs up dissension among the Trojan exiles. Pious Aeneas listens to his father's word in a dream (to meet him at the Elysian Fields) and sails toward Italy. Tragically, Aeneas's helmsman, Palinarus, dies at sea. In Book 6, Aeneas and the remnant arrive in Italy and offer appropriate sacrifices. In his visit to the underworld, he meets Dido, Palinarus, and other souls. He soon crosses the river, Styx, passes by warriors and sinners, and then comes to the Elysian Fields where the righteous exist. Here, Aeneas's father tells him about his future descendants and the destiny of Rome, culminating in the reign of Augustus Caesar.

Books 7–12 take place in Italy, and the narrative tells of Aeneas's conquest of Latium, the future site of Rome. In Book 7, King Latinus, a descendant of Saturn (father of Jupiter), welcomes Aeneas and offers his daughter Lavinia to him in marriage, because the king believes in a prophecy that foretells that his daughter will marry a foreign prince of destiny. Juno stirs up hatred (through Allecto from Hades) by inciting Queen Amata and the citizens of Latium against Aeneas in favor of Turnus, king of the Rutulians. In Book 8, Turnus leads the Italians and the Greeks against Aeneas. Evander, the king of a small Greek community (and former ally of Priam, the king of Troy), his son Pallas, and the newly liberated Etruscans unite with Aeneas. While Aeneas and Pallas are on their way to review the Etruscan troops, Aeneas is supernaturally awarded a splendid and miraculous shield from his mother that depicts the glories of Rome.

In Book 9, Turnus wars against the Trojan troops while Aeneas is away, causing considerable loss. In Book 10, Jupiter calls a council to ensure that destiny is not altered. Juno protects Turnus, though Jupiter warns the goddess that Turnus will die. In battle, Turnus kills Pallas, King Evander's son, and takes his weapon belt. In Book 11, Turnus plans another attack but retreats after hearing that Aeneas and the Etruscan armies are approaching. In Book 12, Lavinia is promised to the winner of the duel between Turnus and Aeneas, but after a spear is thrown into the enemy camp, war is incited, resulting in enormous bloodshed. An arrow wounds Aeneas, and his mother Venus helps heal the wound. Thinking that Turnus is dead, Queen Amata commits suicide. In the final duel, Turnus throws a large stone at Aeneas and misses, and Aeneas wounds Turnus with a spear. Seeing the sword belt of Pallas around Turnus's waist, Aeneas kills Turnus out of rage.

Symmetrical Structure

The structure of the *Aeneid* can be divided into two parts which correspond to Homer's epics—Books 1–6 as the Virgilian *Odyssey* and Books 7–12 as the Virgilian *Iliad*.[5] But a division just as viable is the tripartite division which contrasts the tragic nature of three main characters of the *Aeneid*—the tragedy of Turnus (Books 9–12) paralleling the tragedy of Dido (Books 1–4) with the middle section accenting Rome's destiny through Aeneas (Books 5–8).[6] From a thematic perspective, this division is also useful for understanding the relationships between the Virgilian characters and the gods. In addition, Virgil probably chose to alternate the intensity of his books—the odd numbered books provide dramatic relief for the more intense even-numbered books.

Two other symmetrical propositions seem possible. A basic model compares the parallels of Books 1 and 7, 2 and 8, 3 and 9, 4 and 10, 5 and 11, and 6 and 12. But more likely, Virgil alternated his books around Book 7, a pivotal section integrating Augustan symbolism (Books 6 and 8 are Roman, 5 and 9 are interludes, and Books 1–4 and 10–12 involve the secondary heroes of Dido and Turnus).[7] In particular, Professor Otis argues that Virgil organized his poem around Book 7 to show the inner struggle and spiritual rebirth of Aeneas (and Rome).[8] This theme of resurrection connects the *Aeneid* to Virgil's other works. In the *Georgics* and the *Eclogues*, an evil past opposes the new hope which is embodied in the savior, Caesar-Octavian, who "represents the principal resurrec-

---

5. The second half of the *Aeneid* corresponds to the first half based on a number of parallels; see Conway, *Harvard Lectures*, 139; and Duckworth, *Structural Patterns*, 2–3.

6. Duckworth, "*Aeneid* as a Trilogy," 1–10; and Pöschl, "Poetic Achievement," 290–99. Galinsky sees Book 5 as introducing the "central and most important triad of the epic"; Galinsky, "*Aeneid* 5," 165.

7. See Camps, "A Note on the Structure," 214–15.

8. In this case, Virgil combines Stoic and religious elements; Otis, *Virgil*, 215–17.

tion and rebirth."[9] The central "death-resurrection" motif of Book 7 of the *Aeneid* corresponds to a similar death-resurrection motif (a journey to and from the underworld) in the pivotal portions of the *Eclogues* and the *Georgics* (i.e., *Eclogue* 5 and *Aristaeus*). In the *Aeneid*, Books 1–6 narrate the Odyssean preparatory half, and Books 7–12 reveal the Iliadic fulfillment.[10] Most importantly, Books 6 and 8 show a close, direct relationship with Book 7.[11] In this case, unworthy love and destructive *furor* are overcome through moral action by a reconsecrated and resurrected hero (much like the *Eclogues* and *Georgics*), and in the case of this nationalistic narrative, "inward" struggle represents the Roman-Augustan ideal accomplished by a divine-hero.[12]

For the purposes of this study, the general division of Books 1–6 and Books 7–12 serves as an overall outline for discussion, while the tripartite division (Books 1–4, 5–8, 9–12) is referenced for the purpose of highlighting significant themes and imagery, especially concerning the key character relationships between Dido, Turnus, and Aeneas. And since Virgil embeds and aligns the gospel of Caesar in and around Book 7, important Augustan themes are clarified with this central pattern in mind.

---

9. Ibid., 216.

10. A deliberate parallelism between 1 and 7, 4 and 10, 5 and 9, and 6 and 8 is "quite-unmistakable" with each culminating in a revelation about the future of Rome; ibid., 217.

11. Otis views the alternating contrast of intensity in the first six books ("light" in Books 1, 3, and 5; "dark" in Books 2, 4, and 6) as leading up to the rebirth motif in Book 7; *Virgil*, 218. From a thematic perspective, the death-resurrection theme in Book 6 transitions from the defeat, passion, and uncertainty of Books 1–5 into the victorious nature of Books 8–12; in Book 4, Aeneas escapes his own indignant passion (his own and Dido's); and in Book 10, Aeneas is victorious and shows his reverence for the dead (Pallas); in Book 2, Aeneas recounts the fall of Troy which antithetically parallels the new kingdom in Book 12; and furthermore, in Books 1–5, Aeneas falters, needing Jupiter and Anchises; in Books 8–12, Aeneas never loses courage or resolution; ibid.

12. Aeneas's *katabasis* makes true the θεός ἀνήρ; Virgil is the first to show this kind of *inner* struggle and spiritual rebirth; ibid., 218.

Virgil's Style[13]

Metaphorical pictures spark imagination in a listener's mind, and with Homer, even inanimate things live and move before the eyes.[14] In oral cultures, symbols are less complicated than in written cultures, often more polished, carrying traditional connotation, and they become sacred through repetition. Written story, on the other hand, can limit the reader's participation due to its linear qualities and its capacity for abstraction. In his imitation of Homer's epics, Virgil aimed to surpass the poet's style, too. This means that Virgil incorporated key oral elements of Homer's poetry, and rather than reduce the involvement of the listener through static language, he enhanced participation through purposed emotive metaphors, description, imagery, and dialogue.[15]

Virgil did not passionately concern himself with antiquarian or technical minutiae;[16] rather, it seems that Virgil went against the tendency of his predecessors to use unfamiliar words and wrote to the common man, a literary reaction in harmony with the Augustan idea that the poet had a right and a duty to address the citizens at large.[17] Although Virgil shows respect for early tragedy with his archaisms and neologisms, what stands out most is (1) his use of nonpoetic common words, which were found in prose and used among the educated Romans, and (2) his introduction of new combinations of words.[18] Rather than follow the formal Alexandrian style of monotonous, artificial placement of words, such

---

13. For an excellent review of Virgil's use of sentences and innovations, see Quinn, *Virgil's Aeneid*, 383–93, 414–40.

14. For example, "the shameless rock rolled down into the plain," *Il.* 13.587; "spears standing fast in the ground, though longing to feed on the flesh," *Il.* 4.126; "arched, and crested waves," *Il.* 11.574; G. M. A. Grube, *On Poetry and Style*, 93.

15. For a more in-depth discussion of Virgil's style, language, and meter, see Cordier, *Études sur le Vocabulaire Épique*; Duckworth, *Vergil and Classical Hexameter*; Lyne, *Words and the Poet*; Moskalew, *Formular Language*; O'Hara, "Virgil's Style," 241–58; Sparrow, *Half-Lines*; and Quinn's discussion on Virgil's epic tempo in *Latin Explorations*, 193–238. For a helpful summary of Virgil's style and his use of language and meter, see Horsfall, *Companion to the Study of Vergil*, 217–48.

16. Horsfall, "Virgil," 466–67.

17. Wilkenson, "Language of Virgil," 181–92. Wilkenson examines the vocabulary in Virgil's *Aeneid* and concludes that he uses "ordinary words to a marked degree," offset by clever combinations and abnormal constructions.

18. Conte, *Latin Literature*, 283. Conte lists some of these: "a place fresh with slaughter," *Recentem caede locum*; "blood slain," *caeso sanguine*; and "light of bronze," *lux aena*.

as two adjective-noun pairs symmetrically placed with rigid rhythmic unity, Virgil empowers the hexameter verse with rhythmic structure for flexibility, creating a wide range of expression, whether through calm descriptions or ones that arouse pathetic exchanges.[19]

Virgil advances beyond traditional methods to evoke emotion, connecting the listener more closely to the narrative. Virgil repeats actions and words, such as the fixed epithet "pious Aeneas," and catalogues objects and persons in a similar manner to Homer, but Virgil does so with a new sense. He involves the reader "in the psychology of the persons of the action."[20] For example, Virgil takes great pains to develop verbal and substantive correspondences between his narrative and his similes.[21] A battle is compared to warring winds (*magno discordes uenti proelia ceu tollunt* . . . , 10.356–59), which is closely related to the adjacent military narrative, whereas in 2.415–21, Virgil specifically kept military terms out of the wind simile. Such implicit meanings increase the participation of the listener with the narrator. In other examples of battle descriptions, Virgil often narrates a general slaughter with a little cameo description (like Homer) for the purpose of variety and vividness (especially the scenes in Books 9–12), but his cameos are more poignant than Homer's in that he uses some of them as lead-ins to the climax of the fighting.[22]

Virgil also creatively achieves emotional constancy by giving the listener the opportunity to see and feel through a character's own perspective.[23] For example, in the narrative of the athletic games in honor of Aeneas's father (5.315–42), Virgil shifts the subject ("runners") as little as possible at first, and then shifts to individual runners sequentially (in contrast to Homer who does not preserve logical succession of

---

19. Ibid., 281.

20. Ibid., 283.

21. "Virgil is interested in large structural effects, in emotional colouring, he is also a symbolist: but he is apart from all this a miniaturist, he worked with words singly, polishing them for their immediate settings"; West, "Multiple-Correspondence Similes," 49.

22. Williams, *The Aeneid*, 59. Virgil's guiding principle in narrative speech is concentration: each speech expressing a single emotion or decision; Heinze, *Virgil's Epic Technique*, 321–24.

23. Virgil most often employs imagery that follows from general symbolism to explicit perspective (e.g., the effect of Aeneas's shouldering the responsibility as he carries his father out of Troy, 2.707–25); Bovie, "The Imagery of Ascent-Descent," 339.

subjects) to create empathy within the listener.²⁴ This Virgilian passage is also full of words which describe the feeling of the runners (verbs include: *corripiunt, spatia, emicat,* and *volat*; adjectives and adjectival phrases: *infelix, non ille oblitus amorum, iuvenis iam victor ovans*) in contrast to the ordinary, objective words of Homer.²⁵ It is not surprising, then, that when Virgil refers to the mural paintings on Dido's Temple (1.450–93), he does not give a series of pictures but instead emphasizes their effect on Aeneas's emotions.²⁶ However, this does not mean that Virgil limited artistic detail.

A careful reading of the imaginary illustrations on Aeneas's shield reveals Virgil's poetic ability to demonstrate visual artistry (8.626–27).²⁷ The Battle of Actium and the triple triumph of Octavian commands the center scene (*in medio*, 8.675) of the round clipeus shield, a non-real shield that is visually discernible. Virgil brings to mind metal artwork with his descriptions of a wolf, shrubs, swelling of the sea, dolphins (pictured with color and texture). Some of the common scenes in visual Roman art are also depicted, such as crowd scenes, sacrifices, four-horse chariots, ships, triumphs, and temples. The vivid colors include the dew of blood, the green cave of Mars, a silver goose in gilded porticoes (metalwork), gold hair, gold clothes, gold necklaces, striped cloaks that shine, shores of the Red Sea (*litore rubro*), a flash of flame color (*Stuppea flamma*), and black smoke. Cleopatra's skin is described against the red of her sailor's blood.²⁸

Just as Virgil demonstrates skill in his depictions and in his ability to stir the heart, he also demonstrates skill in not employing such devices. Concerning the speeches in the *Aeneid*, Virgil often leaves out the element of shared suffering.²⁹ This contrasts the Homeric speeches

24. Otis, *Virgil*, 43–44.

25. Ibid., 46.

26. Williams, "Pictures on Dido's Temple," 45.

27. West argues that the shield is more than an appeal to emotion (as in the vision in 6.756–860), and it is different than appealing to conceptual thought (as in the prophecy of the Augustan empire), but it was meant to illustrate a conceivable and effective "real" metal shield; West, "*Cernere Erat*, 295–304. "In almost every line so far there is at least one point which brings vividly before our eyes an illustration which would be conceivable and effective on a metal shield"; ibid., 303.

28. Ibid., 299. West states that such artistic detail may create interest rather than refer to historical, symbolic, or chronological significance.

29. Feeney, "Taciturnity of Aeneas," 167–90.

where dialogue leads to a solution—recognition that brings about grief, perspective, and intimacy.[30] Speakers often share their suffering in Homer's epics, whereas in Virgil's *Aeneid*, one-third of the speeches contain no reply.[31] Conversations are "rigidly undomestic" between husband and wife, father and son, and mother and child.[32] This creates a feeling of uncomfortable isolation, particularly in scenes of pity and fear. While the absence of the reciprocal nature of communication between characters works well for ceremonial scenes (e.g. *Aen*. 5.45–71, 7.120–34, and 8.532–40) and leadership scenes (e.g., *Aen*. 1.198–207, 2.707–20, 8.127–56, and 12.565–73), it does not create a sense of emotional attachment.[33] In this manner, Virgil focuses the listeners' attention on Roman virtue and Aeneas's mission.

Imagery and Theme in Books 1–6

Most of the main themes of the *Aeneid* are expressed in the opening scenes:[34] divine wrath, *pietas*, divine will, sacrifice, kingship, and Rome's destiny. In the first six books, Aeneas's character develops from internal uncertainty as a Trojan leader to a devoted father of a promised nation. He endures divine testing because of his appointed status, and after his delayed mission in Carthage, he obeys the will of Jupiter by sailing on to Italy (at this point in the epic, he begins to personify Rome). Landing in Sicily, the Trojans celebrate the anniversary of Anchises's death with athletic competition; the drum beat of war is foreshadowed, and the themes of Rome, empire, and destiny intensify. Virgil changes Aeneas's common epithet from "pious Aeneas" to "father Aeneas" which reveals his patriarchal responsibility given from heaven. Before landing on Italian shores, Aeneas descends to the underworld where Roman customs and rituals are pronounced with a didactic purpose concerning

---

30. Ibid., 179–80. For examples, see *Od*. 23.85f, 4.113–14; *Il*. 24.134–40 and 485–506.

31. Highet, *Speeches in Vergil's Aeneid*, 23–24.

32. Feeney notes that Aeneas and Anchises only converse in the Underworld; Evander speaks just once to his son while alive, and Aeneas speaks to his disguised mother, but she speaks only briefly to him; "Taciturnity of Aeneas," 180.

33. Ibid.

34. R. D. Williams lists these as: heroic epic, fate and history, human suffering, divine action, and Aeneas's mission; *The Aeneid*, 31.

eternal life. Here Aeneas finds renewal and cleansing from his doubt and uncertainty.

Heavenly Wrath

Virgil imitates the *Iliad* and the *Odyssey* in the opening lines of his poem. "Arms and a man" (*Arma virumque*) imitates the *Odyssey*, and the rhythm and general structure of the first seven lines are taken from the *Iliad*.[35] The Roman poet sings of a Trojan leader who endures heavenly wrath to establish a city called Rome from which the Latin race will come (1:1–7):

> ARMA virumque cano, Troiae qui primus ab oris
> Italiam fato profugus Laviniaque venit
> litora-multum ille et terris iactatus et alto
> vi superum, saevae memorem Iunonis ob iram,
> multa quoque et bello passus, dum conderet urbem
> inferretque deos Latio; genus unde Latinum
> Albanique patres atque altae moenia Romae.

> Arms and the man I sing, who, exiled by fate,
> first came from the shores of Troy to Italy and Lavinian
> shores: many times driven about on land and sea
> by the power of the gods, by Juno's furious unforgiving wrath,
> long-suffering in war, until he founds a city
> and brings his gods to Latium, from which comes the Latin race,
> the Alban fathers, and the walls of noble Rome.

Whereas Homer invokes the Muse right away to sing of Achilles's anger, to sing of the hero's deeds and sufferings, Virgil replaces Homer's theme to "arms" and invokes the Muse to recall the *cause* of divine anger ("... is there such anger in celestial spirits?," 1.8–11):[36]

> *Musa, mihi causas memora, quo numine laeso*
> *quidve dolens regina deum tot volvere casus*
> *insignem pietate Virum, tot adire labores*
> *impulerit. tantaene animis caelestibus irae?*

> O Muse recall for me the causes, how offended in her deity
> or why the grieving queen of the gods causes so many afflictions
> upon a man known for piety, to bear so many hardships;
> Can there be such anger in heavenly minds?

35. Conington, *Works of Virgil*, 2:3.
36. Eve Adler, *Vergil's Empire*, 4.

The divine anger of Juno is considered the highest theme of the *Aeneid*, with "arms and a man" and "the founding of Rome" as secondary themes.[37] Virgil's use of the key word "heavens" (*caelestibus*) indicates his desire to know the reason for heavenly disorder.[38] The omnipotent god, Jupiter, governs the heavens, and the world reflects this order, while *Furie* has its appropriate place in Hades. Virgil immediately creates religious and philosophical interest as to why Juno, through her impassioned anger, creates a disturbance on earth, especially upon an undeserving pious Trojan.

In Virgil's carefully structured plot, the disturbance in heaven actuates different levels of conflict among the characters in the *Aeneid*. The violent storm in the opening sequence drives Aeneas to Carthage and sets the mood for the entire epic (1.8–296).[39] The early introduction of the thematic struggle between two world powers (1.23), Carthage and Rome, increases in intensity (see 4.628). While this world contest represents all Roman wars, including the civil wars, the initial scene of the *Aeneid* introduces the conflict at a higher level—Jupiter, presented as the almighty father whose words are all powerful (10.100), represents order and reverence, and Juno, a jealous goddess, represents chaos and destruction.[40] Furthermore, the contrast between Jupiter and Juno plays itself out in the contrast between Aeneas and Dido and between Aeneas and Turnus.[41] Symbolically, Jupiter, Aeneas, and Augustus conquer the

---

37. Ibid., 4. Virgil's question concerning heavenly wrath is not decorative but "the programmatic text of the whole poem, the statement of the problem whose attempted resolution is to occupy the rest of the twelve books"; MacKay, "Hero and Theme," 165.

38. Servius *ad*. 1.1. Aeneas's devotion to divine duty (*insignem pietate virum*, 1.10) and his trials caused by heaven's wrath raises "the great unanswered question of the *Aeneid*"; Williams, "Purpose of the *Aeneid*," 31. Juno personifies the undeserved forces of ill-fortune which beset the human race because of her stance against Rome's destiny; ibid., 32.

39. Pöschl, *Art of Vergil*, 13. Pöschl finds the closest parallel to this literary device to be the plague which introduces the *Iliad*.

40. Ibid., 17.

41. The contrast between calm Jupiter and chaotic Juno also replays itself out at a smaller level between the gods, Aeolus and Neptune (1.52, 1.148). Pöschl notes five areas where the idea of regulation is expressed: (1) Aeolus holds winds in subjection, (2) Neptune calms them, (3) Aeneas reacts to fortune's blows, (4) Augustus chains *Furor impius* in Jupiter's prophecy, and (5) Jupiter demonstrates his power and control over *fata*; ibid. 22. In the initial sequences, Virgil narrates three levels of reality—divine world order, heroic myth, and history—in which he combined Cicero's platonic philo-

demonic forces of chaos, and Juno, Dido, Turnus, and Antony represent the defeated.[42]

Furor-Pietas

In the *Aeneid*, divine providence and divine wrath bear upon Aeneas, developing and testing his virtue. The overall theme of Virgil's epic can also be explained as a contrast between *pietas* (the acceptance of fate) and *furor* (rebellion against fate).[43] In this light, the first six books narrate the internal triumph of *pietas* (faithful/dutiful) over *impii* (irreverent/undutiful), and the latter six books concern external triumph in military action. Virgil's subjective purpose can be interpreted on three levels of conflict:[44] (1) Fate (Jupiter) and Counter-Fate (Juno), (2) Between Aeneas and his own passions (emphasized in Books 1–6), and (3) Between Aeneas and the *impii* (emphasized in Books 7–12). On each of these levels, the plot centers around a *furor-pietas* concept. Fate (Jupiter) elects Aeneas (Rome), but Aeneas must remain faithful in

---

sophical ideas with Homer's unity of nature; "Even where it involves natural phenomena, the myth of Aeneas is a metaphor of Roman history and its Augustan fulfillment . . . the *Aeneid* is a poem of humanity, not a political manifesto"; ibid., 23.

42. Ibid., 18; Pöschl understands the Roman god, the Roman hero, and the Roman emperor as incarnations of the same idea—human action is embedded in divine action, artistically and factually, a "key to the secret of classical composition"; ibid., 16.

43. Otis, *Virgil*, 223. Virgil attaches fates to individuals (e.g., Aeneas, 1.382, 7.234; Priam, 2.554; Turnus, 10.472; and Latinus, 11.160) and communities (e.g., Troy, 2.34, 3.182). For a more comprehensive list and discussion of the relationship of fates in the *Aeneid*, see Matthaei, "The Fates," 11–26. Matthaei describes how one person's fate can be better than another's (6.546) and how fates can be opposed, such as the fates of the Trojans and Juno's own fates (7.294, 9.133). Interestingly, Venus feels for Aeneas and the "contrary" fates he will face (1.239), and Jupiter weighs the "opposing fates" (*fata diversa*) of Aeneas and Turnus before the final duel (12.725–28). What seems most confusing, is that a person's fate can change to "new" or "different" fates. For example, Venus asks Jupiter if new fates can be made for the Trojans (*nova condere fata*, 10.35), and Aeneas expresses his change of fates (*nos alia ex aliis in fata vocamur*, 3.494) which refers to a new era of glory. On the one hand, it seems that fate stands for the way things "should be, its best possibilities," but on the other hand, fate also refers to a determined misfortune. For example, the Lydians (who were doomed unless they found a leader) freed themselves from their fate when they found Aeneas (10.154). In other words, the fates choose Aeneas and Rome over Carthage, because they exercise "a moral choice and are a moral force"; thus, Virgil reinstates "justice into a disorderly worldview"; ibid., 13–14. Augustus demonstrated this nervous relationship that a Roman might have with fate; see App. *Civ.* 3.48. Suet. *Aug.* 70.2; 75.1, 83; 91.1–2; and 96.1–2.

44. Otis, *Virgil*, 223.

his internal choice of *pietas* over *furor*.⁴⁵ Virgil scripts necessary action of the gods and of nature to create situations for Aeneas that lead to a moral choice, which in turn affects his fortune.

Throughout the *Aeneid*, the forces of justice (the gods Jupiter, Venus, and Neptune) stand antithetically to the forces of *furor* (the gods Juno and Aeolus). These opposing forces can be diagrammed as follows:⁴⁶

> Fate (Jupiter) vs. the sub-Fates (Juno, Venus)
> Rome (Venus) vs. Carthage (Juno)
> Calm (Neptune) vs. Storm (Aeolus)

Venus often intercedes to Jupiter on behalf of her son, Aeneas (Rome's destiny), against the hostility of Juno, who regularly intervenes to hinder and cause suffering to the Trojans. But both Venus and Juno (sub-Fates) are subject to Jupiter (Fate). Furthermore, "wrath" is not to be confused with unjust "*furor*." For example, Neptune's anger is "just" as he calms the troubled waves (1.126–36):

> *Interea magno misceri murmure pontum*
> *emissamque hiemem sensit Neptunus et imis*
> *stagna refusa vadis, graviter commotus; et alto*
> *prospiciens, summa placidum caput extulit unda.*
> *disiectam Aeneae toto videt aecquore classem,*
> *fluctibus oppressos Troas caelique ruina.*
> *nec latuere doli fratrem Iunonis et irae.*
> *Eurum ad se Zephyrumque vocat, dehinc talia fatur:*
> *"Tantane vos generis tenuit fiducia vestri?*
> *iam caelum terramque meo sine numine, venti,*
> *miscere et tantas audetis tollere moles?*
> *quos ego-! sed motos praestat componere fluctus:*
> *post mihi non simili poem commissa luetis . . ."*

> In the meantime, Neptune sensed a great disturbing turbulence at sea,
> and the storm was loosed and the waters
> sprang from the depths; gravely aroused and with care
> for the sea, he lifted his calm face over the high waters.
> He sees Aeneas's fleet scattered across the ocean,

---

45. "One thread runs through the whole complex of forces engaged: *pietas-furor*, the antithetical dyad of moral ideas or feelings related to *fatum* as to the factor which will ultimately use them both to moral ends"; ibid. 233.

46. Ibid.

the Trojans oppressed by the waves and the tumbling sky.
Nor is Juno able to deceive her brother and hide anger.
Neptune calls the East and West winds, then says:
"So great a faith you have in your race?
Do you winds dare disrupt heaven and earth without my
    authority,
and cause so great a burden?
Whom I! But it is better to calm the tumultuous waves:
Afterwards you will atone to me a different punishment for
    your offenses.

Neptune's righteous wrath stands in contrast to unjust *furor* (like that of Dido, the Queen of Carthage).[47] But the focus of the epic rests on how these outside forces bring Aeneas to the point of making internal moral choices, decisions of *pietas* over *furor* (internal calm or storm).[48]

Pius Aeneas

Amidst wind gusts, hurling waves, and the sounds of oars snapping, Virgil introduces Aeneas (1.92–93):

> *extemplo Aeneae solvuntur frigore membra:*
> *ingemit et duplicis tendens ad sidera palmas*
> *talia voce refert: "o terque quaterque beati,*
> *quis ante ora patrum Troiae sub moenibus altis*
> *contigit oppetere! o Danaum fortissime gentis*
> *Tydide! mene Ilacis occumbere campis*
> *non potuisse tauque animam hanc effundere dextra.*

> Immediately Aeneas's limbs grow weak with fear,
> He extends both hands to the heavens,
> crying aloud, "Oh three, four times fortunate,
> were those who died before their father's eyes,
> under the noble walls of Troy. Oh Tydeus's son, the bravest
> of the Greek race, ah! that I could not have fallen in the open
>   fields of Troy,
> and pour out my spirit at your hand.

---

47. One of the basic themes in the *Aeneid* is the storm at sea (1.9–296) which parallels the Allecto scenes (7.286–640); both of these scenes are initial symbols of the *Odyssey* and the *Iliad*; Pöschl, *Art of Vergil*, 24–33.

48. Virgil omits the preamble of the storm (*Od.* 5.299–305) and only uses the personal complaint (*Od.* 5.306–12) which means that Virgil is "obviously" concerned about the inner thoughts and feelings of Aeneas; Otis, *Virgil*, 230–32.

The exiled Aeneas grieves and remembers the fallen glory of Troy, a consistent theme throughout the epic (e.g., 1.372; 4.430).[49] With courage and faith, he encourages the remnant to persevere in their journey to a promised land of rest in Latium, a predestined place for the royal citizens of Troy (1.204–5). Yet, within his heart, Aeneas hides deep sorrow: "he spoke these words, sick with emotional pain; he feigns hope on his face, but represses grief in his heart (*Talia voce refert, curisque ingentibus aeger/ spem voltu simulat, premit altum corde dolorem*, 1.208–9).

Most often, though, Aeneas honestly discloses his emotions. When recounting the battle of Troy to Dido, he does not hesitate to share his grief,[50] to tell of his passionate anger in war (*furor iraque*, 2.314), to express fear, or to describe the burden he feels for those beside him (2.726–29). This emotive personality contrasts the Homeric hero but serves a literary purpose in creating a balance between two conflicting interests, Aeneas's own needs and that of Rome's destiny. This two-dimensional emphasis reveals Aeneas's character (and tests the moral choices of the audience), whether he produces the virtues of *religio* and *pietas* (not Greek philosophical ideologies such as reason or pleasure).[51]

The continuous action in Books 1–4 describes the tremendous grief Aeneas endures and the familial encouragement he receives. First, Aeneas rushes into battle with fury (2.355), and then repeats his passionate response when he learns that his wife has died. His mother confronts him during this rage and questions his emboldened behavior: "My son, what resentment (*dolor*) stirs such ungovernable wrath? Why this rage? . . . Do you first not see where you have left your age-worn father Anchises and whether your wife Creusa and your child Ascanius are still alive?" (2.594–97).[52] Later in a vision his wife appears to him

---

49. In the Homeric parallel, Odysseus grieves his lost glory and honor, but he does not demonstrate love (*Od.* 5.306); Pöschl, *Art of Vergil*, 35.

50. Virgil underscores Aeneas's grief and compassion: Aeneas heaves a deep sigh (*ingentem gemitum*, 1.485) from the depths of his heart concerning the casualties of war; remembering his people and homeland brings about unspeakable grief and sorrow to him (*renovare dolorem . . . lamentabile regnum . . . luctuque*, 2.3–12). He consistently shows pity in Books 5 and 6 also: Aeneas weeps (*flens ipse*) for Hector; and speaks words of sorrow (*maistas expromere*), and he is quick to show pity and compassion for others (*miserari*, 5.350; *miseratus*, 6.332).

51. Fowler, *Religious Experience*, 412.

52. Early in the epic, Virgil makes it clear that grief exists in the heavens—Cupid continually grieves (*nostro doluisti saepe dolore*, 1.669) over Juno's hatred against Aeneas.

challenging his decision to yield to frantic grief (*dolori*, 2.776). At this point in the narrative, Aeneas's *pietas* is only familial and his behavior more like a Homeric hero.[53] It is Anchises, his father, who interprets the forewarnings of the gods to guide his son at each crisis (*omnis curae casusque levamen*, 3.709), and it is Anchises who commands the ships to sail from the shores (*vade . . . felix nati pietate*, 3.480) after the many ocean storms.[54] The death of Anchises tests Aeneas's trust and obedience, virtues that take on greater significance as Aeneas becomes more aware of his universal purpose in establishing Rome.

In Book 4, after Aeneas had opened up to Dido (about his duty to his father, about his mission, the promised kingdom, and his awarded title *pius*, 2.567–68, 701–3; 3.97–98, and 393), he remained in Carthage, which threatened his future. He experiences guilt because of the delay of the mission (4.224–25), and he feels considerable grief for Dido, but eventually makes the correct decision of choosing duty over passion (4.393–96): "But pious Aeneas, though he desired to soothe her grief (*dolentum*) . . . he obeyed the divine command with great loyalty."

Pater Aeneas

The tone changes from tense, relational disruption in Book 4, to peace and celebration in Book 5. Virgil presents Aeneas as a confident leader, who presides over the games with a clear conscience, and as the *paterfamilias*, who carefully performs the ritual of the *Parentalia*. This event involves an annual renewal of the rite of burial with the propitiation of the departed, a necessary aspect for the welfare of the Roman fam-

---

53. "He had to be an old model hero before he could be one of the new"; Otis, *Virgil*, 244.

54. In Book 3, Anchises directs departures from Troy, Thrace, Delos, Crete, the Strophades, Buthrotum, and Scylla-Charybdis, and all of the divine directives are submitted to Anchises for interpretation and action; Lloyd, "Character of Anchises," 48. Lloyd shows how Virgil develops the character of Anchises as a complement to the piety of Aeneas: In Book 2, Virgil introduces Anchises as the *paterfamilias*, a father who will not leave. Aeneas at first does not retreat, but desires to rescue his family. In this case "*pietas in patriam*" seems to come into conflict with the "*pietas in deos*." In Book 5, it is through the rites in honor of Anchises's death that Aeneas renews his *pietas* after his delay of mission (because of his relationship with Dido). The games are more than an interlude between Books 4 and 6, they mark a type of apotheosis before Aeneas visits Anchises's shade in Hades; ibid., 51. In fact, the rites given at Anchises's tomb are close to those given for a deity; Bailey, *Religion in Virgil*, 291–95. After Book 5, Anchises becomes something like an agent of Jupiter.

ily.⁵⁵ After nine days the living members have a lovefeast, forgiving all quarrels. These religious games are associated with the heroic past, and when a participant wins an event, the athlete receives glory and honor, a benefit extended to the family.⁵⁶

The games in Book 5 begin with ship racing, which Virgil describes in great detail: "They press forward with great struggle; the golden stern trembles at the expansive strokes, moving the ocean floor underneath them. Then their rapid breathing shakes their limbs and parched mouths, and sweat streams down" (5.197–200). The other contests follow: a foot race, the energetic wrestling matches, an archery contest; all climax into the final event of the games, the *lusus Troiae*.⁵⁷

Francis Cairns elaborates on how the continuity in *Odyssey* 8 allows Virgil to make the *lusus Troiae*, with all its singing and dancing, the crowning point of his games, and bridges the past greatness of Troy (5.563–67) with the future greatness of Rome (5.568).⁵⁸ The *lusus* underlines the martial significance of the Sicilian games by substituting military maneuvers for the Phaeacian dancing (5.581). Virgil both reverses the Odyssean model and echoes it. More importantly, Homer's account of the Phaeacians as a people given up to the joys of feasting, dance, and song, must, in part, represent a sympathetic appreciation of the enjoyments of peace and prosperity. The Augustans would have found these associated concepts powerfully relevant to Virgil's picture of the Trojans as they watched Ascanius leading his squadrons in the *lusus Troiae* to honor his grandfather and as they observed in the boys' faces the features of their Trojan ancestors.⁵⁹ Virgil traces the continuity of the *lusus* (5.596–603) to a time of peace. Thus, "the multiple ambivalence of the concluding line of the *lusus* description comes into its own: *sanctus pater* of *hac celebrata tenus sancto certamina patri* [as far as these contests have been celebrated for the holy father, 5.603] becomes at once Anchises, Aeneas, and, in foreshadowing, Augustus."⁶⁰

---

55. Fowler, *Religious Experience*, 418. Virgil transforms the Greek traditions, which are wholly transposed from their Iliadic context (*Il.* 23), into new Roman themes. For a discussion of parallels, see Grandsen, *Virgil's Iliad*, 83–84.

56. Cairns, *Virgil's Augustan Epic*, 219.

57. The events in Book 5 foreshadow the battles to come in Book 9.

58. Cairns, *Virgil's Augustan Epic*, 247–48.

59. Ibid., 248.

60. Ibid. The *lusus Troiae* were introduced by Sulla and fully developed by Augustus;

Juno once again intervenes to avert Jupiter's plans by sending Iris to stir up disharmony among the Trojan women.[61] In a frenzy, the women snatch fire from the hearths and set the ships ablaze (5.661). Aeneas rents his garment, lifts his hands, and cries out to Jupiter, "if your loving kindness (*pietas*) of old has regard for human suffering, grant now our fleet escape from the flame, O father" (5.689–90). Aeneas must endure in crisis, but he waivers (5.700–704):

> *At pater Aeneas, casu concussus acerbo,*
> *nunc huc ingentis, nunc illuc pectore curas*
> *mutabat versans, Siculisne resideret arvis,*
> *oblitus fatorum, Italasne capesseret oras.*

> But father Aeneas, struck by the cruel blow,
> turning this way and that with pain in his heart,
> questions whether he should reside in Sicilian lands,
> forgetful of fate, or lay hold of Italian shores.

Then the seer Nautes reminds Aeneas of his divine race (*divinae stirpis*, 5.711) and tells him to allow those who are weak, fearful, and wearied to settle in Sicily. Though encouraged by Nautes's words, Aeneas is torn within his soul, burdened by all his cares (5.719); soon Anchises appears to direct Aeneas by Jupiter's command to adhere to Nautes's prophecy (5.724–25), to lead the brave to Italy and to meet him (Anchises) again in Elysium amid the sweet assembly of the blessed. Before arriving in Italy, Book 5 ends with Palinarus at the helm, falling asleep and flinging headlong into the ocean. Aeneas grieves, not knowing that he will meet his friend again on his descent into Hades.

Aeneas's *Katabasis*

In the opening scene of Book 6, Aeneas weeps over Palinarus, with the remnant fleet landing safely on the shores of Cumae.[62] The fantastic,

---

Virgil connects them with Aeneas to compliment Augustus; Fairclough, *Virgil*, 487.

61. In Book 1, Juno instigated the storm, and in Book 4, she influenced the union of Aeneas and Dido. Otis divides the latter part of Book 5 into three acts of hatred which are followed by a declension of the hero's *pietas* (his forgetfulness of duty); these in turn are followed by counter-interventions of Jupiter (Jupiter sends Mercury in Books 1 and 4; Jupiter speaks through Anchises here); *Virgil*, 274.

62. Aeneas's journey into the underworld in Book 6 transitions the listener from Aeneas's past (Books 1–5) into his and Rome's destined future (Books 7–12). This journey from the cave at Avernus to the Gates of Ivory can be broken down into three main

almost imaginary, descriptions of the journey into the underworld that follow make this episode an unbelievable sight.[63] Dwelling in this mythological-historical region of Hades[64] are evil spirits, beasts, deceased comrades, sinners, and divine souls, with punishments meted our for individuals in specific categories.[65]

Before Aeneas can reach his father in the Elysian fields, he first makes appropriate sacrifices at the Temple of Apollo and listens to the prophecies from Deiphobe about his future battles to come. She discourages him from trying to enter Hades because of its dangers, but Aeneas perseveres. After following the prophetess's instructions, he plucks a golden bough from a tree, and makes sacrifices, after which a chasm to the underworld opens.

At the river Acheron, crowds of dead souls await the infernal ferry to enter Hades. Aeneas first meets Leucaspis and Orontes, sailors who died on their voyage to Troy (1.113–14). Then Aeneas meets Palinarus, Dido, and Deiphobus, who symbolically represent his past (in reverse sequence of the narrative—Books 5, 4, and 2). Palinarus entreats his former leader Aeneas for a proper burial, to which the prophetess promises an eternal tomb. Then he sees in a distance Dido's dim form in the shadows of the forest, and in tears, with tenderness, he reminds her of his obedience to the divine command. She turns away from him, and he pities her as she goes (*prosequitur lacrimis longe et miseratur*

---

themes: (1) life after death (purification from sin and the rewarding of virtue); (2) the future of Rome; and (3) Aeneas's character; his past, present, and future; Williams, "Sixth Book," 191–207. Williams divides the final section as: (a) preparations for the descent, (b) the journey through the underworld, and (c) the explanation of the rebirth and the vision of Roman heroes.

63. This ordeal was a type of initiation or sacrament; Fowler, *Religious Experience*, 420. Fowler notes that Virgil is more geographically descriptive and purposeful (Aeneas renews his call and mission) in his imitation of Homer's *katabasis*.

64. Virgil creatively synthesizes tradition and folklore. He borrows from Orphic sources; see Butler, *The Sixth Book*, 19–36. The assimilation of Orphic ideas, Pythagorean philosophy, and Homeric ideas were developed by Plato and assimilated in Stoicism; see Williams, "Sixth Book," 193–95. See also the *katabasis* of Hercules and Orpheus in *Georgic* 4.

65. The descent into the underworld has been divided into two parts (mythological and philosophical) or three parts (mythological, moral, and philosophical). For two parts, see Norden, *Aeneis Buch VI*, 14–15; for three parts, see Otis, *Virgil*, 289–90; and Norwood, "Tripartite Eschatology," 15–16. For an excellent critical discussion of the literature, see Solmsen, "World of the Dead," 208–23.

euntem, 6.476). Traveling farther, Aeneas reaches the fields where the well known warriors exist. There Aeneas meets Deiphobus, son of Priam, a fallen soldier at Troy, whose face is torn and his frame mangled. As Aeneas confronts these individuals, he experiences the emotions from events in his tragic past—the Trojan war, his journey, and his testing at Carthage—but despite his grief over *fates* casualties, he chooses *pietas* for the sake of Rome.

The connection between the Augustan present and the eschatology of the underworld is intimate and complex, and it is clear that Virgil responds to the end of one *saeculum* and the beginning of another.[66] After Aeneas revisits his past, he reaches a fork in the road. The Sybil describes Tartarus to Aeneas, a place of judgment and punishment. Virgil blends two types of descriptions—the first list of punishments follows the traditional, mythological accounts of afterlife, while the second list of punishments stems from Orphic-Pythagorean milieu (behaviors on earth which merit treatments in the underworld, 6.608–14):[67]

> *Hic quibus invisi fratres, dum vita manebat,*
> *pulsatusve parens, et fraus innexa clienti,*
> *aut qui divitiis soli incubuere repertis*
> *nec partem posuere suis (quae maxima turba est),*
> *quique ob adulterium caesi, quique arma secuti*
> *impia nec veriti dominorum fallere dextras,*
> *inclusi poenam exspectant.*

> Here are those who in their lifetime who hated their brothers,
> struck their parents, and contrived to steal from a client,
> or who hoarded earned wealth to themselves,
>   not setting aside a portion for their own *family* (which is the largest number),

---

66. Zetzel, "*Romane Memento*," 263–84.

67. Ibid., 265. A subtle resurrection motif seems to be present. D. A. West argues that Virgil, in his prophecy of Roman heroes, alludes to Plato (*Republic*, Book 10) and the mythological tale of a living man (named Er) who descends into the underworld, dies, and comes back to life. His experience resembles Aeneas's experience (the judges of the dead, a waiting time, the rebirth of souls, measured punishments, and the nature of the universe); West, "Bough and the Gate," 236–38. In one passage, Er saw the just who were sent on the road to the right which led to heaven and the unjust taking the road to the left to torture (*Republic* 614C). West emphasizes that the Roman people would notice the Platonic allusion; ibid. Herein lies the hope for eternal life—unlike Homer's Elysian plain, which was reserved for the divine, Virgil's groves are reserved for anyone of virtue; Williams, *The Aeneid*, 199.

or who were killed for adultery, pursued impious war,
or who do not fear breaking trust with their landlords;
immured, they await punishment.

In the second list of sins, Virgil adapts common Greek crimes with Roman color. For example, *patraloia* is a standard crime in the apocalyptic tradition; the phrase *pulsatus parens* seems to allude to a Roman law; fratricide reflects Roman concerns (*fraus innexa clienti* is Roman); and there may be similar overtones of greed in keeping money away from one's family.[68] Virgil makes Tartarus Roman and modernized, and "what the underworld supplies for the new age of Augustus, above all else, is the memory of justice."[69]

The purification of souls (which Anchises will soon describe to Aeneas) radically differs from the punishments in Tartarus, which means he brings together what might seem to be incompatible accounts for a specific eschatological purpose:[70]

> The several different types of peculiarity in Virgil's account of Tartarus work together to create a single effect. In the first place, the anomalous versions of traditional legends tend to diminish the authority of the mythological underworld, and that authority is superseded by that of the moralizing versions of Orphic-Pythagorean eschatology. We are given a Tartarus which is not limited to mythic sinners, but has room for all those who violate the universal canons of justice and morality. In the second place, that universal morality is itself given a more specific location in space and time: it applies quite precisely to the citizens of the Roman state, and enforces the morality of Roman law. The underworld is not frozen in the narrative time of the *Aeneid* or of myth. Its burden is historical, and is directed to the concerns of the Augustan age.[71]

---

68. Zetzel, "*Romane Memento*," 271. However, Virgil goes beyond this to identify historical crimes with specific events and individuals—the slave revolt alludes to the war between Octavian and Sextus Pompeius (6.612-13; *RG* 5.1-2), and the second section of crimes (6.621-22) adapts two verses from the poem of Virgil's friend, Varius, to describe the behavior of Mark Antony; ibid.

69. Zetzel, "*Romane Memento*," 284.

70. The judgment process and purification points to a developed Orphic-Pythagorean background; it is not only Platonic; ibid., 267.

71. Ibid., 272.

While the punishments seem strange (e.g., rolling a rock and hanging on a wheel), Virgil separates traditional criminals from traditional punishments, and traditional groups of crimes are illogically separated (categories such as greed, sexual immorality, and family violations overlap, but the arrangement is abnormal, 6.610–22).[72]

Leaving the fields, Aeneas approaches his father, Anchises, who is telling a tale of the fates and fortunes of his people. When he saw Aeneas coming toward him, tears flowed from his eyes. They embraced. Soon Aeneas questions his father about the countless people and tribes along the river banks. Anchises describes to him the process of the rebirth of souls (6.713–14). Here Virgil writes in symbolic terms so that Aeneas lives through his past, and with the poetic version of rebirth revealing the future, the ideas shift from Homeric to Roman (with movement of verse, rapid grouping of names, a more heightened diction, and a unity of presentations of the character of Rome).[73] The Roman parade begins chronologically with Silvia of Alba and builds to the honoring of Romulus, the first founder of the city of Rome. Then comes Augustus, the second founder of Rome, who will restore the Golden Age and bring Rome's dominion to the ends of the world.[74] Anchises makes clear Rome's mission (6.847–53):

---

72. Ibid., 271.

73. Williams, "Sixth Book," 202.

74. The parade of Roman Heroes (6.756–886) divides into two parts (transitioned by Anchises's question to Aeneas, 6.806–7); Williams, *The Aeneid*, 37–38. In the first half, the dramatic energy builds, with Augustus out of chronological order so that he becomes the "second founder" of Rome (placed next to Romulus), and with the military might of Rome supremacy symbolized in Augustus's victory at Actium. Williams notes the special significance of the comparison of Augustus to Hercules and Bacchus (6.800–801): these three civilize the world (Hercules freed the world from monstrous creatures; Bacchus symbolizes the conquest by man of wild nature), and both Hercules and Bacchus are mortals who had become deified because of their services to mankind—Augustus will receive the same reward; ibid., 37. In the second half of the parade, Rome endures suffering in its rise to power, symbolized by its first two kings, Romulus, the conqueror, and Numa, the man of peace and civilization; ibid., 39.

The other significant passage in the first half of the *Aeneid* which prophesies the future greatness of Rome is Jupiter's prophecy to Venus, 1.257–96. Though Aeneas and the Trojans will endure war and suffering, Aeneas will "crush" the opposition and establish an eternal rule (*imperium sine fine dedi*, 1.279). Williams notes that Jupiter only mentions two periods of Roman history (the conquest of Greece and the period of Augustus), and the Golden Age of Augustus is a time of universal peace where *Furor impius* will be tamed; ibid., 36.

excudent alii spirantia mollius aera,
(credo equidem), vivos ducent de marmore voltus,
orabunt causas melius, caelique meatus
describent radio et surgentia sidera dicent:
to regere imperio populos, Romane, memento
(hae tibi erunt artes), pacique imponere morem,
parcere subiectis et debellare superbos.

Others, I do not doubt, will hammer out bronze with softer lines,
drawing out features of life from marble,
plead their causes better, trace with instruments the movement
    of the stars
and record the rising of the constellations:
O Rome, remember to rule the nations by your authority;
these will be the arts for you: to establish the order of peace,
to spare the humble and war against the proud![75]

In the final lines of Book 6, Virgil employs the traditional imagery of ivory gates to provide closure. The imagery and meaning of the gates of horn and ivory ought to be understood in a Platonic context of the doctrine of the soul.[76] In Hades, Aeneas is imprisoned by the body and the illusions of this world. For Virgil, the physical world is a shadow of a purer world, and this concept provides the structure for him to express the "evanescence of mortal aspirations."[77] Interestingly, the parade of heroes and Virgil's emphasis on *gloria*, which differs from the traditional use, exalts Rome in a manner in which the audience expects a Platonic vision.[78] Virgil scripts powerful imagery without the philosophical comfort of immortality and redemption, which means that the meeting of Aeneas and Anchises is a political image of process for the Roman state and its statesman.[79] Not surprisingly, the beginning lines of Book 7 will praise Aeneas's nurse Caeita for honor, glory, and name (7.3–4).

---

75. Romans viewed themselves as servants of the gods to rule the nations; Virgil only mentions Greek oratory as an intellectual, artistic contribution of the Greeks.

76. Tarrant, "Aeneas," 51–55. See also, Johnson, *Darkness Visible*, 105–11.

77. Ibid., 54.

78. Feeney, "History and Revelation," 4:237.

79. Ibid.

Stoic Wrath

Juno's jealousy and her *furor* cause disturbance in heaven, discord on earth, and conflict between heaven and earth. The audience anticipates how Aeneas will overcome *furor* with internal *pietas*, and how Rome will fulfill her purpose of war—peace and security, granting mercy to vanquished enemies.[80] In his presentation of Roman conquest, Virgil alludes to the Stoic ideals where bravery is reasoned; it is not frenzied or irascible. Stoicism shares with the Augustan age the attitude that personal glory is not sought. For the Stoic, vengeful anger as punishment for injustice is equated to "passion," which means that Virgil writes in a Stoic sense when he incorporates a range of violent emotions as *furor* ("madness"), an "inimical polarity" to *pietas*.[81] Rome will bring about a "softened" age where wars will end (*aspera tum positis mitescent saecula bellis*, 1.291). Unlike Juno's passion (1.151–52), Aeneas resembles a Stoic when he turns from his passionate relationship with Dido to follow divine command (4.393–96). For Aeneas, peace and security of all peoples is his destined responsibility, acting mercifully without irrationality (6.851–52).[82]

At first, Aeneas does not show godlike virtue; he develops morally over time, through testing. If Aeneas fails in his trials (in his probation period), he recognizes his moral weakness, which eventually will result in the future glory of Rome.[83] But Aeneas does not fail in his relationship to his people, family, and the gods (justice or *pietas*); rather, he lacks moderation, courage, and wisdom (*prudentia*). Stoics gave specific meanings to these four virtues, and Romans listening to this epic would recognize Aeneas's shortcomings.[84] Aeneas's *imprudentia*

---

80. R. O. A. M. Lyne reviews a considerable amount of Roman literature (e.g, Cicero, Horace, Cato, Livy, Julius Caesar, Sallust, other Politicians, and Augustus) and concludes that Virgil combines the Roman idealized imperialist perspective of methods of war with Stoic sympathies; "Politics of War," 190–91. In particular, Lyne notes Horace's "image" (in *Odes* 3.4) for Augustus's military actions—with phrases such as "regulated force" for Augustus and "irrational force" for the enemy; this "regulated force" is "promoted by the gods" to do something greater (*Odes* 3.66–67); ibid., 193.

81. Ibid., 194.

82. This character contrasts the traditional epic hero; ibid., 195.

83. Bowra, "Aeneas and the Stoic Ideal," 365. Several passages contain Stoic technical terminology (e.g., 3.182; in Stoic terms, *exercite* means "tested by ordeal," 5.725, 6.105); ibid., 365, 370.

84. Ibid., 367.

is exhibited in impracticability in achieving his desired ends. For example, his giving in to temptation to Dido was not a heroic fault, but a forgotten duty, which contrasts Dido's passion and disavowed principle. Mercury chastises him for this, for not knowing right and wrong. But Aeneas's passion, or lack of self control, demonstrates his weakness for not acting in moderation, his lack of subordinating passion to reason. Aeneas openly admits his fury and impulsive nature (2.314–15). In the first five poetic books, Aeneas often acts defensively, and his lack of preparedness in crisis shows his unsettledness and uncertainty.[85] But in Book 6, Aeneas gains the confidence that he needs to begin preparing for the battles ahead.

Human Sacrifice

In comparing sacrifice in Homer with other Greek tragedies, the *Iliad* and *Odyssey* tend to exclude homicide within the family, and exclude imagery drawn from animal sacrifice (three similes do refer to killing a domestic animal: *Od.* 4.535, 11.411, and 413–15); in addition, ritual plays a more positive role in Homer than that of other Greek tragedies.[86] However, a considerable amount of uncontrolled violence occurs in the Homeric battle scenes.

Concerning ancient tradition in some barbarous tribes, a human being was, at times, sacrificed in order to propitiate the gods at the outset of war, but the references to human sacrifice in Roman times are not easily verified.[87] After 97 B.C. the Roman government did not tolerate human sacrifice. Interestingly, it has been suggested that Octavian's proscriptions might be interpreted as a type of sacrifice, but it is believed that his military carried out these executions at will.[88]

---

85. Bowra asserts that Maecenas (Augustus's minister) and his circle of poets are concerned with the regeneration of the Roman character through a popularized Stoic type; ibid., 370.

86. Seaford, "Homeric and Tragic Sacrifice," 87–88. For sacrificial themes in the *Aeneid*, see Bandara, "Sacrificial Levels," 217–39; Feeney, *Literature and Religion*; and Hardie, *Epic Successors of Virgil*. For a complicated argument concerning Aeneas as "priest-king" whose sacrifices of others results in the sacrifice of himself; see Dyson, *King of the Wood*, 139–40.

87. Reid, "Human Sacrifices," 34–52. See App. *Civ.* 5.48–49.

88. Reid, "Human Sacrifices," 42.

In the first half of the *Aeneid*, Virgil describes death in language that suggests the ritual religious killing of sacrificial victims, primarily through minor characters (e.g., Orontes, Laocoon in Sinon's tale, Palinarus, and Misenus), which may provide insight into the final duel between Aeneas and Turnus in Book 12. Regarding Orontes and Palinarus, death is associated with prophecy and sacrifice.[89] Virgil describes the "hidden rocks" (*saxa latentia*) in which Orontes is hurled upon by the wind as "altars" (*Aras*, 1:108–10), the first of many sacrifices in the *Aeneid*. A more conspicuous sacrifice occurs in Book 5 when Neptune foretells the death of Palinarus by saying that one life would be given for the many,[90] before the Trojans arrive in Italy (5.814–15): "There will be only one lost in the tumultuous waves that you will look for; one life will be given for the many" (*unus erit tantum, amissum quem gurgite quaeres; unum pro multis dabitur caput*). Palinarus can be associated with *fortunas* (based on an analysis of the associations in Homer's Odysseus; e.g., storm, sea, seafarer, and *fata*), and with the sacrifice of Palinarus echoing the sacrifice of Cloanthus,[91] it can be demonstrated that a principle of *pietas*, not *fortunas*, is responsible for Aeneas's safe landfall.[92] In this manner, trust in personal *fortuna* can result in disaster, and Virgil seems to contrast this faith in *fortunas* with the *pietas* which brings Aeneas divine favor.[93]

Virgil often utilizes imagery and metaphors in the *Aeneid* taken from the ancient daily practice of sacrifice. In Book 2, Sinon deceives the Trojans with a lying tale, which involves the only actual sacrifice in the *Aeneid* where the intended victim is a human being. But it is Laocoon's death at the altar, while performing a sacrifice to Neptune, which completes the theme of sacrifice.[94] Philip Hardie interprets several elements of sacrificial crisis in the *Aeneid*: "rivalry between similar

89. O'Hara, *Optimistic Prophecy*, 19–21. O'Hara emphasizes how the Alexandrian as well as the Augustan poets choose precise language to communicate allusive meaning.

90. This prompts Aeneas later to call into question the faithfulness of Apollo ("Is this how he keeps his promises?"; *en haec promissa fides est*? 6.346).

91. Palinarus offered a sacrifice of entrails and wine into the sea unto the "storm gods" for safe travel (5.775–76), which parallels Cloanthus who also threw entrails and wine into the sea (5.237–38), propelling him to victory).

92. Nicoll, "Sacrifice of Palinarus," 459–72.

93. Here, it is "impossible to avoid Virgil's view of Palinarus and the Augustan concept of *Fortuna Caesaris*"; ibid., 469.

94. Smith, "Deception and Sacrifice," 503–23. See *Aen*. 2.119–31.

heroes, the sacrifice of one life for many, the escalation of reciprocal violence, and the substitution of one life for another," and concludes that these were views shared by the early Principate.[95]

As Sibyl guides Aeneas on his way to the underworld, the death and burial of Misenus appears to be an integral part of the preparation.[96] The Sibyl says of the dead Misenus (6.152): "Bear him first to his own place and bury him in the tomb. Lead black cattle there; let these be your first atoning sacrifice" (*sedibus hunc refer ante suis, et conde sepulcro; duc nigras pecudes, ea prima piacula sunto*). This text refers to a sacrifice which is part of the burial ceremony where black cattle are offered for the purification of Misenus's death (a death which polluted the fleet). Otis concludes that Misenus's death is a symbol of the soiled mortality common to all the profane (those who have not been purified and initiated into the mystery that protects them from death or gives them life from death), and that Aeneas, both by the piacular sacrifice and by the power of the life-giving branch, is made ritually pure and capable of withstanding death.[97] In this sense, death is itself a sacrifice, and this represents the exchange of a life for a life—his own life for that of Aeneas.

Divine Kingship

Among the gods in the *Aeneid*, Jupiter is most prominently *rex* (e.g., 1.65, 241). References to kingship are significantly greater in Virgil than in Homer, and Aeneas is the character most frequently treated in terms of kingship. From one perspective, King Aeneas and King Jupiter are Virgilian equivalents for earth and heaven respectively.[98] Aeneas and Augustus are ancestors of the Julian house, which makes this kingship tie important to Virgil's contemporaries. In 47 B.C., Julius Caesar

---

95. Hardie, *Epic Successors*, 21. Hardie borrows from René Gerard's social theory, which finds societal institutions at fault for not curbing societal violence; an innocent person becomes a victim (a scapegoat for the community's violence) for community benefit; see Girard, *Violence and the Sacred*.

96. Otis, *Virgil*, 288.

97. Ibid.

98. Cairns, *Virgil's Augustan Epic*, 21. Horace, too, portrayed Augustus as Jupiter's royal agent; see *Odes* 1.12.49–52; see also, Murray, "The Attitude of the Augustan Poets," 241–46. This kind of divine-human relationship finds its origin in Hellenistic philosophy.

issued a coin with Aeneas rescuing his father, Anchises, a reflection of Caesar's *pietas* as ruler.[99] In Rome, leading officials were seen as *de facto* "kings." It makes sense then that this positive view of the "good" kingship would apply to the *princeps* Augustus.[100] The Roman people wield "royal" power (1.21–22); they "rule" the world (6.851). Although Augustus avoided the title "king," historians emphasized his royal birth, and he was honored as a king in places like Egypt and Macedonia.[101]

Aeneas's royal inheritance depended on his mission. Virgil chooses language with precise legal connotations concerning kingdom succession in Italy (4.272, 274–76).[102] Failure to complete the mission would mean a disinheritance of his sonship. Two important prophecies reaffirm the connection of kingship and his purpose: Jupiter reassures Venus about her son's predestined kingdom (1.267–71), and Apollo prophesies the dominion of the House of Aeneas over all lands (3.97–98).

Providential Fates

The terms *fatum* and *fata* have different meanings in the *Aeneid*.[103] Virgil seems conscious of the root-meaning of *fatum* as "the thing spoken" (either of the word of the prophet, word of the oracle, or word of the god), and often employs the plural form to intend the meaning "fate" which governs the lives of men and events.[104] Virgil also borrows from Greek concepts which are not necessarily Roman (e.g., the idea of fates conflicting, fates modified, or fates overruled by a higher fate).[105] But most importantly, the religious idea of divine providence (similar to the

---

99. Cairns, *Virgil's Augustan Epic*, 4.

100. Cairns lists the elements of the good king stereotype from a wide range of scholarship; ibid., 18–21. Also see Rawson, "Caesar's Heritage," 154–57.

101. See chapter 1 of this study, "Background of Caesar Augustus," 3–4.

102. Eidinow, "Dido," 260–67.

103. Fortune is used as an equivalent of *fatum* (e.g., 1.39, 6.95, and 11.43), but it is also used in the sense of chance (e.g., 7.559, 8.15) and destiny (e.g., 2.387, 5.22); Bailey, *Religion in Virgil*, 234–40.

104. Ibid., 205.

105. Matthaei, "The Fates," 14. Matthaei discusses how Juno delays the course of Aeneas, acting out of uncertainty (not knowing whether or not a particular fate is permanent); on the other hand, Jupiter works in harmony with the fates. The fates act through the gods (8.398); the fates and gods work in harmony (e.g., 3.717, 4.713, 7.10, and 7.594); and sometimes the fates themselves are only mentioned; ibid.

Stoic conception of πρόνοια) lies behind the whole poem.[106] This idea contrasts the common Greek meaning of chance (and its vague relationship to the laws of nature), as Virgil employs the term in contexts of divine will and its outcome.[107] Virgil's theology seems to move toward monotheism, with Jupiter governing omnipotently as a "tribal god."[108] In the *Aeneid*, Rome's destiny is the purpose of divine will, a blessing to those under Rome's rule.

The gods intervene at times of direction, serve as mediums of prophecy, and personify aspects of human nature or natural forces.[109] The gods in the *Aeneid*, as in Roman religion, are not separated from nature.[110] The Romans sought the good-will of these divine inhabitants whenever they carried out relevant tasks in agriculture or for the state. For example, prayers were offered for good fortune—every morning, at the main meal of the day, before the flocks were taken out to pasture, and before a journey. The constant occurrence of phrases in Latin literature such as *dis faventabus, dis iuvantzbus* or *volentibus*, reveal that nothing was undertaken until the will of the deities had been ascertained and conscience satisfied.[111] "Let us remember that the whole story of the *Aeneid* is one of the bending of the will of the hero, as a type of the ideal Roman, to the ascertainable will of the powers in the universe."[112]

Virgil understands history (after the battle at Actium) as the result of divine will, for Actium made history potentially intelligible.[113] Characters in the *Aeneid* acknowledge the *fata* when history becomes intelligible, but this is often temporal. For example, Dido and Aeneas (and Turnus in the latter half of the poem) do not see the confrontation of Jupiter and Juno. Jupiter only intervenes when fulfillment of his

---

106. Bailey, *Religion in Virgil*, 232.

107. Ibid., 209–14.

108. Ibid., 234.

109. For helpful works on the role of the gods in the *Aeneid*, see: Boyancé, *La Religion de Virgile*; Coleman, "Gods in the *Aeneid*," 143–68; Kühn, *Götterszenen bei Vergil*; Thornton, *Living Universe*, 144f; Williams, *Technique and Ideas*, 76f; and Wilson, "Jupiter and the Fates," 361–71.

110. For example, the river Tiber in 8.19-40 is the deity; Hahn, "Vergil's Linguistic Treatment," 56–67.

111. Fowler, *Religious Experience*, 251.

112. Ibid.

113. Wilson, "Jupiter and the Fates," 370.

promises are in jeopardy (e.g., he sends Mercury to Carthage to command Aeneas to set sail for Italy). More significant than Juno representing *ira* is Juno's bending to Jupiter's view of history: "the events of the *Aeneid* have the τὰ καθ' ἕκαστον quality which Aristotle predicated of historical events . . . as these events are received by the divine mind, and are there sifted and interpreted in relation to the long-term pattern of history, so each event begins to assume τὰ καθόλου qualities of poetry."[114]

Imagery and Theme in Books 7–12

The invocation in Book 7 begins a new section to the *Aeneid* (an even greater work; *maius opus moveo*, 7.45). Adler interprets the new proem (7.1–45) to answer the three elements of the first proem (Rome-anger-Carthage) with another triad (Rome-anger-Italy).[115] The answer to Rome's becoming "kingdom over the nations" (*regnum gentibus*, 1.17), and the answer to the Roman people becoming "king far and wide" (*late regem*, 1.21), is first to become king over the Italian nations.[116] In this sense, the Odyssean *Aeneid* critiques the Carthaginian regime by pointing out an inadequate understanding of anger which does not secure peace, and the Iliadic *Aeneid* critiques the Italian (or Saturnian) regime, the traditional myth of the Golden Age.[117]

From a different perspective, the major theme in Books 7–12 can be understood as the divine man of Roman destiny (Aeneas), whose mission it is to defeat impious *furor* (represented by Allecto and the Latin wars).[118] In this way, Books 7 and 8 are introductions to the divine man's role against the violent character of war. Books 9–12 display this violence (*furor*) of individuals and the violence of the mass against Aeneas (*humanitas* and *virtus*).[119]

---

114. Ibid., 371.

115. Adler, *Vergil's Empire*, 140–41. In Books 7–12, Juno supports Italy rather than the defeated Carthage.

116. Ibid., 144.

117. Ibid.

118. Otis, *Virgil*, 331–32. The god of old Arcadian Rome was Hercules, and now the future Rome's θεός ἀνήρ is to be Augustus—all three symbolize the eternally Roman struggle of *pietas* and *humanitas* against savage and barbaric violence; ibid.

119. Books 10 and 12 carry the Iliadic main theme (the parallelism of Achilles-Hector-Patroclus with Aeneas-Turnus-Pallas), but they contrast Aeneas and Turnus;

Based on the principal figures and epic structure of the *Aeneid*, Virgil makes his central message (Book 5–8) clear by framing it between the tragedies of Dido (Books 1–4) and Turnus (Books 9–12). Both tragic characters conjure sympathy with the audience, and both meet death, because of their ἁμαρτία and its consequence. The two tragedies do not lack historical significance—Dido's death symbolizes the overthrow of Carthage by Rome (4.669–70), and Turnus's death results in Roman supremacy, the union of Romans and Latins.[120]

Uno Sanguine

In Book 7, Aeneas and his men land on Italian soil and quickly realize that one of the prophecies about their new home in Italy has already been fulfilled. King Latinus gives a great welcome to Aeneas and soon offers his daughter to him in marriage (he did this because he believed an oracle which foretold of a foreign prince who would bring victory). Queen Amata (King Latinus's wife) and Juno favor the Rutulian prince, Turnus, to marry the royal daughter. Juno incites Allecto from Hades to influence Queen Amata, Turnus, and the Latium citizens against Aeneas.[121] What first appeared to be unity between the Latins and Trojans has now turned into discord. In this book, Virgil accents the Roman principle

---

the two episodes of heroism (a Trojan and a Latin) contrast *humanitas-virtus* with battle fury and lust of plunder (which doom such heroes as Nisus, Euryalus, and Camilla); ibid., 317.

120. Duckworth, "*Aeneid* as a Trilogy," 5. Duckworth sees a parallel to Horace's *Odes*. The interlocking of the twelve books of the *Aeneid* (divided into halves and thirds) suggests that "Horace must have known of his friend's structural plans before he composed the Roman Odes . . . [and it] seems hardly accidental that the six friezes in this famous monument [Ara Pacis] likewise have a double arrangement: (1) a tripartite division: two legendary friezes, two of contemporary history and two symbolical friezes; and (2) two halves: one Julian (Aeneas, the imperial family, Italia), the other Roman (Romulus, the senate and Roman people, Roma). Each half likewise divides into thirds, with the historical frieze framed by legend and symbol. The structure of the *Aeneid* and the Roman Odes must certainly have been in the mind of the artists as they planned the monument"; ibid., 9–10.

121. Four similes (whipped up, boiling, progressively surging, seething uncontrolled upon its course) mark three stages in which fury escalates to a climax, where Allecto incorporates all the aspects of violence and fury of Books 1, 2, and 4; Otis, *Virgil*, 327. For Virgil's creation of Allecto as a monster identical to Ennius's description of Discordia, see Fraenkel, "Aspects," 1–14.

of revenge against Rome's enemies, and he includes considerable detail reflecting the customs and attitudes of Augustan Rome.

The elements of Tragedy are also carefully scripted. Virgil introduces Turnus as appearing at midnight (7.414), and it is Allecto, who bears war and death in her hands, who comes to Turnus and incites him with "frenzy of war" (7.462).[122] Turnus stands in the way of Aeneas's mission.[123] The poet also portrays Turnus as a courageous hero (7.473), a man of nobility (7.55, 7.650), and an innocent victim (similar to Dido in that he draws respect and sympathy from the audience). The symbols on Turnus's armor (7.783–84)—an image of the metamorphosis of Io and a fire-breathing Chimaera—punctuate the dilemma of whether Turnus is to be perceived as a victim of the gods or as an irrational enemy of the future of Rome.[124] Turnus's passion, like Dido, transforms him into a "beast," which is signified in the emblem of Io (an animal metamorphis by the work of the gods),[125] and in the mythical demon Chimaera (see 6.288). As the gods influence Turnus toward *furor*, the suspense builds concerning his final outcome (particularly, the role of *pietas* in his end and whether Turnus will be a victim of the gods).

The mood changes to unity again in Book 8. Based on a dream, Aeneas sails up the Tiber river with two ships to meet with Evander, king of a small Arcadian Greek community who lives on the future site of Rome. With an attitude of humility and without fear, he comes to King Evander extending an arranged branch (*ramos*, 8.128) as a sacred headband.[126] Aeneas acknowledges Evander's lineage (*stirpe*, 8.130) from Atreus and reminds him of their shared origin (8:132–42):

122. Galinsky compares Cacus with Turnus and does not believe Virgil symbolizes Cleopatra and Antony with Turnus. Virgil casts Turnus in a context of darkness and fire; both symbols are typical of Hades; Galinsky, "The Hercules-Cacus Episode," 26–27.

123. Turnus commands the army, which includes Mezentius (the abrogated leader of the Etruscans) and Camilla, a violent female warrior.

124. Gale, "The Shield of Turnus," 176–221. Concerning passion, Turnus's character development resembles that of Dido (Books 1–4). Gale explains that the fire-breathing monster and the defenseless woman are transformed into an animal through the desires and jealousies of the gods; this parallels the metamorphosis and passion of Dido. Pöschl notes how Virgil often compares his characters to animals when the behavior is aggressive or dishonorable (e.g., lion: 9.792–96, 10.454–56, and 12.4–9; tiger: 9.730; wolf: 9.59–64 and 565–66; and eagle: 9.563–64); *Art of Vergil*, 98–9.

125. Ibid.

126. Theodore Williams translates this line as "lifting this olive-branch with fillets

cognatique patres, tua terris didita fama,
coniunxere tibi et fatis egere volentem.
Dardanus, Iliacae primus pater urbis et auctor,
Electra, ut Grai perhibent, Atlantide cretus,
advehitur Teucros; Electram maximus Atlas
edidit, aetherios umero qui sustinet orbis.
vobis Mercurius pater est, quem candida Maia
Cyllenae gelido conceptum vertice fudit;
at Maiam, auditis si quicquam credimus, Atlas,
idem Atlas generat caeli qui sidera tollit.
sic genus amborum scindit se sanguine ab uno.

Our fathers being related; your fame that is known throughout
  the world
has bound me to you, and has led me to be obedient to the fates.
Dardanus, first father and founder of the Trojan city,
born of Atlantean Electra (as the Greeks claim) and
carried to the Trojan people; Electra was begotten of mighty
  Atlas,
who sustains the heavenly spheres on his shoulders.
Your ancestor is Mercury, whom beautiful Maia conceived
and gave birth on the Cyllene's cold summit;
but Maia, if we believe in the things we have heard, is the child
  of Atlas,
the same Atlas who holds up the heavenly stars.
In this way, both of our races branch from one blood.

Evander and Aeneas are related through their ancestors, Dardinus (leader of Troy) and Atlas.[127] Virgil uses the phrase "branch from one blood" to reveal their shared origin.[128] Even though the Romans have supremacy over the Greeks (6.836-37), the road to safety will come

bound"; *Aeneid of Virgil*, 262. Virgil also uses the stem (*stirpe*) of a sacred olive tree (*oleaster*) in 12.766-80.

127. For a helpful discussion on pre-Virgilian traditions, see Gruen, *Culture and National Identity*, 6-51; particularly see Dionysius of Halicarnassus, *Roman Antiquities* 1.31.1-2. For genealogical diagrams, see Clausen, *Virgil's Aeneid*, 119-20. Most of the Latin and Trojan names appear in the Homeric poems; Saunders, "Names of Trojans and Latins," 537-55. When Augustus defeated Antony (a Philhellene) at Actium and conquered Alexandria, he ended any Hellenistic hope for the East to dominate the Roman West. Here Virgil reduces the tension between Greek and Roman pride.

128. See also 3.163-64. *Stirpe* means the lower part of the trunk, stock, stem, shoot, or root; Andrews, Freund, Lewis, and Short, *Latin Dictionary*, s.v. "*stirpe*." Two significant parallels in the *Aeneid* use the word *stirpe* and *sanguine*: 7.98-99 (*stirpe* and *sanguine*) and 11.394 (Trojan blood, *sanguine*, to King Evander's lineage, *stirpe*).

first through a Grecian city (6.96–97). Virgil restructures the legend about Aeneas's arrival in Latium so that no people are excluded from Italy's origins.[129] He fuses the different war stories into a single war between the Trojans and the Latins, followed by reconciliation. By uniting the Greek Arcadians with the Trojans, Virgil brings together two traditional adversaries (Greeks and Trojans) as well as the Etruscans. Virgil's selection of Homeric material accents his dramatic and political purposes.[130]

Virgil accents the humble bond between the Trojans and the Arcadians. Aeneas looks for a humble home for their country's gods (7.229) and finds this in Evander's Greek community. The poor immigrant, Evander, lives on the Palatine (8.456) in an "exiguous cottage, the prototype of Augustus's own house on the Palatine . . . modest and humble, a collection of huts . . . his own house is called angustus, confined, cramped."[131] Virgil then contrasts this simplicity and humility with the enemy's "arrogant" power and "proud" race (8.483–84).

Rome's Greatness

At the end of Book 8, Venus demonstrates her love for her son in the battles ahead by having her husband, a divine craftsman, make a suit of armor for Aeneas. The shield is not needed for battle, but serves as literary strategy for Virgil, since the coming wars in Italy play a significant role for the Roman state, the *gens Iulia*, and the Augustan Principate (8.627–28).[132] This narrative has two sections: the scenes centering around the edge of the shield (8.626–70) and Augustus's victory at Actium (8.675–728).[133] Virgil thrusts to the forefront visual imagery

129. Conte, *Latin Literature*, 280–88.

130. Ibid.

131. Grandsen, *Virgil's Iliad*, 56. Pöschl interprets this lowly connection as a purification process where Aeneas is ". . . cleansed of the odium of his Asiatic origin and imbued with Italo-Roman contempt for *luxuria*. In leaving the Oriental world, Aeneas becomes a Roman in his heart. This then is the deeper meaning of the eighth book as it concerns Aeneas's inner pilgrimage"; *Art of Vergil*, 60.

132. West, "Shield of Aeneas," 295–304. The Homeric parallel simply uses the shield to portray Greek life (*Il.* 18.478–79). In 27 B.C., the Senate honored Augustus with a golden shield (*Clipeus Virtutis*).

133. The outer scenes do not record history beyond 390 B.C.; this spotlights the central scene of Actium and present-day events (8.678–81); Williams, *The Aeneid*, 45. Williams explains the third of six scenes which depicts the story of King Tullus

of fleets, Augustus and Agrippa, and Cleopatra behind Antony in the middle of the Antonine forces (8.675–696). Oriental and Olympian gods are also depicted (8.697). This passage uses a technique familiar in Roman art where phases of a narrative are demonstrated in the same picture with different pictures of the character (e.g., Cleopatra bears down on the enemy, Apollo stretches his bow, and the Oriental forces turn and flee).[134] In this artistic display, the Augustan panel is most prominent.

This central scene portrays Augustus leading Italians into battle, representing Augustus's victories over the East. But Augustus defeats the Trojans, too, which contrasts the story line of Aeneas, a Trojan, preparing to go to war against Italians. Virgil simplifies Homer by concentrating on warfare and centers the visual imagery around Rome.[135] At the end of the *ekphrasis*, Virgil takes the listener East (Asia and the Euphrates), West (Rhine), North (Gaul and Scythia), and South (Africa). Interestingly, Augustus carries into battle the very same household gods that Aeneas took with him from his ravaged city, so that what is most sacred and intimate of Troy survives in Italy, sending a message of continuity and consolation.[136] In essence, the shield of Aeneas visually concludes Book 8 and "holds up the narrative and sums up the meaning of the poem."[137]

Tragic Turnus

Books 9, 10, and 11 narrate individual battle scenes. At first, Turnus acts piously in his prayers to the gods (9.22), but Juno's influence provokes Turnus to war against Aeneas's troops, while Aeneas is away seeking the support of the Etruscans. Like a wolf tormented by the fury of famine, he rides around the walls wildly, with bloodless jaws, and iron hot

---

Hostilius who breaks his word (*fides violata*) in punishing the Alban Mettus.

134. West, "Shield of Aeneas," 302.

135. Ibid., 302–3. The final scenes on the Shield may represent the survival of major dangers to the city of Rome (through divine destiny and the virtue of its citizens); see Harrison, "Survival and Supremacy of Rome," 76.

136. West, "Shield of Aeneas," 303. Williams notes the parallel between 8.679 and 3.12 which describe the departure of Aeneas from Troy—what Aeneas began centuries before is brought to its final conclusion by Augustus at Actium; *The Aeneid*, 47.

137. Grandsen, *Virgil's Iliad*, 95.

resentment in his bones (9.59–60). Turnus enters the walls of the Trojan camp murdering and terrorizing with a thirst for blood (9.731, 757).

At night, an experienced veteran, Nisus, and a young soldier named Euryalus, slip behind enemy lines to carry a message to Aeneas. Eventually they are killed by returning enemy cavalry which causes great grief among the Trojans.[138] Jupiter calls a council to ensure that destiny is not altered, and warns Juno that Turnus will die. Still, Juno protects Turnus as he continues to fight savagely. Turnus kills Pallas, King Evander's son, and takes his weapon belt. Upon hearing that Aeneas and the Etruscan armies are approaching, Turnus and his forces retreat.

In Book 12, Lavinia is promised to the winner of the duel between Aeneas and Turnus. Father Aeneas, origin of the Roman race (*Romanae stirpis origo*, 12.166), stands with his blazing starry shield and celestial arms extended and prays that he does not selfishly reign alone, but that he would enter into an everlasting covenant with both nations (Trojans and Italians). Turnus despairs. A spear is thrown into the enemy camp inciting war. Then an arrow wounds Aeneas, weakening his knees and impeding his speed. Turnus suddenly burns with fire and hope. With anger, terror, and ambush, Turnus guides his galloping horses over bodies of blood (12.336–37).[139] Venus comes to her son Aeneas's aid and helps heal the wound (12.411–12). Not having heard from Turnus, Queen Amata commits suicide in her palace thinking that he is dead (12.593–94).

After hearing of the news and realizing the disaster upon him, Turnus, like Dido, accepts his death and glory gracefully, without retreat (12.648). With shame, madness, grief, and a love tormented by fury, he decides to meet Aeneas in a final duel. Turnus frantically throws a large stone at Aeneas and misses. Aeneas hurls his spear with all of his might and wounds Turnus. Denied by Juno and filled with fear, Turnus has nowhere to escape (12.913–17) and makes his plea (12.930–36):

---

138. Nisus and Euryalus both make tragic mistakes. Duckworth makes the comparison between the tragic death of Nisus and Euryalus (at the beginning of the Turnus books, 9–12) with Turnus, who is characterized by *furor, violentia, ira*, and his reckless desire for booty; Duckworth, "Significance of Nisus and Euryalus," 129–55.

139. Turnus kills savagely (staking severed dripping heads on his chariot), but does so with Roman justice; Aeneas, on the other hand, kills for the "bitter fulfillment of duty"; Pöschl, *Art of Vergil*, 122. Aeneas only enters battle three times (to retaliate against a violated treaty, to avenge the death of Pallas, and to respond to the Latins' violation of a pact); ibid., 123.

ille humilis supplex oculos dextramque precantem
protendens "equidem merui nec deprecor" inquit;
"utere sorte tua. miseri to si qua parentis
tangere cura potest, oro (fait et tibi talis
Anchises genitor) Dauni miserere senectae
et me, sea corpus spoliatum lumine mavis,
redde meis.

In humility he lowered his eyes and extended his right hand:
"I deserve this and do not ask for mercy," he said,
"Seize your destiny. If any concern of a parent's
grief is able to touch you (for you had such a
father in Anchises) I beg you to pity Daunus's old age,
return to me, or if you prefer, return my lifeless body back to
my people.

Aeneas hesitates, but then sees Pallas's sword belt around Turnus's waist, and out of rage sends him to the underworld (12.945–52):

ille, oculis postquam saevi monumenta doloris
exuviasque hausit, furiis accensus et ira
terribilis: "tune hinc spoliis indute meorum
eripiare mihi? Pallas te hoc vulnere, Pallas
immolat et poenam scelerato ex sanguine sumit."
hoc dicens ferrum adverso sub pectore condit
fervidus; ast illi solvuntur frigore membra
vitaque cum gemitu fugit indignata sub umbras.

Aeneas, after drinking in with his eyes the spoil *of his friend*,
a memorial of cruel grief, is set on fire with fury and terrible
  wrath:
"Will you, clothed in the spoils of one of my own,
be snatched from me? Pallas it is, Pallas sacrifices you with this
  wound,
and takes retribution from your defiled blood!"
Saying this in burning rage he buries his sword deep into
  Turnus's chest.
His limbs became limp and cold,
and with a groan his indignant spirit fled to the Shades below.

As an agent of vengeance, Aeneas sacrifices Turnus for the cause of Rome.

Virgil scripts the actions and words of Aeneas and Turnus (Books 9–12) to complete the larger singular plot (which involves a significant parallel to the tragic story of Dido) to influence his listeners toward a universal message of Rome's promised age of peace. Here the Roman attitudes of war and historical influences of the past connect to the present as the noble and ignoble actions of the Rutulian prince and the elected Trojan king unfold. Juno uses Turnus as an agent of her own jealousy and wrath, but Jupiter and Anchises (and at times, Venus) providentially guide Aeneas to fulfill his glorious mission. In contrast to the traditional Turnus legend, but remaining consistent with epic tradition, Virgil portrays Turnus as an enemy but does present some of his qualities as honorable (e.g., compassion for comrades and *pietas*).[140] Turnus, like Dido, is not aware of the gods actuating the events. He too makes a mistake (ἁμαρτία) in ignorance[141] and expresses his guilt. His love for glory turns into unbridled fury. His situation changed unexpectedly from passionate chauvinism to sadness (reversal) with a simultaneous awareness (recognition) at the end of Book 12.

Turnus's blindness intensifies the emotional effect, which means that the conclusions he draws about the future are based on improbability (false premises). Turnus moves from ignorance to some recognition, which brings about fear, pity, and amazement among the listeners of the *Aeneid*. The Trojans do not rejoice (12.919–20), and the Rutulians grieve as Carthage did for Dido, which creates a compassionate moment

---

140. There is something of the grandeur of Achilles in Turnus, which makes this ending more tragic; Pöschl, *Art of Vergil*, 138. All three main characters (Aeneas, Dido, and Turnus) personify the three cardinal virtues in the *Aeneid*, but Turnus lacks the noble glow of Aeneas and Dido, and is possessed with the fury of Hell; ibid. Anderson argues that (1) Virgil unites the personalities of Achilles, Agamemnon, and Menelaus in Aeneas, so that the supreme moral justification motivates the leader and finest warrior of the Trojans, and (2) he made Turnus a poignant combination of Paris and Hector, so that the defeat and death of Italy's noblest warrior will also remove the need for war; Anderson, "Virgil's Second *Iliad*," 27–28. The *furor* and *ira* of both Turnus and Aeneas are depicted against a background of allusions to Achilles, but Aeneas also shares with Achilles a certain resignation to fate which is lacking in Turnus until the very end of the poem; Nortwick, "Aeneas, Turnus, and Achilles," 303–14. Nortwick suggests that it might be that Aeneas puts to rest in Turnus and in himself that anachronistic Achillean heroism which is to be replaced by *pietas*, the cornerstone of the new civilization of Rome.

141. Turnus's *culpa* is his ignorance of his fate and fortune, equated with immoderateness in his hour of success (10.501–2); Otis, *Virgil*, 356. His *inhumanitas* condemns him, and he disrespects the *virtus* of an enemy and shows his contempt for human suffering and *pietas*; ibid.

for the weak-willed Turnus.¹⁴² Aeneas sends Turnus to the underworld, and the audience has already been warned in Book 6 about what lies ahead for those who act dishonorably. For Turnus, his violence results in a broken relationship (φιλία) with the political purposes of heaven and the ordered age of peace through Rome. Literary tension is consistently maintained because of the consequences caused by the decisions of the gods which affect the choices of Turnus.

Wrathful Aeneas

Aeneas hesitates (12.939) before he avenges Pallas's death by sacrificing Turnus. The audience knows that Aeneas's political destiny is providentially determined (necessary action), but the issue now centers on whether Aeneas will act in obedience (tension between choice and necessity). Generally speaking, Virgil's ending falls into three interpretive possibilities: (1) Aeneas reacts out of unjust anger, creating a tragic but realistic message about humanity, (2) Aeneas acts justly in a heroic manner, promoting an Augustan ideal, or (3) Virgil does not answer the *furor-pietas* dilemma, stimulating internal debate over a relevant, ambivalent philosophical issue.¹⁴³ How one interprets Aeneas's rage colors the meaning of the whole epic and reveals one's view of Virgil's political intentions. A closer look at the sociological context may clarify the significance of the ending of Virgil's poem.

142. Pöschl, *Art of Vergil*, 135. Heinze interprets Turnus's request for mercy as unheroic character; *Virgil's Epic Technique*, 180. Pöschl defends the tragic nature of Turnus's actions, especially since he sees Turnus as fulfilling the obligations of the treaty; *Art of Vergil*, 78. Elain Fanthem stresses that this does not mean that Turnus deserves compassion or that his virtue is to be remembered; "Fighting Words, 259–80.

143. For representative views: for "unjust anger," see Quinn, *Virgil's Aeneid*, 272; Putnam, *Poetry of the Aeneid*, 193f; for "just anger," see Otis, *Virgil*, 379f; Heinze, *Vergil's Epic Technique*, 180; and Galinsky, "Anger of Aeneas," 321–48; for the view of "unanswered dilemma," see Beare, "Invidious Success," 18–30; Nortwick, "Aeneas, Turnus, and Achilles," 314. Wendell Clausen notices an interesting parallel between the ending in Books 6 and 12; "Interpretation of the *Aeneid*," 139–47. Clausen points out that Virgil chooses to end Book 6 by honoring the deceased Marcellus, the nephew of Augustus, rather than praise Augustus. When Aeneas meets Marcellus in the underworld, he asks Anchises who this man is. Anchises with tears responds that Aeneas should not ask about the great sorrows of his people (6.868). The parade of heroes also includes a somber note about Brutus, who killed his seditious son for the cause of liberty (6.822). Clausen concludes that Virgil's depiction of Rome is "a long Pyrhic victory of the human spirit" which includes a certain realism, not merely propaganda. Thus, when Aeneas kills Turnus, the ending is not bright, and the "light is hard and clear"; ibid., 146.

The martial display of anger out of revenge or the emotional showing of pity was perceived as weakness by the Stoics, which differs from Augustan ideals. C. Bowra writes specifically concerning Virgil's intentions: "In particular, it seems that in these angry scenes Virgil must have had Augustus himself in mind, not the statesman of the later years but the merciless avenger of Julius' death."[144] In other words, Virgil attributes the anger of Augustus to Aeneas, adapting the Stoic model with a historical adaption of an Augustan warrior, an inconsistency which brings "the good man of Stoic theory to the level of the Roman world."[145] It is important to recognize that pity and anger are not Stoic, but Roman, which is why Aeneas shows more compassion as a military leader than Augustus did, and this is why Augustus portrays such an image after Actium.[146]

This does not mean, however, that Virgil's adaptation of Stoic ideals warrants Aeneas a badge of "just anger." Turnus brings dishonor upon himself for his attitude of self-glory and his choice of taking the *spolia* away after killing Pallas. Virgil passes judgment on Turnus for his Homeric agitation (e.g., 12.101–2), not for an immoral fault.[147] In fact, Aeneas's vengeful anger against Turnus does not fit neatly into Stoic principles.[148] In his preparation for the duel with Turnus (12.107–8), Aeneas focuses his mind on peace (12.109), further demonstrated by

144. Bowra draws several parallels between the mercilessness of Aeneas and Augustus: After Philippi, Augustus exacted vengeance much like Aeneas did after the death of Pallas. Aeneas refuses burial to Tarquitus, telling him that he would be left to the birds, and the fishes would lick his wounds; Augustus answered a man who begged humbly for burial and told him that birds would settle that question (see Suet. *Aug.* 13). Aeneas is so angry that no appeal to the names of Anchises and Ascanius move him to spare Magus or Lucagus; Augustus made sons play a game with their fathers to decide who should live, and then looked on while both died (see Suet. Aug. 13). Aeneas sacrificed the sons of Sulmo at Pallas's pyre; Augustus had three hundred prisoners-of-war after Perusia sacrificed on the Ides of March at the altar of Julius; Bowra, "Aeneas and the Stoic Ideal," 18–19. For a framework of Book 12 with respect to Roman attitudes, see Nisbet, "Aeneas Imperator," 50–61.

145. Bowra, "Aeneas and the Stoic Ideal," 373–74. For Stoic ideas in relation to Roman life, see Arnold, *Roman Stoicism*, 380–81.

146. See *RG* 3, 13.

147. Lyne, "Politics of War," 195.

148. Aeneas shows sympathy for the slaughter of Italians (1.101 and Book 8), but he does so with a calm exacting sense of justice, without extreme passion; ibid., 190. Lyne describes his request for a truce to bury the dead (11.108–19) as "measured sympathy."

his level-headed speech (12.176–77). Though Aeneas stands for peace in victory and expresses his policy of magnanimous *clementia*, he also enacts vengeance like a Homeric hero (12.494–99), and without a sense of justice (12.565–73). In other words, he abandons the Stoic ideal, but does not let go of his "high minded aim" (12.466–67).[149] From this perspective, Aeneas kills Turnus dishonorably, since Turnus has been humbled and begs for mercy (which qualifies him for *clementia*, 12.930–38). Aeneas must maintain peace in spite of his act.[150]

Yet, a closer look at Greco-Roman culture reveals that Aeneas's impassioned action can be considered unequivocally moral. In a Roman's mind, Turnus deserves capital punishment:[151] (1) He cuts off the heads of his slain enemies (suspending them from his chariot with dripping blood), (2) he violates the peace by taking up army *impia* (12.31; a crime which Virgil refers to earlier in the epic, 7.647, which has a place in Tartarus, 6.612–13), and (3) he rejoices in the breaking of a sacred peace agreement. Turnus's death results from his act of *devotio*, where he vows to sacrifice his own life to restore the peace of the gods if he is defeated (11.440–43), the final indication of the *ira deorum* (12.694–95). When Turnus asks for his life, he violates his pledge to the gods. So when Aeneas lets his anger carry out the penalty for the way in which Turnus treated Pallas's body after the battle death, Aeneas acts justly.[152]

---

149. Ibid., 202.

150. Lyne concludes: "Vergil has constructed a hero with whom any founder or refounder of Rome must be and would no doubt like to be compared. Vergil's hero understands and espouses the high imperial ideals sung by Horace. But he finds that . . . *inclementia* is often irresistible, and High Motives clash with high motives . . . Vergil's hero demonstrates the truth (we might say) of imperial ideals, what actually happens to them in practice . . . Vergil does not obscure the reality. The wars that gain empire involve ugly violence, and less than perfect motivations will sometimes direct even the greatest hero"; ibid., 203.

151. Galinsky, "Anger of Aeneas," 323–25.

152. Galinsky, "Anger of Aeneas," 325. Galinsky responds to the overwhelming criticism of Aeneas's rejecting Turnus's petition for mercy and his angry killing of him (12:946–47), and argues against the narrow focus of the Stoic moralizing of Aeneas's "irrationality" (or the Christian tradition of withholding mercy; see Lactantius, *Divine Institutes* 5.10–11). "The final scene is a microcosm of the epic in that it is complex and has multiple dimensions. While several responses are possible—and that is always the attraction of a classic—it does not drift off into the grey area of moral irresolution. In the end: Aeneas has to make a decision, and clues are freely given that his impassioned action can be considered as unequivocally moral . . . There is an exquisite balance between Aeneas's subjective volition and the objective causation . . . its fulcrum again

112   Part 1: The Gospel of Augustus in the *Aeneid*

Karl Galinsky illuminates Aeneas's *furor* and *ira* in this final scene and investigates the different philosophical attitudes to anger in antiquity.[153] Aristotle's view of anger is representative of the orators (*Rhet.* 1378a31) when he defines ὀργή as oriented toward revenge or punishment ("an impulse, accompanied by pain, to an apparent revenge for an apparent slight which was directed, without justification, towards what concerns oneself or towards what concerns one's friends," 1378a30 and 1378b-80a).[154] "Slight" (ὀλιγωρία) means causing another shame for the pleasure of it. Turnus kills Pallas, mistreats the corpse, and wishes that Evander, Pallas's father, could be present to witness the killing and the taking of the armor (10.490–91). While there is justice in a victorious battle (10.459), there is no justification for hybris (*Rhet.* 1378b23–28), which contrasts Aeneas's treatment of Lausus.[155] In this way, Aeneas acts out of *pietas* and *fides* when he seeks revenge on his slighted friend.[156]

Revenge should be obvious to the offender so that he knows why he is receiving punishment (*Rhet.* 1380b20),[157] and the intensity of anger should be appropriate to the person and situation. In this case, emotions should avoid extreme (*Nic. Eth.* 1106b20–24) and be "felt at the right time, on the right occasion, towards the right people, for the right purpose and in the right manner, [it] is to feel the best amount of them, which is the mean amount—and the best amount is of course the

---

is the anger theme"; ibid., 322–23. The next several paragraphs summarize pertinent sections of Galinsky's article, "Anger of Aeneas," 321–48.

153. Ibid., 332–33.

154. Quotations from Aristotle in this section are translated by G. Karl Galinsky.

155. At the end of Book 10, Aeneas kills the young warrior, Lausus (son of Mezentius and fellow warrior of Turnus), and is moved to pity. Aeneas does not strip him of his armor, but promises the Latin people that he will be given a proper burial.

156. Galinsky, "Anger of Aeneas," 332.

157. Since anger was an important component in meting out punishment, and since mercy without just wrath worked against the law, Roman orators (like Cicero and Tacitus) sought to arouse the *ira* of the judge (e.g., Cicero *De Or.* 1.220 and Tac. *Dial.* 31); Galinsky, "Anger of Aeneas," 333. Galinsky finds St. Paul's characterization of the last judgment as the day of the coming of ὀργή (1 Thess 1.10), the *dies irae*, to be associated with punishment, and finds the tradition of δικαία ὀργή to be related (a phrase that is used by Dio to characterize one of Caesar's reactions to Pompey, *Rom. Hist.* 40.51.2); ibid. It is Aeneas who decides the just punishment of Turnus, and "only the Stoic audience would find anger repugnant here"; ibid., 334.

mark of virtue."¹⁵⁸ In other words, the response may vary depending on different obligations.

It is important to distinguish the relationship between anger, hatred, and compassion. Anger and compassion are linked (*Rhet.* 1382a14); hatred and compassion are not.¹⁵⁹ Turnus realizes that Aeneas is exhibiting enmity (12.938), and Virgil clarifies this by having Aeneas motivated by *ira*. Galinsky argues that Virgil also stresses the association of anger and pain (*Rhet.* 1832a13)¹⁶⁰ and points out that hate is free from pain (*Pol.* 1312b32–34). Aristotle's discussion began by quoting Homer's Achilles on the pleasure of revenge-oriented anger (*Il.* 18.109–10 and *Rhet.* 1378b6–7) but discards the nexus between anger and pleasure. It is the absence of the connotation of pleasure in Aeneas's emotions which differentiates his anger from the anger of Achilles (and from Turnus). "In the Aristotelian sense, then, Aeneas is an example of the morally perfect man."¹⁶¹

This philosophical view also aligns with Virgil's use of the function of anger in the *Iliad*, especially with reference to Achilles. The *Aeneid* ends with echoes of the main themes of the Homeric parallel (22.330–60): Achilles acts without sympathy against Hector, who warns Achilles of the wrath he will incur from the gods, and soon Achilles's anger results in separation from his community. Not so with Aeneas. He hesitates and considers Turnus's plea based on their fathers (10.43–46; for parallel of reference to parents, see *Il.* 22.338, 345). His compassionate and impassionate response places Aeneas at the center of his society, because he acts on behalf of his community, an inversion of the Iliadic episode.¹⁶² Aeneas becomes the instrument of *deum ira* rather than its object.¹⁶³

158. See also *Nic. Eth.* 1125b31–32.

159. Galinsky, "Anger of Aeneas," 334.

160. This follows the preceding argument in the same concluding passage of Aristotle's discussion of anger.

161. Ibid., 335. Galinsky also shows how Aeneas's anger fits within the Epicurean philosophical view, and finds the Stoic perspective too narrow for Virgil's audience; "Anger of Aeneas," 338–39.

162. Ibid., 343.

163. Ibid., 345. Cairns argues that in all ancient philosophical and moral systems *furor* was a vice; *Virgil's Augustan Epic*, 255–56. Cairns analyzes the semantic usage in Virgil of the cognates *furor, furo/furens, furiae* and *furibundus*, and finds 12.946 to be fired by *furiae* and not by *furor*, noting the parallel between Aeneas's *furiae* before he

Human Sacrifice

In the *Aeneid*, Virgil uses slaughtered bulls (*caesi iuvenci*) to symbolize both the *pietas* of sacrifice and the *impietas* of murder, a possible reminder to the listener of human sacrifices, which probably echoed the historical accounts of Octavian's subjugation of Perusia during the Civil Wars.[164] Of the three instances of *caesi iuvenci* in the *Aeneid*, two demonstrate this connection. The first occurrence simply refers to Helenus making a routine sacrifice before prophesying about Aeneas's future (3.369–71). But in Book 5, the blood from a bull-sacrifice causes Nisus to slip at the end of the footrace (5.327–33).[165] Virgil chooses the sacrificed animal's blood for Nisus to slip on rather than dung, as in the parallel scene in Homer (and Virgil uses the phrase *sacer cruor* which darkens Homer's account). Interestingly, in Book 5, it is the blood of slaughtered bulls that causes the downfall, but in Book 9, it is the blood of slaughtered men.[166] In other words, Euryalus and his friend will be sacrificed. Virgil continually "probes the boundaries between man and beast, symbolically substituting one for the other as Nisus slips in the blood of sacrificed bullocks, later to become both a sacrificer of men and a victim himself."[167]

---

kills Turnus and the *furiae* of his great predecessor and exemplar, Hercules. The *furiae* of Aeneas and Hercules are virtuous, while the *furor* of Turnus is evil. For Aeneas's just anger, see also Thomas, "*Furor* and *Furiae*," 261–62.

164. Dyson, "CAESI IUVENCI," 277–86. Dyson begins her argument by examining the phrase *caesi iuvenci* in the *Georgics* that elucidates Virgil's use of verbal ambiguity to create moral ambiguity: (1) his reference to the end of the Golden Age and the passing of the torch from Saturn to Jupiter is used to show impiety in a nonsacrificial sense, which Virgil uses ambiguously to provide an unsettling echo when the phrase appears subsequently in contexts of sacral piety (*Georg.* 2.536–38), (2) his reference to slaughtered bulls is part of the pious trappings of the temple (*Georg.* 3.21–23), (3) purifying blood of the slaughtered bulls gives birth to bees in which Virgil spares no detail of the bull's suffering as it suffocates (*Georg.* 4.299–314), and (4) while bulls are not mentioned, Virgil substitutes buffaloes where men are expected at the end of Book 3 which "will have important ramifications in the *Aeneid*" for understanding animal and human sacrifice.

165. Dyson notes the similar elements of the plague in the *Georgics*: a description of the victor and the phrase *labitur infelix* (3.498–99), which occurs nowhere else in Virgil's works; "CAESI IUVENCI," 279.

166. The *sacer cruor* of the bulls had wet the grass (9.333–34); Dyson mentions that the blood-soaked ground occurs only once more in the *Aeneid* (immediately before Turnus summons Aeneas to the final combat); ibid.

167. Ibid., 280.

The final occurrence of slaughtered bulls (*caesi iuvenci*) occurs when the center of the shield of Aeneas is described, which fulfills Virgil's promise in *Georgics* 3.[168] On the shield, Augustus dedicates three-hundred temples (8.714–19) and *caesi iuvenci* are part of the celebration. While these three-hundred temples, equipped with altar and sacrificial beast, are poetic fiction,[169] "three-hundred" may refer to Augustus's slaughter of knights and senators at the altar of *Divus Iulius* after the capture of Perusia (40 B.C.),[170] one of the greatest atrocities of his reign. It is very likely that these historical events stood out in the minds of the Roman population, and not surprisingly, these events are displayed on the shield of Aeneas, implicitly conveying the harmony and discord and the triumph and murder of civil war.[171] Virgil ends his prophetic gospel with a victorious sacrifice, the last victim of Aeneas's *saeva dolor*.[172]

Summary

As a poet-prophet writing under the influence of Augustus, Virgil writes an epic to supersede the "sacred scriptures" of Greek heritage, Homer's *Iliad* and *Odyssey*. The Roman poet's intricate design and grand symmetry center his message on Rome's greatness and the fulfillment of a promised faithful servant, Aeneas, and his descendant, Caesar Augustus (Books 5–8). Virgil creatively brings together elements of oral tradition and written style to reach the common citizen for a moral, didactic purpose. His style of writing places the listener in a position to feel with the characters and experience the movement of the poem through effective visual description, and at the same time, he limits shared suffering in many of the character dialogues to keep his listeners' attention focused on Roman virtue and Aeneas's mission.

---

168. Dyson draws these parallels: *Georg.* 3.16 and *Aen.* 8.675; *Georg.* 3.22–23 and *Aen.* 8.719; and *Georg.* 3.26–33 and *Aen.* 8.722–28; Dyson, "*CAESI IUVENCI*," 281.

169. Augustus built twelve temples and restored eighty-two; *RG* 19–21.

170. Suet. *Aug.* 15.

171. Dyson, "*CAESI IUVENCI*," 281.

172. Putnam, "*Aeneid* 7," 426. It is worth repeating that *immolat* (12.949) is the same word used when Aeneas offers the sons of Ufens as human offering on the pyre of Pallas (10.519); the sacrifice is made in 11.81, and the only other use of *immolo* is at 10.541; ibid.

Virgil begins his epic with a philosophical question concerning "wrath from heaven" (*caelestibus irae*), asking why it would fall upon a pious Trojan leader, the son of a god. In the opening scenes, the major themes are introduced (e.g., *pietas*, providence, sacrifice, kingship, and Rome's greatness) and the mood of the whole poem is established. The contrast in heaven between Jupiter (representing justice, order, and calm) and Juno (representing fury, chaos, and destruction) is acted out in the conflicts between Dido and Aeneas (Books 1–4) and between Aeneas and Turnus (Books 9–12). The plot centers around a *furor-pietas* theme, with the first half of the *Aeneid* narrating the development and inner struggle of Aeneas and the second half narrating the external battles between Aeneas and his impious foes.

In the first six books, Aeneas endures considerable grief on behalf of his people and his mission, but also learns about the divine plan and eschatological purpose for himself, the remnant, and Rome. In the continuous action of the first four books, Aeneas mourns the loss of his homeland, his wife (Creusa), Dido, and his father. After his delay in Carthage, Aeneas and the Trojans land in Sicily on their way to Italy. Here, in Book 5, Aeneas leads the honorific games as the confident *paterfamilias*, foreshadowing the great Augustus. But the mood changes when Juno incites internal strife. The book ends with the sacrificial death of Aeneas's helmsman, Palinarus. In Book 6, Aeneas descends into the underworld and experiences again the tragic emotions from his past (e.g., the Trojan war, his journey, and his testing in Carthage). In Hades, Aeneas sees souls being punished for sins committed while they were alive, and in Elysium, he learns from his father about the purification of souls and the divine plan in history for the future glory of Rome.

In the last six books, Aeneas defeats *furor* with *pietas*, fulfilling the word of Jupiter, which prepares the way for the appointed savior, Augustus. In Book 7, Virgil introduces the Rutulian prince, Turnus, which builds suspense for the battles ahead, and he demonstrates through Aeneas the Roman principle of revenge against Rome's enemies. In Book 8, Aeneas makes an alliance with Evander, a humble Arcadian Greek king, emphasizing the shared origin of the Trojans and the Greeks (descending from "one blood"). Aeneas's mother, Venus, gives her son a symbolic shield which portrays the historical imagery of Rome's greatness and Augustus's crowning victory at Actium, a thematic summary of the poem. In the final books of the epic, Juno influences

Turnus to the point of demonic rage (he openly displays the heads of his enemies and instigates enormous bloodshed among the Trojans). Aeneas also responds with fury at times (rekindling the listeners' tragic emotions of the civil wars), but in the end acts morally, with justice and *pietas*. Turnus is sacrificed for the future of Rome.

PART 2

❧

The Gospel of God in Romans

4

Paul's Gospel of Salvation to Rome

The Lord said to him [Ananias], "Go, for he [Paul] is a called vessel to me, to carry my name before the nations, kings, and sons of Israel."
(Acts 9:15)

WHEN PAUL WROTE HIS LETTER TO THE CHRISTIANS WHO WERE meeting in house churches in the judicial, financial, and religious center of the empire, he proclaimed a message that directly countervailed the imperial gospel. His recipients, as well as people throughout the empire, observed the political and religious symbolism which portrayed the emperor as the source of peace, unity, and provision, a personification of Roman virtue.[1] Decades before, provincial peoples began placing faith in the emperor by honoring the victorious Augustus as a "savior who put an end to war and established all things" and as "son of god,"[2] and inhabitants and citizens worshipped in their private homes at banquets by pouring out libations on behalf of his name.[3] In the early years of

---

1. Virtues assumed a prominent place on Nero's coinage: Salus, Victoria Augusti, Concordia Augusta, Securitas Augusti, Annona Augusti, and Pax; Fears, "The Cult of Virtues," II.17.2:895–96.

2. Brent, *Imperial Cult*, 19–20.

3. The Senate decreed this in 30 B.C.; see Dio *Rom. Hist.* 51.19.6–7.

Nero's reign, the time of Paul's writing sometime between A.D. 55–58), literature and art had experienced a renewal, a return to the Golden Age of Augustan ideology and cultural superiority.[4]

Paul's audience, considered by society to be a sect of Judaism, seems insignificant in number compared to the Jewish population in Rome (approximately fifty thousand), and especially against the city's larger population of one million.[5] The Christians, like other foreign religious cults, had to adjust their activities so as not to challenge imperial ideology in a city where elected officials and public servants kept a close watch over all activities in each of the 265 districts.[6] In his message to Christian Jews and converted Gentiles,[7] Paul reinterprets Jewish beliefs, and he redirects misplaced Roman values that were propagated from the heart of the empire.[8] In this case, the socio-historical Roman setting becomes an important element in understanding Paul's gospel (in addition to Paul's foundational and primary Old Testament support).[9]

---

4. Wallace-Hadrill, "The Golden Age," 24–25. For celebration of Nero's accession as the beginning of the Golden Age, see the Neronian Einsiedeln Eclogues. See also Jewett, *Romans*, 48–49.

5. Based on 130 inscriptions, Tellbe concludes that the Roman Jewry was not a homogeneous body; they were probably individually structured congregations; Tellbe, 150. For Jewish congregations as associations, see Meeks, *First Urban Christians*, 79–80. Concerning the population of Rome during the time of Augustus, see Garnsey and Saller, *The Roman Empire*, 83; Stambaugh, *Ancient Roman City*, 114.

6. Tellbe, *Paul Between Synagogue and State*, 142–47; also see Robinson, *Ancient Rome*, 9–10.

7. Paul's immediate audience is not purely Jewish or Gentile. While Paul supports his arguments in Romans with Hebrew Scripture, he does not seem to be writing primarily to Jewish Christians; see Munck, *Paul*, 200–209. For the most part, Paul speaks to non-Jews concerning his people, and at the same time, he speaks to a Jewish Christian minority; Kümmel, *Introduction*, 309–10. Also see Dunn, "The Recipients," xliv.

8. Richard Horsley understands some of Paul's use of language as being closely associated with the imperial religion for the purpose of presenting the Gospel as a "direct competitor of the gospel of Caesar"; Horsley, "Paul's Counter-Imperial Gospel," 140. However, it does not seem that Paul thinks his gospel must "compete" or even "counter"; rather, he establishes the truth.

9. "Languages have their meaning because they are grounded in the social practices, shared meaningful activities, of particular communities . . . a person must understand both the wider language and a specific context . . . A competent reader must share realms of discourse and cultural codes with the author . . . Paul was both fully Jewish, absolutely dedicated to his people, and fully a person of Hellenistic culture inhabiting the life of the early Roman empire. The correlate to Paul's theological problem of God's justice toward Jews and the other peoples is the sociological problem of Jews relat-

Chapters 1–3 of this study have shown that Virgil's *Aeneid* was one of the most prominent prophetic sources in first-century Rome, which strengthened Roman ideology and proclaimed the promised salvation to the Roman people through a divine descendant. The *Aeneid* served as a basic reading text for Roman education, much like Homer's works did for the Greek classroom, and public readings of the *Aeneid* were a common form of entertainment, which means that the plot and prophecies of Virgil's epic were well known, especially to the learned in Rome.[10] Chapters 4 and 5 do not assume that Paul read the *Aeneid*, though he may have,[11] but seek to know whether Paul framed his letter or chose specific content based on shared philosophical and moral constructs of thought (themes and imagery) that his audience would recognize (and that he himself was aware of based on what he heard in his travels concerning Virgil's universal story).[12] This analysis follows a sequential progression based on the literary divisions in Paul's letter: After discussing important elements of the prologue and thanksgiving section (1:1–7, 8–15), the possible shared themes and imagery between the first half of the body of Paul's letter (1:16—5:11; 5:12—8:39) and Virgil's *Aeneid* are evaluated.

Appointed Son of God, Rom 1:1—1:15

With unique style, Paul extends the limits of the epistolary genre when he pens his letter to the Romans, educating the Christians concerning the past, present, and future of God's elected people and the salvation that comes through Jesus Christ, the appointed Son of God. The prescript of his letter (1:1–7) gives his listeners clear direction as to the tone and content of the gospel of God that he proclaims, countervail-

---

ing to non-Jews in the highly interactive polyethnic environment of the early empire"; Stowers, *Rereading of Romans*, 6–7, 328.

10. Virgil's works had an immediate and powerful effect on his audiences; see Tac. *Dial.* 13.2.

11. This is not a far-fetched proposition; Polybius translates Virgil's poetry into Greek in the mid-first century; see Seneca, *Consolatio ad Polybium* 11.5. It is a logical conclusion to believe that Paul would be aware of the major themes of the *Aeneid*, especially because of his calling to "kings" and "nations" and because of his diplomatic ability to communicate to the churches in the socio-religious contexts of their own cities.

12. It is important not to minimize the "upward mobility" of the most active and prominent members of Paul's circle; Meeks, *First Urban Christians*, 73.

significant themes of the gospel of Caesar (themes that are most clearly expressed in the *Aeneid*).[13] With pious devotion, Paul offers thanksgiving (1:8–15) for the faithfulness of the believers in Rome, and he reminds them of their mission, an obedience of faith to the nations in the name of Christ Jesus.

Letter Genre

Paul's theological argument and use of universal themes distinguish his letter to the Romans from his other letters, so much so that this missive may be considered a compendium of Christian doctrine.[14] On the other hand, the admonishments in Rom 12:1—15:13 and his personal and familial tone in the greetings and throughout the letter, limit this possibility. Paul deals with a concrete situation, and in order to understand the meaning of the letter, the first step of analysis must include this assumption.[15] Traditional commentators view the situation to be a conflict between Jewish and Gentile Christians,[16] with recent rhetorical studies producing similar conclusions.[17] Socio-political analyses center on Paul's political apologetic, with most of the attention on Rom 13:1–7.[18] None of these arguments adequately account for the thematic structure behind the letter to the Romans.

---

13. The Pauline use of εὐαγγέλιον (denoting the act and content of proclamation) has no parallel in the LXX, and its closest parallel comes from the plural use in extrabiblical Greek, particularly in reference to Augustus; Georgi, "Romans, Missionary Theology," 149.

14. Melanchthon, *Loci Communes*, 69.

15. Donfried, *Romans Debate*, 103. Paul writes to Rome; see Metzger, *Textual Commentary*, 505–6, 533–36.

16. For a review of the major issues, see Wedderburn, "Circumstances," 44–65.

17. For rhetorical analysis based on Paul confronting Christian Jews, see Elliott, *Rhetoric of Romans*, 61–62. For the view that Paul confronts Christian Gentiles, see Stowers, *Rereading of Romans*; Campbell, *Paul's Gospel*; Wright, *Climax of the Covenant*; and Nanos, *Mystery of Romans*. For an up-to-date bibliography on rhetorical analysis of Romans, see Witherington and Hyatt, *Paul's Letter to the Romans*, xix-xxv.

18. For a comprehensive socio-political work with a helpful bibliography, see Blumenfeld, *The Political Paul*. For representative works on 13:1–7, see Elliott, "Romans 13:1–7," 184–205; Pöhlmann and Stuhlmacher, "Zur historischen Situation," 131–66; Dunn, "Romans 13:1–7," 55–68; and Borg, "A New Context," 205–18.

While Paul's letter can be classified as part of the ancient letter genre,[19] no comparable model to Romans has been found in first-century Greco-Roman letter writing, and neither do the early handbooks provide helpful explanations to help make sense of Paul's unique style and form.[20] Furthermore, Paul's arguments do not fit neatly into ancient rhetorical categories. While his literary pattern seems consistent with his other letters (opening, thanksgiving, body, paraenesis,[21] and closing), much of the body (1:17—11:36) resembles a theological treatise of some kind, written in universal tone, with the final section of the body (12:1—15:13) expressing loving, authoritative imperatives. Paul writes to influence his audience toward a moral, religious, and political aim by centering his message around the single action of Christ's redemptive work (3:21–26), which provides a model for believers as they live out their faith among each other and their communities. Paul links the past to the present with an aim to explain the future redemptive plan for the people of God (Israel) through Jesus Christ. This redemption involves an internal process, one which Paul describes using the first person singular (7:7–25). Even though Paul's literary style and form are quite different from an epic, the major elements—universal consequence; the past, present, and future of an elected people; the singular focus around a laudable god-man hero; and a didactic message for moral imitation—are shared with the *Aeneid*.[22]

19. See Exler, *Form of the Ancient Greek Letter*; White, *Form and Function*; Byrskog assumes that the hearers/readers of Romans had some epistolary and rhetorical training and suggests that the sociocultural situation particular to the ancient hearers/readers provides an answer; Byrskog, "Epistolography," 45; White sees an overlap in the general categories of Greco-Roman letter classifications (introduction letters, petition letters, family letters, and royal letters of diplomacy); White, "Ancient Greek Letters,"85–105; for Paul's use of formulaic and nonformulaic devices in Romans which resemble the Greco-Roman letter tradition (disclosure formulas; expressions of reassurance; responsibility statements; and grief statements), see White, *Form and Function*, 5–9.

20. See Schnider and Stenger, *Studien zum neutestamentlichen Briefformular*, 12–13. Jewish letter writing was not the normative expression for Judaism as it was for Christianity; Dion, "The Aramaic Family Letter," 59–71. The basic aspects of Aramaic letters from the first century can be categorized into only a few specific types, which do not closely follow Greek literary style; Fitzmyer, "Aramaic Epistolography," 27–30.

21. Paul's letters show a complex paraenetic style which resemble hortatory philosophical letters; Stowers, *Letter Writing*, 42. Stowers notes that ever since Aristotle's famous Proteplicus, a tradition existed which placed philosophical exhortations in the form of letters.

22. Concerning Paul's style, he employs common philosophical terms and common

Letter Prescript

In the opening address (1:1–7), Paul uses a common Greek form of writing but develops his own style by placing his name before his recipients, greeting them with an independent familial address: "Beloved . . . grace to you and peace from God our Father and our Lord Jesus Christ" (1:7).[23] This substitution, in place of "greetings," and his concern for his recipients' welfare in the thanksgiving section show his formal wish for health in a religious context.[24] It appears that Paul combines epistolary conventions with the language of thanksgiving, blessing, and prayer to officiate and participate in a worship service with them.[25] He has reason for thanksgiving because of the progress of the gospel within the Christian community in Rome.[26]

In his salutation, Paul not only foreshadows the tone[27] of his letter, but he also outlines the content that follows. Only in Galatians[28] and

---

language (often from the LXX) to reach his Hellenistic Jews and Christian converts; Cranfield, *Romans*, 1:25. Paul incorporates key oral elements, involves the listener through carefully structured argument, and enhances participation through the use of several literary devices: an imaginary interlocutor (to create a sense of dialogue), diatribe, liturgical elements, personal address, and allusions to fixed points in Israel's history; ibid.

23. For aspects of friendship letters (a letter maintaining the affection and social relationships of the household), see Stowers, *Letter Writing*, 71; White, "Ancient Greek Letters," 96–98. The transitional phrases within the body of Romans exhibit the family and friendship letter tradition; even so, Romans should not be classified as a family letter; Stowers, *Letter Writing*, 101–3. Frequently those in prominent positions were expected to write in a friendly manner to their inferiors and to equals for the purpose of persuasion; Malherbe, *Ancient Epistolary Theorists*, 33. Agosto sees Romans as a parallel to a commendation letter, but more so Paul writes to strengthen the cohesion of his communities (at the opposite end of the political-economic spectrum) to better survive repression and persecution by local and imperial rulers (Paul "undermines" the traditions of Roman patronage, power, and the imperial order); Agosto, "Patronage and Commendation," 123.

24. Stowers, *Letter Writing*, 100.

25. Ibid., 101.

26. Doty, *Letters in Primitive Christianity*, 27–28.

27. To the Corinthians, Paul emphasizes their sanctification in Christ Jesus (1 Cor 1:2), to the Ephesians he mentions their faithfulness (Eph 1:1), and to Timothy and Titus he reiterates that his authority comes from God's command (1 Tim 1:1; Titus 1:3).

28. In Galatians, Paul defends his apostleship through Jesus Christ; he highlights the Father as the source of Christ's resurrection and then summarizes his gospel as the powerful, redemptive work of Christ in the present evil age (1:1–4).

Romans does Paul include greetings with notable detail which introduce important themes on which he elaborates in each of these letters. In writing to the Roman believers, Paul provides a thematic synopsis of the major sections of his letter: being separated for the Gospel of God (a message he defines in 1:17—5:11); the appointed Son of God in power, according to the Holy Spirit, by the resurrection from the dead (in the life of the believers, 5:12-8:39); the promise of Scripture concerning the seed of David (9:1—11:36); and the grace and apostleship that Paul and the believers have received in obedience of faith into all nations on behalf of His name (12—15:13).[29]

When reading Romans from the perspective that Paul countervails the gospel of Caesar, it is interesting that the opening verses of Romans negate the main tenets presented in the *Aeneid* (Virgil considers himself a "poet-prophet," and he prophesies the fulfillment of divine will through an elected people, the Romans, from whom comes a royal descendent, a son of god who ushers in an eternal age of peace). Paul introduces himself in his letter as God's servant separated for the holy task of communicating the Gospel, an allusion to the Levitical consecration of divine service on behalf of Israel.[30] By stating that his message has been proclaimed by the Hebrew prophets and Holy Scriptures, he emphasizes the inspirational source of his words and reaffirms God's *promise* of a divine son from royal Jewish descent, the seed of David.[31] Jesus Christ, the "appointed Son of God" (τοῦ ὁρισθέντος υἱοῦ θεοῦ) in power,[32] ushers in a new age, the renewal of God's creation.[33]

---

29. A common rhetorical device, the *Aeneid*, too, includes the main themes in its opening scenes (e.g., divine wrath, *pietas*, divine will, sacrifice, kingship, and Rome's destiny).

30. Cranfield, *Romans*, 1:53.

31. The absence of the article before the adjective "holy" (1:3) stresses the writings as "holy"; Mounce, *Romans*, 60.

32. "Romans was written at the very beginning of Nero's rule, when propaganda based on such prophetic and theological speculations, with intense eschatological expectations, enjoyed great popularity. For Paul, Jesus is what the princeps claimed to be: representative of humanity, reconciler and ruler of the world"; Georgi, "Romans, Missionary Theology," 154.

33. This redemptive act is directly connected to Christ's "resurrection" (Rom 1:4); Moo, *Romans 1–8*, 43. Interestingly, as argued in chapter 3 of this study, a resurrection motif is present in the *Aeneid*. It seems that Virgil organizes his poem around Book 7 to show the inner struggle and spiritual rebirth of Aeneas (and Rome). This resurrection theme connects the *Aeneid* to Virgil's other works, the *Georgics* and the *Eclogues*,

When Paul refers to Christ as "the appointed" Son of God (Rom 1:4), he also confronts the "messianic" ideology attributed to Augustus.³⁴ As discussed in chapter 1 of this study, stories abounded concerning the divine birth and the messianic qualities of Octavian Augustus. After his victory at Actium in 27 B.C., which established him as the sole ruler of the Roman empire, the Senate honored him with the office of *Pontifex Maximus*, commissioned him as "Father of His Country," and erected a golden statue of him with an inscription crediting him for establishing universal peace. Images portrayed the emperor with his toga drawn over his head and pouring out a libation before an altar, sending a new pictorial message of the union of religious and political powers that were united in the "monarch."³⁵ Paul's terminology in Romans directly contrasts this false gospel.

---

where an evil past opposes the new hope which is embodied in the "savior," Caesar Augustus, who represents the principal resurrection and rebirth. Aeneas descends to the underworld where Roman customs and rituals are pronounced with a didactic purpose concerning eternal life. Here Aeneas finds renewal and cleansing from his doubt and uncertainty. This resurrection motif is also represented in Virgil's prophecy of Roman heroes when he alludes to Plato's *Republic* (Book 10) and the mythological tale of a living man (named Er) who descends into the underworld, dies, and comes back to life. Aeneas's experience resembles Er's (e.g., judges of the dead, a waiting time, the rebirth of souls, measured punishments, and the nature of the universe). Virgil borrows from Orphic sources, Pythagorean philosophy, and Homeric ideas that were developed by Plato and assimilated in Stoicism. Unlike Homer's Elysian plain, Virgil conveys that eternal life awaits those who practice virtue.

34. The primary meaning of "Son of God" in 1:4 refers to Davidic messiahship (Ps 2:7; and 2 Sam 7:14). But, "the exegete must explain why a text like this [Rom 1:3–4] should be cited in a letter addressed to the seat of Roman power"; Georgi, "Romans, Missionary Theology," 150. For Augustus as an eschatological figure, see Harrison, "Augustan Age of Grace," 83–90; and Georgi, "Who Is the True Prophet," 36–46.

35. Nero ordered a general assembly of all the Greeks and spoke of how many more would have benefited from his grace if his benefaction was received when Hellas was at its prime. The chief priest of Augusti for life made the motion: "Whereas Nero, Lord of all the Cosmos, Supreme Imperator, designated Tribune for the thirteenth time, Father of his country, New Sun that brightens Hellas, who has chosen to be the benefactor of Hellas, and with piety requites our Gods, who are always at his side and look out for safety is unique in the annals of time and as Supreme Imperator has proved himself the friend of Hellas, [Nero] Zeus Liberator, and has granted to us our liberty that from of old was so characteristic of us and germane to our land, but then was snatched from us; (and whereas this liberation) is his gift to us, and he has restored (to Hellas) its ancient autonomy and freedom . . ."; Danker, *Benefactor*, 284. For Nero as "messianic" figure, see Suet. *Nero* 57 and Dio *Rom. Hist.* 64.

Dieter Georgi points out that Rom 1:3–4 reflects the two-phase structure of the biblical law of kingship:[36] (1) The future king was first declared God's elect by prophetic designation, and (2) then he was adopted as God's son, the king. Georgi notes that the phrase "seed of David" applied to the entire dynasty after the prophet Nathan, so Paul may be introducing the true king against the antagonist, the Roman Caesar. In this way, Paul's royal terminology speaks beyond Jewish nationalism to supplant imperial ideology concerning a Caesar who achieved universal peace after Actium. Yet, Augustus set a clear precedent by not portraying himself as "king." This is relevant, since it is Virgil who places significance on "kingship" by frequently referring to Aeneas in royal terms (the earthly equivalent of the heavenly king Jupiter[37]), and Virgil implies that the failure of Aeneas to complete his mission would mean a disinheritance of sonship.

It makes cultural sense that Paul's use of "Son of God" and the appositional phrase "Jesus Christ as Lord"[38] might also counter the theological concepts prominent in the imperial cult. Allen Brent demonstrates that a parallel relationship between Christian Monarchianism and pagan monotheism of the imperial cult had fully developed in the second century,[39] but it is too difficult to draw *significant* sociological conclusions based on a comparison of the early Christian house-church structure in Paul's day to the imperial administration of Nero. It is probable, however, that an initial "embryonic" relationship existed between the social and political existence of the early Church and the imperial establishment, and if this is true, some socioreligious principles may be applicable to this discussion concerning Romans and the *Aeneid*.[40]

---

36. Georgi, "Romans, Missionary Theology," 151–52.

37. In the *Aeneid*, Jupiter is the founder of the Roman race (7.219) and is considered the all powerful father (7.770); he is the father of the gods (10.2, 100), king of all (10.112), and reigns from his golden throne (10.116).

38. For "Jesus as Lord" in relation to Roman political concepts, see White, *The Apostle of God*; also see Deissmann, *Light*, 362–63. The significance of κύριος is multifaceted; it is Paul's favorite title for Christ (used 230 times in the Pauline corpus); Dunn, *Romans 1–8*, 16.

39. Brent, *Imperial Cult*, 10.

40. Brent uses Cohen's sociological model in his contra-cultural theory to examine the interaction between Church and State as they developed alongside each other. For this model, see Cohen, *Delinquent Boys*; and "Sociological Research," 781–88. Cohen theorizes that a subculture can be known based on its interaction with its wider cul-

By analyzing a subculture's response to its wider culture (or host culture), particularly in the way truth is established in an inverse manner (contra-culture), sociologists are able to reconstruct and postulate some of the values of that subculture. They look for a system of privilege or honor that has been reversed.[41] In this light, Paul responds not only to the influence of Judaism in the Roman church, but he also responds to the wider culture of Roman imperial values—a "two-front approach."[42] Paul primarily uses Old Testament support to realign the value system of the believers in Rome, but he also, simultaneously, establishes truth in an inverse manner against the symbolism and precepts of Roman imperialism. To accomplish this, Paul may have chosen a "contra-literary" approach rather than a contra-culture approach, since the organizational dynamic of the early church in Rome was at an incipient stage of development. If so, Paul chooses an "interactive" framework which echoes the key themes and values of the *Aeneid*, reversing and establishing important principles and values for the "upwardly mobile"[43] Jewish and Gentile Christians.

Such a literary decision would make sense for several reasons. Having not visited the Roman congregation, Paul diplomatically draws from a common domain of bold philosophical and moral concepts within the frame of reference of the body of believers in Rome. As an apostle to the Gentiles, one called to preach to "kings" as well as "the sons of Israel," Paul expects his letter to be circulated,[44] and his content demonstrates a broad and lasting theological purpose. He supplants the gospel of Caesar with the true gospel of God.

---

ture: "More positively the contra-culture was produced by an interaction that redefined the demands of the host culture, accepting some of them and reformulating others"; "Culture of the Gang," 11. Furthermore, certain sociological principles may apply to all cultures; A. Cohen, *Self Consciousness*, 170. Gary Burnett positively affirms Anthony Cohen's distinctions between individualism and selfhood when he writes, "Clearly, it is possible to argue for the importance of selfhood and individuality, whilst recognizing that a society is not characterized by individualism, or is more collectively oriented, as the Hellenistic world clearly was"; Burnett, *Paul*, 29.

41. Brent, *Imperial Cult*, 16.

42. This concept of a "two-front approach" is taken from Harrison; "Augustan Age of Grace," 80.

43. See Meeks, *First Urban Christians*, 73.

44. See Botha, "Verbal Art," 409–28; Dewey, "Textuality," 37–65; and Ward, "Pauline Voice," 103.

From an overall perspective, it seems that Paul reverses the central theme of the *Aeneid* in a manner similar to Virgil's reversal of Homer's epics. When Virgil scripts the gods as having elected the Trojan Aeneas (and his Roman descendants) to establish a Latin nation, Virgil counters Homer's epics which narrate a Grecian people ruling the world. Paul, on the other hand, overturns the overarching political-religious values of the *Aeneid* when he proclaims Jesus Christ as the "appointed son of God in power." Paul absolutely rejects the idea that God elected a Roman descendant to establish a Latin nation which brings peace to the world; instead, God's order of election comes through the Jew first, a message Paul develops in more detail in Romans 9–11.

Thanksgiving Section

Paul's thanksgiving section reveals his religious devotion, his desire to visit, and the purpose of his mission.[45] He gives thanks first for the "faith" of the Roman church that is being proclaimed throughout the world. In this context, and throughout the letter, "faith" connotes a sense of "faithfulness" or "duty."[46] Paul serves (λατρεύω) with his whole heart in proclaiming the gospel of God's son (1:8–9) and prays continually for the Roman believers (1:10–11). Paul desires to strengthen

---

45. See O'Brien, *Introductory Thanksgivings*, 259–65. O'Brien outlines two basic structural types of Paul's introductory thanksgiving sections based on common material: (a) a thanksgiving report, (b) a petitionary prayer report, and (c) personal and apostolic details concerning his relationship to the addressees. J. M. Robinson discusses Paul's thanksgivings as a product of several interacting backgrounds (e.g., epistolary and liturgical, hellenistic, Jewish, and Christian); "Historicality of Biblical Language," 143–44. Gordon Wiles believes that established prayer traditions which were connected to the synagogues existed in Paul's day, and in addition to these synagogue forms, Paul incorporated Greek liturgical language derived from the LXX; Wiles, *Paul's Intercessory Prayers*, 17–18. Based on a survey of Greek papyrus letters from 260 B.C. to the 8th century A.D., Schubert finds that Greek letters containing introductory thanksgivings are rarely linked to prayer assurances; Schubert, *Form and Function*, 143–44.

46. "Faith" (πίστις) conveys a sense similar to the concept of Roman *pietas*. It is interesting that Paul restates what he means in 16:19 when he rejoices that everyone has heard of their "obedience" (ὑπακοή). These two parallel verses help make sense of what Paul means in 1:5, when he says that "we have received grace and apostleship into the 'obedience of faith' (ὑπακοὴν πίστεως) for all the nations on behalf of his name." For various views on "obedience of faith" in 1:5, see Cranfield, *Romans*, 1:66. Georgi defines the word πίστις as "faithfulness" or "loyalty" based on the Latin synonym "*fides*"; "Romans, Missionary Theology," 149. Augustus discovered the "faith" of the Roman people; see *RG* 32.

(τὸ στηριχθῆναι) them with a gift of revelation, which must be delivered in person (1:11) with an attitude of humility (1:12).[47] He makes them aware that he has been hindered from seeing them several times, implying that a divine plan is at work to reap a harvest of firstfruits among the Christians in Rome and in the rest of the nations.[48] Paul makes clear his duty—the universal aim of evangelizing those in Rome, whether "Greek or Barbarian" (1:13–14).[49]

Power of God unto Salvation, Romans 1:16—5:11

Unlike his other letters, in Romans, Paul introduces the body of his letter with a thematic statement (1:16), emphasizing God's elective, salvific process in history: "to the Jew first and then to the Gentile."[50] Such a statement raises the question concerning God's impartiality (an important subject upon which Paul elaborates in this letter). Paul then clarifies two sides of God's righteousness—righteousness through faith

---

47. Paul's thanksgivings are inextricably linked with the Gospel; O'Brien, 268–69. Thanksgiving is made for the present and the past, and is connected with God's faithfulness toward an eschatological emphasis; ibid.

48. In 1 Thess 2:18, Paul refers to Satan as having hindered him, but here Paul uses the passive which means that Paul had God's action in mind; Cranfield, *Romans*, 1:82.

49. The stress of 1:14 falls upon Paul's "obligation" to be fulfilled concerning his mission to the nations; Murray, *Romans*, 24; Matthew Black reads this as "to have a duty to"; Black, *Romans*, 42. Paul's address to "Greeks and Barbarians, the wise and the ignorant" (Rom 1:14) should be understood in the bilingual context of Rome; "Greek" meant "Greco-Roman," and "Barbarian" refers to alien tribes who cannot speak Greek or Latin; Jewett, "Response: Exegetical Support," 62–63. Jewett explains Paul's use of "obligation" as indebtedness to God, and he suggests that Paul reverses the social system here by stating that he is indebted to Barbarians; ibid., 65. Mark Reasoner argues that "obligation" in Greco-Roman society involved a "reciprocity ethic" to the gods, gratitude for gifts received; *Strong and the Weak*, 176–86. Georgi interprets Paul's obligation to both Greeks and Barbarians as a typical formula in Hellenistic propaganda, especially political propaganda, for the unity of the human race; "Romans, Missionary Theology," 151.

50. The principal emphasis is on the saving power of the Gospel (1:16b); Dunn, *Romans 1–8*, 37. Paul expresses his relationship to the Sovereign whom he represents to prevail against opposing forces, a political relationship (1:16); Jewett, "Romans," 15. Paul's use of σωτηρία (1:16, 10:1, 11:11, and 13:11) would have been understood as an "alternative" to Augustus and his successors; Horsley, "Paul's Counter-Imperial Gospel," 141.

and righteousness demonstrated in wrath (1:17-18)[51]—which frame the first section of the theological argument.

Jewish Race

When Paul says that he is not ashamed of the Gospel, he implies (1) that he wants others to share his view,[52] and (2) that his message stands in contrast to another message (or messages). His silence concerning "another message" and his firm belief in "the" Gospel, show that he is not "countering" or "competing" against other gospels; rather, he establishes his gospel as the only true gospel.[53] Paul begins by affirming the salvific power of God and his selected order—"first to the Jew . . . ."[54] This phrase is more than a rhetorical device, it emphasizes divine providence on behalf of Israel and humankind.[55] Scholars often comment on the theological and historical emphasis of this text, but neglect the intensity for which this document cries out "Jewish race!" against an imperial community where the dominant reality is "Roman race!" In other words, Paul supplants Roman ideology in his theme, rejecting a false gospel that salvation to the nations comes through Roman lineage.

51. Paul's own specific theology on the revelation of God's justice and of justification by faith owes much to the theology of Isaiah and the Psalms concerning the kingship of Yahweh; see Yinger, *Paul, Judaism, and Judgment*, 332–33. Also see, Chilton, "Aramaic and Targumic Antecedents," 378–97. Also, *RG* 34 speaks of δικαιοσύνη (*Iustitia*).

52. Olson, "Epistolary Uses," 587–89.

53. For a representative view that Paul "competes" with the gospel of Caesar: "If the terms chosen by Paul for his Roman readers have associations with the slogans of Caesar religion, then Paul's gospel must be understood as competing with the gospel of the Caesars. Paul's gospel enters into critical dialogue with the good news that universal peace has been achieved by the miracle of Actium. This was a prodigious miracle that brought respite and new life to a world tortured by a century of civil war. Even a devout Jew like Philo could celebrate this marvel, secured by the law and might of Rome. The *sōtēria* represented by Caesar and his empire is challenged by the *sōtēria* brought about by Jesus"; Georgi, "Romans, Missionary Theology," 152.

54. Since Paul speaks of the theological and historical decision of God concerning the Jews and the Gentiles, Paul may be including the specific reference of σωτηρία to the deliverances of Israel (Exod 14:13 and 15:2; and Babylonian Captivity in Isa 45:17 and 52:15); Black, *Romans*, 43–44. He could also be referring to the Greek concept of preservation that includes the eschatological meaning of deliverance from final destruction; Dunn, *Romans 1–8*, 39. The cognates of σωτηρία are widely used in the Greek world and in the LXX; see Moo, *Romans 1–8*, 61–62.

55. It also provides a practical theological model for Paul in his ministry before evangelizing Spain (15:22–32); Brindle, "To the Jew First," 221–33.

This does not necessarily mean that Paul directly confronts Virgil's message. Paul writes nearly three-quarters of a century after the publication of the *Aeneid*, which means that the values laid down in this Roman epic enjoyed decades of political and religious assimilation and social ratification. To determine a close connection between the ideology presented in the *Aeneid* and Paul's theological framework in Romans, the unique themes and traditions to which the *Aeneid* contributed most, concerning Roman ideology within Roman society, need to be made clear.

Virgil harnessed the current philosophical, religious, and historical issues of his time by uniquely depicting, in mythical and poetic detail, the sacred themes of Rome: (a) revealing the nature of wrath from heaven (a theme introduced in the prologue, *Aeneid* 1.11), (b) the linking of the past to the present through the inner struggle of a god-man (part of a resurrection motif), and (c) the prophetic account of the future savior and descendant son of god, Augustus Caesar, and his eschatological impact on the destiny of the Roman people. The general framework of Paul's letter has general similarities to these main thematic elements: wrath revealed from heaven (1:18—3:26), past history (concerning sin) and the believer's inner struggle (the resurrection of Jesus Christ acted out in believers, 5:12—8:39), and the salvation of God's elect (9:1—11:36).

Heavenly Wrath

Paul introduces two characteristics of God's justice (δικαιοσύνη) that are continually being revealed (1:17a and 18a):

> 17 <u>For the righteousness of God is being revealed</u>
> from faith into faith
> even as is written, "The just shall live by faith."
>
> 18 <u>For the wrath of God is being revealed from heaven</u>
> upon all ungodliness and wickedness of men
> who suppress the truth by their wickedness.

Justice from heaven is understood as a contrast between the righteousness of God revealed "from faith into faith" and his wrath which is revealed upon all "ungodliness and wickedness" (17b and 18b).[56]

---

56. The preposition γάρ links God's justice (1:17) to God's anger (1:18–19); Stowers, *Rereading of Romans*, 92.

Likewise, the clause "the just will live by faith" stands antithetically to those "who suppress the truth by their wickedness" (17c and 18c).[57] In these opening verses of the body, Paul responds to an unanswered theological-philosophical question concerning the relationship between justice and wrath: righteousness comes from heaven revealed through "faith," and righteousness is also revealed through God's wrath.[58]

From a philosophical perspective, Bruno Blumenfeld presents a theory that Romans displays the influence of Hellenistic Pythagorean political philosophy—a divine βασιλεία and πόλις organizational structure with the pivotal concept in each of the two configurations of δικαιοσύνη qualified by πίστις in the case of the πόλις, and by θεός in the case of βασιλεία.[59] He finds common ground between metaphysics and theology when he argues that the grand, intricate theological discourse of Romans is formally structured after the model of classical political tracts (such as those of Plato and Aristotle). For the ancient political philosophers, politics and piety were inseparable, with divine truth manifested in an ordered society.[60] In this case, the structure frames a comparison to the ideal state and its counterpart in the psychological dimension, a reordering of the flawed soul.[61] Blumenfeld

---

57. Rom 1:17b can be seen as a messianic prooftext: Dodd, *According to the Scriptures*, 51; Brownlee, "Messianic Motifs," 29; Sanders, "Habakkuk in Qumran," 233; Hays, *Faith of Jesus Christ*, 150–57; and Campbell, "Romans 1:17," 265–85.

58. The noun δικαιοσύνη denotes the quality of being δίκαιος; the adjective δίκαιος means "observant of duty" and describes the person whose conduct conforms to δίκη; see Cranfield, *Romans*, 1:93; Dunn, *Romans 1–8*, 40–41. Δικαιοσύνη is one of the four cardinal virtues (as well as courage, wisdom, and temperance). Augustus is honored for his "righteousness and faithfulness" (*iustitia et pietas*); *RG* 34. *Iustitia* was one of the virtues on Augustus's golden shield (27 B.C.), and it became linked with imperial power so much so that it sometimes acquired the title "*Augusta*." For the relationship of δικαιοσύνη to the covenant, see Black, *Romans*, 44. For Jewish theology behind δικαιοσύνη, see Moo, *Epistle to the Romans*, 79–90. For the Jewish context of righteousness of God as referring to God's own faithfulness, see Wright, "Romans," 184–213.

59. Blumenfeld, *The Political Paul*, 302–414. Blumenfeld believes that Paul transforms the relation between δικαιοσύνη and νόμος by deconstructing νόμος and supplanting with πίστις. Unlike νόμος, πίστις is a universal law; its personification is Christ; ibid., 372.

60. Blumenfeld recognizes an overlap in certain key themes and terminology with patterns of Paul's ideas and "reminiscent" configurations in classical and Hellenistic political theory, particularly Hellenistic Pythagorean political theory; ibid., 414.

61. Ibid.

argues that the world already has an impeccable model of order in the divine; if only a proper power (a philosopher, a king, and in this case, "Christ") could be found to bring earthly disorder into conformity with the divine blueprint. For Paul, πίστις is the bond of the πόλις. While these conclusions are received with caution, Blumenfeld's political ideas concerning Paul's intentions in the letter to the Romans share similarities with the *Aeneid*.[62]

Virgil's epic proclaims a divine truth manifested in an ordered society. The *Aeneid* does not separate politics and piety. The divine kingdom (e.g., Jupiter and the gods) determines the organizational structure of the πόλις with the pivotal concept in each of the two configurations as justice, qualified by *pietas* in the case of Aeneas and his community and θεός in the case of βασιλεία. The plot structure of the *Aeneid* borrows elements from Platonic and Aristotelian philosophy, particularly Hellenistic Pythagorean political philosophy. Virgil demonstrates the testing of Aeneas's inner psychological dimension against the ideal state (from heaven), a reordering of his imperfect soul. The heavens (through Jupiter) provide the perfect model for which pious King Aeneas brings earthly disorder into conformity with the divine plan. For Virgil, *pietas* is the bond of the πόλις. It is the thematic virtue of Aeneas which demonstrates his faithfulness to divine will.

It is interesting that Paul begins the body of his letter by elaborating on the nature of God's wrath from heaven,[63] a topic that Virgil introduces in his poem (a desire to understand the *cause* of divine anger against a righteous god-man, *Aen.* 1.11). Divine wrath (the highest theme of the *Aeneid*)[64] directly intervenes in human conflict, often deceptively, delaying the outcome of the establishment of Rome and

---

62. Georgi also interprets these verses in light of kingship, concerning God's loyalty (πίστις) affirmed in God's solidarity (δικαιοσύνη) with the human race: "The good news of Jesus refuses to employ threats and the exercise of power and violence—even the law—as instruments of rulership . . . the *sōtēria* of the God Jesus has made loyalty a two-way street (*ek pisteōs eis pistin*, 1:16): it demonstrates and creates loyalty, but demands loyalty as well (1:16–17)"; "Romans, Missionary Theology," 152.

63. Paul begins his letter by giving a theological-historical perspective concerning the fall of humanity. Virgil, on the other hand, gives a mythical-historical perspective by retelling the fall of Troy (ἁμαρτία in epic tragedies refers to a mistake made out of ignorance, not moral sin).

64. Adler, *Vergil's Empire*, 4. The resolution of heavenly wrath occupies the entire *Aeneid*; MacKay, "Hero and Theme," 165.

her elected people.⁶⁵ However, Paul characterizes God as acting justly in both configurations of justice—righteousness revealed through faith and righteousness revealed through wrath. Virgil symbolically scripts Jupiter, Aeneas, and Augustus as conquering the demonic forces of chaos. For Paul, justice comes through the sacrifice of Jesus Christ (Rom 3:25-26).

When Paul quotes Hab 2:4 (Rom 1:17), he expresses confidence, influencing his listeners to take on similar virtue (which probably reveals the lack of confidence on the listeners' part).⁶⁶ Habakkuk 2:4 provides an important matrix for Paul to justify his gospel because it "draws attention both to God's faithfulness and to the reciprocal need for the obedience of faith and perseverance on the part of the hearer as the path to life."⁶⁷ The prophet Habakkuk used the term "faith" in the sense of "faithfulness"; those who are loyal and steadfast will be preserved in difficult times.⁶⁸ Paul further develops this meaning in relation to Christ in the second section of his letter (Rom 5:12—8:39).

While Paul does not explicitly mention the fall of Adam in Rom 1:18-32, he does refer to the creation story. Humanity is subject to God's truth, because the knowledge of God is revealed in them ("for God has made himself evident in them"), and the invisible attributes of God are clearly understood in his created order and design by the things he has made (1:19-20). The wrath of God is being revealed against all of creation, against those who suppress the truth with their wickedness (1:18), and against those who approve of others who do evil (1:32). Paul does not seem to be referring to those who have specific knowledge of the Law, but he exposes those who, in their passion, irrationally worship creation rather than give glory to the Creator. God hands them over to their passion (ἐπιθυμίαις, 1:24). Although the just wrath that Paul describes in Romans 1 does not parallel the irrational *furor* from the heavens in the mythical account of the *Aeneid*, the topic of irrational passion is an important theme in both Romans and the *Aeneid*.

Paul's theology, rooted in the Old Testament, contrasts some of the social and religious values in Rome. By the end of Augustus's reign,

---

65. Virgil portrays Juno as a destructive goddess of *furor*; he portrays Jupiter as the "almighty father" and as the "god of order" whose words are true.

66. Olsen, "Epistolary Uses," 589.

67. Watts, "'For I Am Not Ashamed,'" 24.

68. Mounce, *Romans*, 74.

the themes of primeval degeneration, the sinful age, and the wrath of God had become well-known in relation to the return of the Golden Age.[69] Paul's critique of Gentile depravity logically implies criticism of part of the ideological basis of imperial rule (even though he may not have been intentional in this purpose).[70] In Greco-Roman society, desires in and of themselves were not bad, but when practiced outside of rational control, they were dangerous. About the time that Paul wrote Romans, Seneca (an adviser to Nero) speaks of the great multitude of the people as "unruly, seditious, without self-mastery, ready for mutual destruction if it throws off the yoke of rule . . . We have all sinned; some in serious ways, some in less serious ways; some by deliberate intent, some impulsively or led astray by the wickedness of others."[71] Roman rule intensified an ancient Mediterranean ethic of self-restraint, where virtue was honored and vices were shamed. Philosophy became a science of self-mastery, and this was also true in some circles of Hellenistic Judaism (e.g., Philo, Josephus, and other Hellenistic Jewish authors understood the Torah as teaching an ethic of self-mastery).[72]

Paul employs a vice list (1:29–32), a common literary device in the New Testament and in Greco-Roman culture, especially among the Stoics.[73] Paul seems to arrange his list for rhetorical purposes, in some cases choosing synonymous words. In comparison to Virgil's sin list (6.609–10), Paul names more types of sin which would readily be known by Jewish Christians; whereas, Virgil's list adapts common Greek crimes that reflect Roman concerns. Although both lists emphasize wickedness, only a few sins overlap: covetousness (*aut qui divitiis soli incubuere repertis*, 6.610; πλεονεξία, 1:29) and enmity against par-

---

69. Stowers, *Rereading of Romans*, 42–82. Stowers reviews the cultural and philosophical attitudes of self-mastery in Greco-Roman culture, and he discusses the principles of self-mastery practiced in Judaism. He interprets self-mastery as a personal, social, and theological problem that is "the most palpable issue" of Romans 1–8; ibid., 43.

70. Price, "Response," 182. Price moves the emphasis to "structures of power" rather than Rome itself.

71. *Clem.* 1.1.1; 1.6.3–4; 1.22.2, as in Stowers, *Rereading of Romans*, 124.

72. Ibid., 55, 58–74.

73. See Engberg-Pedersen, "Paul, Virtues, and Vices," 608–33. Dunn references *Aen.* 2.164–67 and discusses Paul's Stoic terminology; see *Romans 1–8*, 75–76.

ents (*pulsatusve parens*, 6.609; γονεῦσιν ἀπειθεῖς, 1:30). In each text, judgment awaits the sinner.[74]

In his descent to the underworld in Book 6, Aeneas sees the punishments for sinful acts. Aeneas also sees the rewards for good works (virtue) which include honor and eternal life. Because Virgil didactically communicates a unique message concerning eternal reward, and because Paul does not preach a doctrine of "works" salvation, it is important that Paul's theology concerning "good works" and "eternal life" in Rom 2:6–11 be examined more closely.

Eternal Reward

In Rom 2:6–7, Paul states that "God will repay each according to his works, to the ones persevering in good works—glory, honor, and eternal life." Paul's terminology here seems to contrast his argument of "justification by faith"; thus, it is important to know: (1) what Paul means in these verses and (2) what sources he might be using to instruct his listeners.

Paul does not qualify or explain in detail what he means when he writes about judgment, works, and eternal reward.[75] The lack of discussion concerning the difference between "justification by faith" and "judgment according to works" points to the probability that Paul builds upon a construct of thought which was familiar to him and his audience.[76] Furthermore, there does not seem to be theological tension on this subject in Paul's letters, yet scholars hold to a wide variety of opinions as to what Paul means by "judgment according to works."[77]

---

74. Virgil blends two types of descriptions—a traditional list of punishments (concerning mythological accounts of afterlife) and a list of punishments for behaviors on earth which merit treatments in the underworld (from an Orphic-Pythagorean milieu); see *Aen.* 6.608–14.

75. The terms "deeds" and "works" are used interchangeably in this section.

76. See 1 Cor 4:4–5, 6:9–11, Gal 6:7–8, Col 1:23–33, and Phil 2:12–13.

77. Joseph Burgess reviews the literature for Paul's view of "reward and works"; "Rewards," 94–110. Burgess places the many different positions in ten separate categories. In 1977, E. P. Sanders questioned the generally held belief that salvation by faith (not works) contrasted the belief of first-century Judaism which based salvation on obedience to the law (acceptance based on merit); *Paul and Palestinian Judaism*, 550. Sanders's theology of "covenantal nomism" defined covenant membership as a dependence on God's grace with "works of the law" serving as a demonstration of inclusion. If a Jew continued to disobey, he or she could lose their salvation. According

"Reward based on works" is not an independent theme for Paul. Apparently, he uses judgment material in a disparate manner,[78] and he reinterprets judgment material for a particular purpose.

After Paul describes God's continual wrath, as it is revealed from heaven to all those who disobey (1:17-32), he makes the claim that those who make judgments, both Jew and Gentile, will in turn receive God's judgment (2:1-5).[79] Since mankind deserves death on the day of judgment,[80] how can one man judge another man? In Greek literary style, Paul speaks to an imaginary interlocutor who represents mankind (2:1, "Oh man . . .") and pronounces God's wrath against those who practice deeds which they themselves judge others for doing.[81]

---

to Sanders, Paul did not attack Judaism for a self-righteousness based on deeds done before God; rather, Paul developed a new form of covenantal nomism in order to reach both Jews and Gentiles where the law was not a condition for salvation—"a covenantal religion which one enters by baptism, membership which provides salvation, which has a specific set of commandments, obedience to which . . . keeps one in the covenantal relationship, while repeated or heinous transgression removes one from membership," ibid., 513. This view provided an important theological framework for scholars after 1977 who wished to support or defend their suppositions centered around a theology of "works" (merit). Some modify Sanders's conclusions while others directly contradict them. I. Howard Marshall finds Sanders's view of salvation to be inappropriate because "covenantal nomism" contradicts the nature of the believer—to be saved through dying with Christ and gaining a new life; "Salvation, Grace and Works," 342; particularly, see Hooker, "Paul and Covenantal Nomism," 47-56.

78. For example, God, Christ, angels, and Christians become the judge at the last judgment, and the standard by which people are finally judged can be works, worship, obedience, and attitude; in some passages, believers escape the final judgment, while in other passages, all will be judged on that final day; Burgess, "Rewards," 100.

79. Stowers argues stylistically and rhetorically that 2:1 does not begin a new section; διό is an important transition; *Rereading of Romans*, 12.

80. This corresponds to the "Day of the Lord" which the Old Testament prophets foretold (e.g., Amos 8:2; Isa 2:12; Jer 46:10, 50:31; and Ezek 7:10).

81. Stowers explains Paul's warning in Romans 2 as the literary device of "speech-in-character" (speech that represents another person; e.g., 2:1-5, 3:31-4:2, 3:1-9, and 7:7-8:2); *Rereading of Romans*, 126-58. The apostrophe to the person in 2:1f introduces the future day of judgment; Paul particularly alludes to: Zephaniah and God's wrath, the arrogance of Israel and the nations, and the salvation of Israel and the nations; ibid., 118-20. Also, when Paul elaborates on the eschatological day of wrath in Rom 2:6-11, he may be using a chiastic arrangement of seven parallel phrases to emphasize the core phrases: ὀργὴ καὶ θυμός and θλῖψις καὶ στενοχωρία; see Grobel, "Chiastic Retribution-Formula," 257.

When Paul writes that God "will repay each according to his works," the emphasis is on God's impartiality (1:6, 11)—a central argument.[82] Whether Jew or Gentile, when one chooses to "do evil" or "do good" the rewards will be apportioned without favoritism—trouble, hardship, and wrath for the disobedient, and glory, honor, and eternal life for those who obey. This aspect of God's nature leads Paul to highlight the hypocrisy of the Jews who judge others and violate the very Law that they preach ("For through you, the law of God is being blasphemed into all of the nations"; 2:24).[83] Paul condemns the "circumcised" for their sin (2:27), and at the same time he reasons that the "uncircumcised Gentile" can be justified by keeping the Law and be credited for it (2:26). According to Paul, a person is "a Jew inwardly, circumcised in the heart, by the Spirit, not by the written Law; so praise is unto God, not men" (2:29).

Thus, Paul cannot mean that "good works" result in salvation. In 2:6–7, Paul states that God will repay "each person according to his deeds" (ὃς ἀποδώσει ἑκάστῳ κατὰ τὰ ἔργα αὐτοῦ). To those who persist in doing good works (ἔργου ἀγαθοῦ), seeking glory, honor, immortality, he will render eternal life (δόξαν καὶ τιμὴν καὶ ἀφθαρσίαν ζητοῦσιν ζωὴν αἰώνιον).[84] Understanding the semantic significance in this verse to mean "eternal salvation" contradicts Paul's following argument in Rom 3:9–20. Here Paul uses Scripture from Psalms and Isaiah to argue that no one is righteous and that all works of the Law will not be justified before God. Rather, righteousness comes by faith in Jesus Christ, without distinction, to all who believe (3:23). It may be that Paul borrows Greek philosophical terms (or from Roman theology) to appeal to Hellenistic Jews or converted Gentiles when he discusses

---

82. Jouette Bassler establishes the thematic centrality of Paul's affirmation of divine impartiality (2:11) both for the opening argument of the letter and for the letter as a whole; Bassler, "Divine Impartiality," 43–58. Based on the internal structure of Rom 1:16–2:29, Bassler finds 2:11 to emerge as the thematic pivot point of the argument. The emphasis here is impartiality in the message of grace (impartiality in judgment, Romans 1–2; which is matched by impartiality in grace, Romans 3–4).

83. Paul cites Isa 52:5 (Rom 2:24) where God deals positively with the nations; Shum, *Paul's Use of Isaiah*, 179.

84. Paul's use of ἀποδώσει carries the connotation of rendering, reward, or recompense in both good and bad senses; BDAG, s.v. "ἀποδίδωμι." In Rom 2:8–10, Paul repeats the rewards for "good works" and "evil works," but he adds his theme, "to the Jew first and then to the Gentile."

reward for "works."[85] Additional contextual background is needed to understand Paul's meaning.

Kent Yinger analyzes the recompense motif—judgment according to deeds—in the Old Testament and finds its widespread use within the writings and the prophets, but not in the Pentateuch.[86] Overall, this motif functions in several ways: (a) praise to God, (b) comfort to those who "manifest" covenant loyalty, and (c) a warning to the disobedient.[87] While the Old Testament most often refers to God's work through collective Israel, it is also apparent that God judges individuals: the patriarchs base their faithfulness on the covenant, wisdom literature accents God's calling an individual into account for his or her "good"

---

85. For "doing good" as part of the ancient Greek virtue system, see Blumenfeld, *Political Paul*, 324–28.

86. Kent Yinger examines the theme "judgment according to works" according to writings of early Judaism (including Pseudepigraphical writings, Qumran literature, Targums, Midrashim, and Philo); *Judgment According to Deeds*; 22–138. In some instances the Pseudepigrapha reveal the impartiality of God to the Jew and Gentile, but most of the references regarding "judgment according to works" speak collectively to those within Israel—punishment for wickedness. The reward on the day of judgment for those observing the covenant is mercy. Deeds are not measured in terms of a "summation" of "good works" compared to "bad works," and individual effort is understood in the context of one's confidence as a Jew resting on God's faithfulness. Similarly, in Qumran literature, "judgment according to works" means punishment of the wicked, but there does not seem to be a reference to a future event of measure. Targumic literature contains distinct phraseology concerning "works" that is not found in the Old Testament. The Targums "rewrite" biblical texts—inserting "merit" in place of "righteousness." The children of Israel are saved due to the unfailing source of grace from the patriarchs. In addition to the emphasis of God's covenant with the patriarchs, the concept of "merit" in the Targums includes a sacrificial context—intercession, perfect offerings, and priestly reward. Furthermore, Philo discusses the blessings and curses at the end of the Mosaic legislation in Deuteronomy, and he mentions rewards and penalties experienced in this world, but he does not speak about life after death as the realm when divine sanctions come into effect.

87. Ibid., 60; for examples of above motifs see Jer 32:18–19; Ps 18:20–24; and Hos 4:9. Yinger understands Paul's language choices as "echoes of Scripture" which draw from the "storeroom of materials" from biblical tradition. In other words, the divine recompense according to deeds became an important theological axiom for Judaism in which the varying situation of the hearers could bring about different applications. "Works of obedience are not viewed as merits, each to be recompensed in atomistic fashion, but instead are the observable manifestations of the covenant loyalty of the unseen heart," ibid., 62.

and "evil" works, and Jeremiah accents an individualistic sense within Israel's covenant relationship to Yahweh.[88]

However, based on the following analysis of key words and phrases that Paul uses in Rom 2:6–11—"works," "eternal life," and "each according to . . ."—Paul's theme concerning reward for "good works" can be interpreted in light of a priestly context. It seems that Paul alludes to the language of Levitical imagery—sacrifice, mercy, and judgment.

Priestly Context for "Works"

It is clear that Paul incorporated priestly sacrificial imagery in his letter to the Romans. Paul introduces himself in his letter in the context of holy service when he writes as a called apostle "separated" (ἀφωρισμένος, 1:1)[89] unto the Gospel of God. Then in his thanksgiving section, Paul writes that he continually prays for the believers in Rome as he "serves" (λατρεύω, 1:9)[90] God in his spirit in the Gospel of his Son. Paul goes on to describe the Son of God as a just payment of sin, using Old Testament atonement imagery—"the one whom God presented as a mercy-sacrifice (ἱλαστήριον)[91] through faith in his blood as a demonstration of his righteousness" (3:25). It is in this context of priestly reward that Paul's meaning in Rom 2:6–11 should be understood.

---

88. Ibid., 31.

89. This priestly terminology, that Paul employs, parallels the language which describes the Levitical duties and requirements concerning offerings (ἀφορίζω, Exod 29:27 and Lev 20:25). This section compares key phraseology in Rom 2:6 to the LXX. For Paul's priority on the Greek vocabulary of the LXX and for the general difficulties of the text, see Ellis, *Paul's Use of the Old Testament*, 11–16.

90. In Ezek 45:4, the holy portion of the land was for the priests, the ministers of the sanctuary (ἱερεῦσιν τοῖς λειτουργοῦσιν ἐν τῷ ἁγίῳ), who minister unto the Lord. They were separated for holy service (ἀφωρισμένους τῷ ἁγιασμῷ αὐτῶν). But specifically, "ministering" (λειτουργέω) refers to Levitical or priestly service (λειτουργία) in the tent of meeting. Also see Exod 28:43, 29:30; Num 3:6, 31; 4:1–43; 7:5–10; 8:22–26; 16:9; 18:2–32; 1 Kgs 8:11, and 1 Chr 28:20–21.

Paul continues his sacrificial theme when he exhorts believers: "Based on the mercies of God, present your bodies as a living sacrifice, holy and pleasing to God, which is your spiritual service" (λατρείαν; 12:1). Paul believes that his service (λειτουργὸν) to Christ unto the nations is a priestly duty (ἱερουργοῦντα) to carry out the Gospel of God in order that the offering of the Gentiles might be pleasing and sanctified, (ἡγιασμένη, 15:16).

91. For Mercy Seat, see Exod 25:17–22; 31:7; 35:12; 38:5–8; and Num 7:89.

For Tabernacle and priestly service, Yahweh designed specific requirements and specific tasks. These activities and services centered around the Tabernacle and are often phrased as "according to (all) works." For example, God speaks to Moses concerning a man from the tribe of Judah who was filled with the Spirit of God to devise skillful "works" in gold, silver, brass, stone, and wood "to work in all kinds of workmanship" (ἐργάζεσθαι κατὰ πάντα τὰ ἔργα) to make what God commanded concerning the Tabernacle (Exod 31:5).[92] It is interesting that the "work" of the sanctuary took place based on freewill offerings "so that all the skilled men came who did every kind of work on the sanctuary (τὰ ἔργα τοῦ ἁγιοῦ), each according to his task (ἕκαστος κατὰ τὸ αὐτοῦ ἔργον, Exod 36:4–5), and this was done based on God's command. Furthermore, priests and the children of Israel performed services of the Tabernacle (κατὰ πάντα τὰ ἔργα τῆς σκηνῆς, Num 3:8). Yahweh tells Moses to reward "each man according to his Tabernacle service": πρὸς τὰ ἔργα τὰ λειτουργικὰ τῆς σκηνῆς τοῦ μαρτυρίου καὶ δώσεις αὐτὰ τοῖς Λευίταις ἑκάστῳ κατὰ τὴν αὐτοῦ λειτουργίαν (Num 7:5).[93]

In the *Aeneid*, Virgil depicts Aeneas as a pious father who leads his people in religious devotion and Roman tradition. In his descent to the underworld, Aeneas witnesses the punishments meted out for individuals based on their sins—crimes with Roman color and violent consequence (6.610–22). These illogical, mythical images portray Tartarus as a grand and dark place, resembling an eternal Roman state that carries out its universal will on individuals. For those practicing virtue, everlasting spring and shady groves await them, a blissful place with its own sun and stars (6.541–42). Little, if any, correlation exists between Paul's Levitical allusions to "works" and Virgil's vision of afterlife. However, since the phrase "eternal life" (ζωὴν αἰώνιον) does not seem to have a close parallel to the Torah or early Judaism, it is important to examine the meaning and source of this phrase.[94]

---

92. Also, see Exod 31:1–7, 35:32–34, and 36:1.

93. This is also true of Solomon's temple (κατὰ τὸ ἔργον τοῦτο, 1 Kgs 7:45; and 1 Chr 23:24), and service of musicians unto the Lord (1 Chr 25:1).

94. The conclusions in this section are congruent with Paul's theme of "judgment according to works" in 1 Cor 3:1—4:5 and 2 Cor 5:1–10. The theme of "judgment according to works" in 1 Cor 3:1—4:5 shares a similar context of (a) God's mercy, (b) sacrificial imagery, and (c) a final judgment day. In 1 Cor 3:5–8, Paul describes Apollos

"Eternal Life"

Paul employs terms in Rom 2:6-11 that do not closely parallel literature from early Judaism. The mention of eternal life places this passage in contrast to Qumran literature which mainly stresses punishment,[95] and to the Pseudepigraphal writings which stress punishment for those who do wrong and chastisement for those who are shown mercy.[96]

---

and himself as servants whom the Lord gave to each his task, and "each will receive his own reward according to his own labor." The parallel thought underscores a thematic echo of 5b to verse 8, which makes sense then that only God would receive boasting. "Wages" (μισθὸς, 3:8) used in a positive sense with "according to works" places this concept outside of the traditional uses in Qumran literature and the Pseudepigrapha. It is also interesting that Paul describes himself as an expert builder according to the grace God has given him (1 Cor 3:10), and this same adjective "expert" (σοφὸς) is used in Exodus to describe the skilled persons (σοφὸς τῇ καρδίᾳ) who made the materials for the Tabernacle and the skilled persons who built the Tabernacle (see Exod 35:10, 25). It is not surprising that Paul uses "temple" terminology which echoes the "Levitical-Tabernacle" imagery of the Old Testament concerning the people of God (1 Cor 3:11-16). "Works" is understood in a priestly context of obedience, God's mercy, and the revelatory quality of God's judgment (1 Cor 3:17). In this sense, no one can boast in men. Later in 1 Cor 4:5, "praise" for service does not come from the community, but from God for priestly work he designed, to servants who serve in faith.

In 2 Cor 5:1-10, eternal reward is also presented with Levitical imagery centered around a sacrificial life. In 4:7-10, Paul utilizes the Levitical imagery of "earthen vessels" (the phrase σκεῦος ὀστράκινον finds its meaning of purity in Lev 6:21, 11:33, 14:50, and 15:12; see also 2 Tim 2:20) to refer to himself and his companions as "crushed . . . struck down, but not destroyed." In this manner, Paul understands that he and his companions always carry in them the sacrificial death of Jesus. In 2 Cor 5:1-2, Paul refers to the body as an "earthly tabernacle" that will be torn down, and believers have an eternal building made by God. The believers' lives are pleasing (εὐάρεστοι) to Him (5:9). Their service is holy, out of fear of the Lord (5:11). In fact, Paul and his companions present themselves as God's suffering servants for the day of salvation (6:1-4).

95. Bockmuehl's findings concerning Qumran material are fundamentally compatible with E. P. Sanders' study of 1977; Bockmuehl, "1QS," 381–414. However, Bockmuehl disagrees with Sanders's treatment, based on recent findings over the past twenty-five years, in that a great many of the newly released Dead Sea Scrolls have no significant sectarian sense; see Sanders, 320. Thus, in the Qumran literature, "judgment according to works" means punishment of the wicked; it does not refer to a future event of measure, but a sentence of those who disdain God; Yinger, *Judgment According to Deeds*, 138.

96. The Pseudepigraphical writings continue the Old Testament tradition of "judgment according to works," but in the Pseudepigrapha this phrase might better be stated as "*punishment* according to works" for the purpose of warning; ibid., 89. Clear distinctions are made between the righteous and the wicked within the nation of Israel (e.g., 1 En. 100:7; Jub. 5:15); the concept that God promises a positive reward to the righteous according to their works is not found in the Pseudepigrapha; ibid.

Furthermore, the writings of early Judaism address collective Israel, which means Paul might be introducing a radical perspective by implying that Jew and Gentile have a means to glory, honor, immortality, and eternal life.[97]

By using the words: glory (δόξαν), honor (τιμὴν), immortality (ἀφθαρσίαν), and eternal life (ζωὴν αἰώνιον), Paul does not directly reference the Greco-Roman sense of reward for virtue. Neither does Paul refer to the concept in Hellenistic Judaism of the free will in abiding by the law of nature in acquiring virtue. Rather, Paul uses these words in Rom 2:6–11 to refer to resurrection.

Paul uses the terms "life" and "immortality" in his other letters to signify the resurrection of the body (e.g., 1 Cor 15:42; and 2 Tim 2:10–11). These terms denote eschatological gifts of God already firmly associated in Jewish thought with the "resurrection life of the blessed."[98] It is interesting that the LXX records the phrase "honor and glory" (τιμὴν καὶ δόξαν) only twice: sacred garments were made for Aaron and his brother for the purpose of serving as priests, and these garments gave Aaron "honor and glory" as he represented Israel (Exod 28:2).[99] For Paul, eternal life points to Christ's holy service and sacrifice.

"Each According to..."

Based on the terms discussed thus far in Rom 2:6–11, this passage indicates the sense of God's mercy in a context of sacrifice and judgment. Paul's phrase "each according to..." (Rom 2:6) repeats language from prophetic literature concerning the "measure" of judgment based on one's works. Variations of the phrase "each according to... works (ways,

---

97. This is especially true since Paul defines a Jew as one who is a Jew "inwardly circumcised in the heart by the Spirit" (2:29). Paul is not the only author to discuss God's impartiality to Jew and Gentile; see *Jub.* 5:12–16; *Pss. Sol.* 17:8–9.

This inward emphasis of the heart echoes the Sinaitic covenant. "Circumcision in the heart" involved obedience to the Sinai covenant, and in the Old Testament divine intervention changes the human heart; Gowan, *Eschatology*, 75. See Deut 30:6 and 10:16. In addition, Paul may be echoing wisdom literature concerning God's judgment of hidden things (e.g., "Wisdom is glorious and unfading... obeying the law assures imperishability [ἀφθαρσίας], and imperishability makes one near to God"; Wis 6:12a, 18–19).

98. Cranfield, *Romans*, 1:147; also see 1 Pet 1:7.

99. The other use of "honor and glory" in the LXX refers to Aaron's sons, the priests. Tunics, sashes, and headbands were made to bring "honor and glory" as they served in the tent of meeting (Exod 28:40).

doings, etc.)" reveals the nature of God's judgment—he warns Israel and other nations, holding both Israel and the Gentile nations accountable, individually and corporately.[100] The Old Testament prophets, with the exception of Hosea, often understand God's judgment according to works in relation to God's mighty acts of deliverance for Israel.[101] God's judgments exceed the "amount" or "measure" of deeds done by Israel or the Gentiles. In other words, God does not seem to operate on a "deed-equals-deed" basis where he measures good works and compares them to the amount of bad works.

The phrase "each according to . . ." refers to a measurement, but the measurement reveals a contrast of abundance, not equality.[102] God abundantly rewards those who respond to him in obedience. This kind of measurement makes clear the context of Rom 2:6–11. God's continual wrath is being revealed from heaven upon the wicked (1:18), and the wicked will receive hardship and trouble. Likewise, for the sacrificial behavior of those who do good, God's righteousness is revealed and eternal life is given. When Paul writes that God will repay those who do good works, he draws upon Old Testament imagery to reveal God's character of mercy in a sacrificial context on the day of judgment, *concerning God's elect and the nations*. It makes sense that he would restate his theme immediately after repeating the reward for

---

100. For example, Yahweh warns that he will repay the lawless for the evil done according to the works of his hands (κατὰ τὰ ἔργα τῶν χειρῶν αὐτοῦ, Isa 3:11); when Yahweh speaks to Judah, he speaks to the individual in a corporate context, "I, Yahweh, search the mind, I try the heart, even to give every man according to his ways, according to the fruit of his doings (ἑκάστῳ κατὰ τὰς ὁδοὺς αὐτοῦ καὶ κατὰ τοὺς καρποὺς τῶν ἐπιτηδευμάτων αὐτοῦ, Jer 17:10); to Babylon, Yahweh says he will repay her according to her works (κατὰ τὰ ἔργα αὐτῆς; Jer 50:29 [LXX Jer 27:29], for she has come against the Holy One of Israel. It is also important to see that this accountability and judgment reveal the merciful character of God. In Jer 32:18–20 [LXX Jer 39:18–20], Yahweh shows his mercy when he repays the iniquity of the fathers unto their children after them.

101. Richard Adamiak understands the history of Israel as containing a consistent system of divine retribution in which the Sinai covenant occupies a position of decisive importance; Adamiak, *Justice and History*, 84–85. In this system of retributive theology, the unconditional promise of the land to the patriarchs is rendered conditional, dependent on the fulfillment of the covenant.

102. In Isa 56:11, the phrase ἕκαστος κατὰ τὸ ἑαυτοῦ is translated as "only more so" (NASB), "great beyond measure" (RSV), "much more abundant" (KJV), and "or even far better" (NIV).

good works: "glory, honor, and peace, *first to the Jew and then to the Gentile*" (Rom 2:9).

For Virgil, the physical world is a shadow of a purer world, and in the *Aeneid*, Anchises describes the process of the rebirth of souls to Aeneas (6.713–14), which markedly differs from the punishments in Tartarus where there is room for all who violate the universal canons of justice and morality. The ideas shift from Homeric to Roman as the epic poet uniquely joins what might seem to be incompatible accounts for a specific eschatological purpose. Aeneas experiences the sight of a Roman parade, emphasizing the *gloria* of Rome and Augustus, the second founder of Rome who will restore the Golden Age and bring Rome's dominion to the ends of the world. Virgil's exultation of Rome deviates from the audience's expectation of a Platonic vision. Instead, Virgil scripts powerful imagery of honor and glory without the philosophical comfort of immortality and redemption, which means that the meeting of Aeneas and Anchises is a political image of process for the Roman state.

Divine *Fides*

After Paul defines a "Jew" as one who is circumcised in the heart by the Spirit, he places himself in a situation where he must make sense of what it means then to be an ethnic Jew, one circumcised in the flesh. One advantage: God entrusted the Jews with his Word (Rom 3:3). Such a statement then raises another issue—God's faithfulness (Rom 3:4). If some of the Israelites did not have faith, does this mean that their unfaithfulness nullifies God's commitment to his covenant people? When Paul addresses Israel's election, he implicitly draws upon a Roman context regarding the virtue of "*fides*" (which is also a prominent theme in the *Aeneid* concerning the gods).[103] He declares that God is true and supports this statement with a verse from the Psalms, "so that you might be justified in your words and victorious in your judgments."[104] Paul will return to this topic of God's faithfulness toward his elect people in

---

103. Simply, *fides* refers to keeping one's word. It is interesting that Aeneas complains that Palinarus's death makes Apollo appear to be a liar ("Is this how he keeps promises?" *en haec promissa fides est*? 6.346). *Fides* was formally honored by the Romans as a goddess around 250 B.C.

104. Paul quotes Ps 51:4b [LXX: 50:6b]. Cranfield notes that the LXX translator took *zākāh* (be pure) to mean "conquer," *Romans*, 1:182.

Romans 9–11; at this point in his letter, he pronounces judgment on Jews and Gentiles (3:10–18) and reveals the sacrificial atonement for sin (3:21–26).

Faithful Christ

While the *Aeneid* is replete with sacrificial acts and imagery,[105] there is no comparison to Paul's declaration of propitiation for sinners through Christ's blood. Unlike Virgil's message,[106] Paul's gospel contains no deception. The gospel of God has previously been proclaimed by the Law and the Prophets. Paul explains in specific terms that the one who is just is also the justifier—Christ is the sacrificial agent.

Virgil does, however, implicitly script death as sacrifice.[107] In chapter 3 of this study, it was shown that the wrath of the gods and moral justice combine when Aeneas sacrifices Turnus for the cause of Rome. In order for Aeneas to establish peace, the *furor-pietas* concept works itself out with Turnus as an agent of heaven's jealous wrath, and Jupiter and Anchises (Aeneas's father) providentially guide Aeneas to fulfill his duty as a son to complete his glorious mission. In the climax and final passage of the *Aeneid*, Aeneas hesitates before avenging Pallas's death by killing Turnus, which shows Aeneas's just action and heroic manner (promoting an Augustan ideal). Aeneas's impassioned action can be considered unequivocally moral, acting out of *pietas* and *fides* as the instrument of *deum ira* rather than its object.

In addition, Virgil uses slaughtered bulls to symbolize both the *pietas* of sacrifice and the *impietas* of murder. Most interesting is the

---

105. For representative sacrifice and atonement passages, see *Aen.* 2.183–4; 2.293–97; 3.118–20, 176–8; 3.403f; 4.58–59; and 6.250.

106. Also, in Book 5, before the Trojans arrive in Italy, Neptune foretells the death of Palinarus (Aeneas's helmsman) by saying that "one life would be given for the many" (*unus erit tantum, amissum quem gurgite quaeres; unum pro multis dabitur caput*, 5.814–15). Even though *pietas* depends on trust, an element of deception takes place, because Apollo had told Aeneas that he would arrive safely on the Ausonian shores (6.343–46) without warning him that Palinarus would die at sea.

107. In the first half of the *Aeneid*, Virgil describes death in language that suggests the ritual religious killing of sacrificial victims, primarily through minor characters (e.g., Orontes, Laocoon in Sinon's tale, Palinarus, and Misenus). In Book 2, a tale is told about a human sacrifice (2.116–17). In Book 6, black cattle are offered for the purification of Misenus's death, a death that represents the exchange of a life for a life; his own life for that of Aeneas (6.152).

blood from bull-sacrifice which causes Nisus to slip at the end of the footrace (5.327–33). Virgil chooses the sacrificed animal's blood for Nisus to slip on (rather than dung as in the parallel scene in Homer). In Book 9, however, it is Nisus's blood that is shed as a type of sacrifice; he becomes a victim himself. Here Virgil symbolically substitutes a human sacrifice in place of animal sacrifice.

The relevance here is not whether Paul parallels the sacrificial imagery of the *Aeneid*, it is whether Paul's description of Christ's death (without mentioning the cross, 3:21–26) is meant to countervail the message of the *Aeneid* (concerning the wrath of the gods, sacrifice, and a god-man) for those listening to the reading of Romans who might be familiar with Virgil's "sacred" epic. Paul is arguing that God is the God of the Gentiles too (3:27), and it is not unlike Paul to relate his message in words that reach the minds of his Greco-Roman listeners. However, more shared themes need to be demonstrated between Paul's letter and Virgil's epic before significant conclusions can be drawn.

Father Abraham

Paul reiterates that reward for works is according to what one owes (4:4), and that righteousness is credited to those who believe, just as Abraham was credited righteousness in faith before circumcision (4:9–10) and before the Law (4:13). Abraham became the father of the Jews and Gentiles (father of the circumcised and uncircumcised; father of those of the Law and those of faith), having believed in the resurrection power of God (4:17).

Abraham serves as a prototype of Christian faith in Romans 4. Textual links between 1:18–25 and 4:1–25 demonstrate a structural contrast between Abraham's faith and Gentile disobedience which demonstrates a model of Gentile acceptance.[108] Abraham's faith can also be interpreted as a reversal of God's wrath, since he gives glory to the Creator. The crucial issue in Romans 4 is not how Abraham was justified,[109] but rather whose father he is and in what way his children

---

108. Adams, "Abraham's Faith," 47–66.

109. "Good works" do not give reason for "boasting." Paul gives a specific reason why boasting is excluded—"Abraham believed God, and it was credited to him as righteousness." Jan Lambrecht understands the two alternatives in vv. 4–5 as once again placed against each other: (a) the one who works has a right to wages; and (2) the one who does not work, but believes, is justified by God freely by means of a gift;

are related to him.[110] Abraham is the father of Jews and Gentiles from "all nations." Abraham's obedience is not only a paradigm for the faith of Christian believers, but is first a prefiguration of the faith of Jesus Christ (3:22): "The story of Abraham would lie in the fact that he finds there a precedent within Scripture for the idea that the faithfulness of a single divinely chosen protagonist can bring God's blessing upon 'many' whose destiny is figured forth in that protagonist's action. In this respect, Abraham serves for Paul not just as an exemplar of Christian believing but also as a typological foreshadowing of Christ, the 'one man' (Rom 5:19) through whose obedience 'the many were constituted righteous.'"[111] In other words, "credit goes to Abraham and his descendant, Jesus Christ, who founded lineages carrying God's grace and promises."[112]

In Book 5 of the *Aeneid*, Aeneas's title changes from "pious Aeneas" to "father Aeneas" when he resides over the games in honor of his father, Anchises. Aeneas is the *paterfamilias* and carefully performs the ritual of the *Parentalia*. Virgil makes the *Iusus Troiae* the crowning point of the games and traces the continuity of the *Iusus* to a time of peace. At that time, Augustus had fully developed the *Iusus Troiae*, so Virgil compliments Augustus when he connects them with Aeneas. In the final lines of Book 5, the *Iusus* description distinguishes the "sacred father" (5.603), referring to the grand patriarch Aeneas (and his father, Anchises), as well as the divine descendant from his lineage, Caesar Augustus.

Pax Christi

Romans 5:1–11 serves as a transition passage between the first two main sections of Romans (1:17—4:25; and 5:12—8:39). Some scholars see this section as an ending to chapters 1–4, while others regard

---

Lambrecht, "Boasting Excluded," 368. In this way the first alternative never became a reality, while the second already took place in Abraham's life based on faith, available to both Jew and Gentile.

110. Hays, "Reconsideration of Rom 4:1," 97.

111. Ibid., 98.

112. Stowers, *Rereading of Romans*, 230. Eisenbaum postulates Abraham as Paul's missionary model. He serves as a symbol of Israel and the "point of contact between Israel and the rest of the peoples of the world," Eisenbaum, "Paul as the New Abraham," 145.

this passage as the beginning to the next section.¹¹³ Pertinent to this discussion are the overlap of Jewish and imperial terms—faith, peace, glory, salvation, Lord, enemies, and reconciliation.¹¹⁴ Paul reaffirms the kingship of Christ and the benefits that a Christian experiences because of his death: "Having been justified by faith, we have peace with God through our Lord Jesus Christ, through whom we have the freedom to enter in faith into this grace in which we stand; we boast in the hope of His glory" (5:1–2).¹¹⁵ Paul then states that perseverance produces character, which leads to hope, because the love of God is being poured into believers' hearts through the Holy Spirit (5:4–5).¹¹⁶

Harrison discusses several characteristics that this passage shares with imperial propaganda.¹¹⁷ First, Augustus's clemency to the nations might evoke images for Christ's initiative to reconcile those who were, at the time, enemies through an act of acquittal (Rom 5:6, 8, and 10). Second, the imperial propaganda portrays Augustus as an eschatological figure who represents the culmination of Providence in the universal history of mankind. This is evidenced by the language of excess (ὑπερβάλλω, ὑπερβολή) which is similar to Paul's language of abundance (περισσεύω).¹¹⁸ The fact that Paul emphasizes "at the right

---

113. For representative arguments: 5:1–11 as an ending to chapters 1–4, see Talbert, *Romans*, 129–30; 5:1–11 as the beginning of the second part of the letter, see Longenecker, "The Focus of Romans," 49–69.

114. For the Old Testament context and the Pauline tradition for Rom 5:1–11, see Martin, "Reconciliation," 36–48. For imperial propaganda, see Elliott, "Paul and the Politics of Empire," 17–39; and Wright, "Paul's Gospel," 160–83.

115. It is interesting that throughout Isaiah, righteousness results in or is closely connected to peace as Israel's eschatological blessings from Yahweh occur, and it plays a significant part in Israel's restoration; Shum, 193; "There is no reason to reject the suggestion that Paul's theological reflection on the effect of justification may have been inspired and directed by this Isaianic motif as a whole or Isa 32:17 in particular"; ibid. See also Dunn, *Romans*, 1:262.

116. One of Aeneas's defining traits is perseverance.

117. J. Harrison, "Augustan Age of Grace," 79–91.

118. A letter to the Asian League from a Roman proconsul (Priene: 9 B.C.) reads: "It is subject to question whether the birthday of our most divine Caesar spells more of joy or blessing, this being a date that we could probably without fear of contradiction equate with the beginning of all things (τῇ τῶν πάντων ἀρχῇ) if not in terms of nature, certainly in terms of utility, seeing that he restored stability, when everything was collapsing and falling into disarray, and gave a new look to the entire world that would have been most happy to accept its own ruin had not the good and common fortune of all been born: Caesar. Therefore people might justly assume that his birthday spells the

time" (κατὰ καιρὸν, 5:6) suggests a final eschatological event.[119] Third, Augustus, with his cosmic status as an eschatological figure, establishes a worldwide reign of fruitfulness and peace that models quintessential Roman values. "Paul's portrayal of Christ as the eschatological Figure of world and cosmic history would have registered with Romans imbued with the Augustan eschatology (and who may well have been alienated by imperial successors such as Caligula and Nero)."[120]

In Rom 5:6–8, Paul does not refer to traditional formulas when he speaks of Christ's death. He proclaims the Christ event in association with all humanity (including the weak and the ungodly in 1:18—3:20):

> He becomes a strange first among equals, a very singular sort of princeps. The ruler of the world joins company with those in rebellion against him. This claim defies both Jewish and Roman moral principles, not only as phenomena of individual or religious morality, but as phenomena of social and political ethics and administrative efficiency . . . [In Rom 5:6–8] Paul declares an end to the deadly cycle of power, privilege, law, justice, and violence. The unilateral preemptive act of Christ brings about the deliverance of all human beings—not only from sin, but also from the law and the alienation and corruption brought about by the law.[121]

In addition to the principal meaning of atoning sacrifice for sin in 5:1–12, Paul writes that "for the good [τοῦ ἀγαθοῦ] someone might dare to die" (5:7). Clifton Black sees this statement as coming from the classic Greek motif in literature of the heroic death; in other words, Paul plays one understanding of death against the other.[122] Reconciliation comes through the death of Christ, and even more so with salvation through his life, a foreshadowing of the death and resurrection imagery in 5:12—8:39. "For Paul, Jesus is what the princeps claimed to be: representative of humanity, reconciler and ruler of the world. Jesus is all this

---

beginning of life and real living (ἀρχὴν τοῦ βίου καὶ τῆς ζωῆς) and marks the end and boundary of any regret that they had themselves been born"; Ehrenberg, *Documents*, §98a (*ll.* 4–11), as in Harrison, "Augustan Age of Grace," 84.

119. Ibid., 87.

120. Ibid., 90.

121. Georgi, "Romans, Missionary Theology," 153.

122. C. Black, "Pauline Perspectives," 420. Of the ninety-five occurrences of death (θάνατος) in Paul's letters, forty-nine appear in Romans; all but seven of these occur in Romans 5–8.

because he demonstrates the association and identification of God with those in rebellion against God."[123]

The Age of God's Eschatological Grace (Romans 5:12—8:39)

In the first section of the body of the letter, Paul juxtaposes Christ's faithfulness (3:21–26 and 5:1–11) and Abraham's faithfulness (4:1–25) against the sin of humankind (1:17—3:20). In 5:12—8:39, Paul continues the theme of righteousness (5:17, 21; 6:13, 16–20; and 8:10), especially in relation to God's grace and the function of the Law (5:13, 20; 7:1–25; and 8:1–8) concerning sin in the believer's life. In this second section of his letter, Paul directly addresses his audience without the interlocutor, and the theme of πίστις (faithfulness) is absent.[124] Rather than enter into a lengthy exegetical discussion, this part of the study identifies terminology or imagery that might relate to imperial ideology which would then shed light on possible parallels between Romans and the *Aeneid*.

Eschatological Grace

In 5:12–21, Christ represents the new age and new humanity. Paul argues that grace reigns over sin and death and makes the distinction that sin is not the Law. Sin entered through Adam and reigned (ἐβασίλευσεν) until Moses (5:12–14), but grace through Jesus Christ abounds; his obedience results in justification for the many (5:15–21).

J. Harrison proposes that Paul worked on two cultural fronts—Jewish apocalyptic eschatology and imperial eschatological associations—in describing the reign of grace in Rom 5:12–21 (and the new creation in 8:18–39).[125] Traditionally, the interpretation of these two passages in Romans has been limited to Jewish apocalyptic imagery concerning the "age of the fall of Adam" and the "age of the new cre-

---

123. Georgi, "Romans, Missionary Theology," 154.

124. This change of address begins in 4:24. While Paul does not tell a "story" in Romans 5–8, it is important to recognize the poetic and narrative qualities of Paul, especially concerning prophetic texts; Hays, *Faith of Jesus Christ*, 255–56. Also, see Wright, "New Exodus," 26–35. In addition to the Exodus story, see Christoffersson, *Earnest Expectation*, 144–45.

125. Harrison, "Augustan Age of Grace," 79–80.

ation." However, the Roman readers (living in a city known as the city of the "Cosmic-Savior-Benefactor Augustus") probably understood Christ's reign of grace against the echoes of an Augustan age of grace and his benefaction.[126]

Concerning Jewish apocalyptic eschatology expressed through the Adam-Christ typology in 5:12–21, Harrison summarizes three important features.[127] First, when Paul speaks of "grace," "death," and "sin" as reigning powers (5:14, 17, and 21), he refers to the theological concept of dominions ("ages"), a familiar concept within the Jewish eschatological tradition. In this context, the new age of grace and righteousness (5:17b and 21b) supplants the present age of sin and death (5:14a, 17a, and 21a). Second, some Jewish apocalyptic works, such as 4 Ezra and 2 Baruch, connect Adam's sin to death and eternal punishment. Third, it is possible that Paul "reflects" Jewish eschatological traditions when he writes about creation eagerly awaiting the sons of God to be revealed (Rom 8:18–25).[128] An important distinction with Paul, however, is that he contrasts Jewish apocalyptic traditions when he proclaims the new age of Christ as an event that has already begun.[129]

Harrison questions whether there is an overt allusion to Caesarian beneficence in Rom 5:21.[130] Since Augustus and his beneficiaries avoided regnal imagery in describing the principate (the Caesars emphasized their superiority to both client-kings and the monarchs of enemy na-

---

126. Paul uses an intentional rhetorical strategy to show how Christ surpasses "the very best the Caesars had to offer"; ibid., 79. See chapter 1 of this study for the historical descriptions of Augustus which portray him as generous to his benefactors, yet humble and simple in lifestyle.

127. The eschatological newness of grace and the use of the verb "to abound" (περισσεύω) underscore the echatological fullness of God's grace (5:15, 17, 20; 6:20); similarly, the contrasts of death and life accent this fulness (5:12, 14, 17, 21); Harrison, "Augustan Age of Grace," 80. For key passages concerning "two ages," see 4 Ezra 4:2; 6:9; 7:13, 50; 8:1; and 9:19.

128. See Isa 65:17, 25; and 66:22.

129. Russell explains the triumph of God in the prophetic writings as "in the present," and the triumph of God in apocalyptic writings as "beyond history"; Russell, *Method and Message*, 94–95. Concerning the *Aeneid*, Aeneas's suffering evokes a confession of faith (1.204–7) and the future holds what he believes (1.258–60), but it is not yet (1.263–64), but will be fulfilled in the distant future (1.278–79, 283–91). This is a social fulfillment, not an individual one, where his sufferings affect generations; Mullens, "Tragic Optimism," 137–38.

130. Harrison, "Augustan Age of Grace," 84–85.

tions), it is likely that Paul may have evoked the Old Testament portrayal of God as king.[131] But, if Paul is speaking on two cultural fronts, he might be supplanting the ideology established in the *Aeneid* as well, since Virgil emphasizes kingship, particularly in reference to Aeneas, and heralds royal prophecies concerning Augustus.

In chapter 6, Paul communicates the principle of grace using death-life imagery (6:1–14) and slave imagery (6:15–23). When Paul writes that "we might walk in newness of life,"[132] he refers to the old man, who experiences the resurrection of Christ by the glory of the Father (6:4–6), being crucified with Christ.[133] This life is lived under grace which means sin does not reign in the "disobedience of its passions" under law (6:12, 14).[134] Paul reminds the believers that they have been set free unto righteousness which leads to eternal life (6:15–23).

Furor-Faith

At this point, Paul moves the discussion to the inner workings of "passion" and the function of the Law.[135] He says that "I would not know passion if the Law did not say, 'Do not covet'" (7:7), and he then describes an internal struggle (7:18b-20, 22–24a):

> For I desire to do the good that is present at hand
> but I do not do that which is good
> For I do not do the good that I desire to do
> but the evil that I am not desiring to do, this I do
> But that which I am not desiring to do, this I do
> and it is no longer I who do it but sin which dwells in me . . .

---

131. See 1 Sam 8:7; Isa 6:5; Ps 24:7; and Jer 51:57.

132. Collins understands 6:1–14 and the ritual of baptism as the reenactment of the death and resurrection of Jesus; Collins, *Cosmology and Eschatology*, 237. A distinctive feature of Romans 6 is that Paul avoids saying "we have risen" with Christ; rather, he speaks of "newness of life." Collins considers the transformation as incomplete, an actualization that requires continued commitment and grace; ibid.

133. The idea of eschatological newness of life contrasts the Roman god-like ruler and his family's accession to the throne; Harrison, "Augustan Age of Grace," 91.

134. The prophecies of Jeremiah and Ezekiel had already been fulfilled concerning the new creation, but this did not negate the internal change and requirement of full obedience (Rom 6:6, 12); Gowan, *Eschatology*, 91.

135. For the major proposals concerning Paul's meaning of "I" in Romans 7, see Lambrecht, *The Wretched "I,"* 59–91. Lambrecht concludes that one must not defend a single proposal to the exclusion of others.

> For I delight in the law of God according to my inner man,
>   but I see another law at work in my members waging war in
>   the law of my mind
>   and taking me captive by the law of sin which dwells
>   in my members
> I am a wretched man.

Stanley Stowers interprets the above verses (and much of Romans) in light of the Greco-Roman ethic of self-mastery.[136] Particularly in 7:7–8:2, Paul uses the device of "speech-in-character"[137] to depict the internal struggle that was first announced in Romans 1—the refusal to acknowledge God and his sentencing of sinners to be handed over to their desires (ἐπιθυμίαις) and passions (πάθη). Stowers does not find it to be a coincidence that Romans 6–8 explains how freedom from desires (6:12; 7:7, and 8, 13) and passions (7:5 and 8:18) become possible for those who are in Christ; the Spirit of God reverses the sentence pronounced in chapter 1, with sinners appropriating the faithful obedience figured forth in Jesus.[138]

If Stowers is correct, then Paul's rhetoric in 7:7–25 would resemble a tragic soliloquy of a person in a tragic situation:

> Epictetus says that tragedies which have the phrase "wretched man that I am" concern suffering for admiring external things. The cry of despair 'oh wretch that I am' is first made prominent in literature by the tragedians and comedians themselves . . . Such language is not typical of the Hebrew Bible/Old Testament (for example, the Psalms) or earlier Jewish literature but rather of what scholars often call the fragmented personality of Homer and the Greek poets . . . In Hellenistic and Roman times, philosophers and moralists usually rationalized that language. The powers were not really external but internal . . . Thus in 7 one meets a well-known and highly developed kind of rhetoric that was employed by moralists and philosophers to treat the very issues that Paul discusses.[139]

---

136. Stowers argues that Paul's dialogue with the ethic of self-mastery suggests a certain "social location," particularly in relation to themes connected with imperial rule; *Rereading of Romans*, 328. He sees a Greco-Roman influence from Aristotle's principle of virtue and reason concerning the actualization of the soul. See Aristotle, *Nic. Eth.* 1098a7–8, 16–17.

137. Stowers, *Rereading of Romans*, 264–84.

138. Ibid., 251 and 253.

139. Ibid., 271–72. For Epictetus's support, see *Diss.* 1.12.28 and 3.13.4. Stowers

158 PART 2: THE GOSPEL OF GOD IN ROMANS

Interpreting Romans 7 in the context of "self-mastery" and tragedy allows for a reasonable comparison to be made with the *Aeneid*. As previously discussed, Aeneas overcomes desire (*furor*) with faithfulness (*pietas*) for the sake of his people and the future of Rome. In Romans, Christ overcomes desire in the people of God, a present and future event which brings about salvation for his people.

Revealed Glory

Robert Jewett sees an implicit imperial context behind Rom 8:18–23, where Paul's message assumes a Caesarean view of the Golden Age.[140] Paul's letter differs from the imperial vision of "the redemption of Mother earth" which provides a "suitable foil" for re-reading Rom 8:18–23:[141]

> For I consider the sufferings of this present time not worth comparing to the coming glory to be revealed
> For creation earnestly awaits to receive the revelation of the sons of God
> For creation has been submitted unto decay, without having a choice, by the One who subjected it
> Upon hope that creation will be set free from the slavery of decay into the freedom of glory of the children of God
> For we know that all creation groans and suffers great pain up until the present time but not only this we also have the first-fruits of the Spirit and we within ourselves groan as we eagerly await sonship, the redemption of our bodies.

---

also believes that Paul echoes Old Testament motifs in Rom 8:14–30 to affirm God's faithfulness. A narrative context behind Romans 8 advances the thesis of this study. If Paul is telling the story of the people of God from an Old Testament narrative substructure, then Romans takes on a more poetic and story-like purpose. See Keesmaat, "Exodus and the Intertextual Transformation," 29–56. Paul transforms the tradition found in Isaiah and Jeremiah (who also addressed God's faithfulness to Israel) to extend beyond the land and people of Israel. The Exodus narrative becomes the story of all God's people; ibid., 48–49. Sylvia Keesmaat develops this further in *Paul and His Story*, 1–153. Keesmaat ties the function of the Exodus tradition against the circumstances of the church in Rome (e.g., Claudius's expulsion of the Jews in A.D. 49) where Jewish Christians may have been under persecution from the Gentiles. Also see Wright, "New Exodus," 26–35.

140. Jewett, "Corruption and Redemption," 25–46

141. Ibid., 31. Jewett notes that the term παθήματα appears in Rom 8:18 with the article, indicating that the topic is known to the audience.

Jewett finds significance in Paul's expression "to be revealed" (8:18) as a parallel to the thesis of Romans: "conveying an apocalyptic disclosure of the triumph of God over adversity and the corruption of the cosmic order."[142] However, the concept of "glory" does not carry a Greco-Roman sense.[143] God's glory advances in the world through the triumph of the revelation of the Gospel, not military arms. Paul's vision of Edenic hope stresses the "children of God" (8:19), a glory shared by every Christian, which contrasts "a Caesar with a sunburst about his head."[144]

In 8:22–23, humanity and creation suffer and groan.[145] Jewett argues that the personification of creation and birth metaphors of travailing resonate with Greco-Roman images of Mother Earth. In the *Ara Pacis*, Mother Earth represents fertility with her two children and fruit on her lap. On Roman coins, the imagery of Mother Earth with *pieta* was combined to pronounce that the Golden Age had arrived.[146] The expression πᾶσα ἡ κτίσις (the whole creation, 8:22) includes the entire range of animate and inanimate objects on earth and in the heavens. However, Paul does not hear nature's joy and Augustan deliverance, but only groaning, alluding to the Old Testament.[147] Paul's emphasis on

---

142. Ibid., 30.

143. Jewett sees the connection in Rom 8:18 between "revelation" and the restoration of "glory" coming from prophetic and postexilic expectations—"glory" in this context means "a fiery phenomenon issuing from radiance and brilliance, and an abstract meaning of honor, worthiness, and majesty"; ibid., 33–34.

144. Ibid., 40. Jewett discusses other terminology that does not fit neatly into a Roman parallel, such as "confident expectation" which stands in contrast to the relaxed depictions of Mother Earth in the *Ara Pacis*. It is important to recognize the interconnectedness of Paul's passage here between the creation which awaits the "apocalypse of the sons of God" in 8:19 and the chapters that follow; ibid., 35–40. Susan Eastman finds that this phrase in 8:19 concludes the revelation of the righteousness of God in chapters 1–8 (summed up with the promise of "life" in 8:11), and it transitions into the same righteousness as "the apocalypse of the sons of God" in chapters 9–15 (summed up with the promise of "life from the dead" in 11:15); Eastman, "Whose Apocalypse," 277.

145. The wording, "for we know that" (οἴδαμεν δὲ ὅτι, 8:22) makes clear that Paul assumes the Roman believers are acquainted with the idea of nature's corruption; Jewett, "Redemption of Creation," 40. Lambrecht points out that Paul personifies creation as a living, human reality. A solidarity between nature and human beings exists, especially in apocalyptic texts; Lambrecht, *The Wretched "I,"* 128.

146. Jewett, "Redemption of Creation," 41.

147. Jewett understands a similar idea of groaning in Job 31:38–40 (linked to Gen 3:17–18); Isa 24:4–7; and Hos 4:1–3; ibid., 41. He also notes the birth pangs as a metaphor for divine judgment—Isa 13:8, 21:3, 26:17; Jer 4:31, 22:23; Hos 13:13; and Mic 4:9–10.

the groaning lasting "until now" contrasts the premise that Augustus had already inaugurated the Golden Age with the Saecular Games in 17 B.C.[148]

Paul communicates to all Christian believers, not only to persons of status.[149] Paul first refers to "awaiting sonship" as a future fulfillment that confirms a present sonship of believers (8:15). Paul continues his theme in verse 23 from verse 19 (ἀπεκδέχομαι), which had been used to refer to awaiting the "revelation of the sons of God." The future hope is that God's children will one day have dominion in the context of a restored creation.[150] Paul hopes for a redemption that is no longer subject to corruption for the whole community of believers.[151] In a Roman context, only the elite could expect this kind of redemption.[152]

Victorious Love

Even though God's graciousness and love through Christ, expressed in 8:31–39, has no real parallel to the *Aeneid*, Paul does accent the grace of God through Christ which draws upon the nature of benefaction in first-century culture. The language of "abundance" ("He gave his son . . . how much more will he not, with him, graciously give us all things?," 8:32) and "victory"[153] ("in all things we are more than conquerors through him who loved us," 8:37) may echo the virtues attributed to Caesar, but the emphasis on love and intimacy is unique. The idea of intercession in the heavens (Christ intercedes, 8:34) is also not wholly

---

148. Ibid., 43. More specifically, some animate and inanimate objects of nature were considered supernatural and godlike in the *Aeneid*. This contrast is underscored when understanding how the material monism of Stoicism allowed the Romans to apply divination to nature so as to determine the provnoia ("reading the world's soul"); Brent, *Imperial Cult*, 24.

149. Jewett, "Redemption of Creation," 44–45.

150. Ibid., 45.

151. The noun, ἀπολύτρωσις, often has a military connotation, referring to the redemption of prisoners of war (either by victory or by ransom); ibid.

152. Augustus restores the Golden Age and brings Rome's dominion to the ends of the world. Rome's mission—"Remember to rule the nations by your authority; these will be the arts for you: to establish the order of peace, to spare the humble and war against the proud!" (6.851–53).

153. For the emperor as source and personification of victory, see Fears, "Theology of Victory," II.17.2:737–827.

distinctive to Romans,[154] and Paul's graphic description of "slaughter" (8:36; and Ps 44:22), victory, and power in this concluding section of Romans 8 would not be unfamiliar to Roman listeners.

Summary

It is possible that Paul framed his arguments in Romans to countervail the significant themes raised in Virgil's *Aeneid* as a "contra-literary" rhetorical strategy. This in no way suggests that Paul borrows his content from the Roman epic. But the shared themes of "heavenly wrath" and the "inner struggle against passion" in Romans and the *Aeneid* deserve examination. Virgil introduces his epic with a dilemma concerning justice and how heavenly wrath can come against a righteous god-man. Paul's initial theme of heavenly wrath answers Virgil's dilemma by showing how God's wrath is just in his sacrificial gift of his son, Jesus Christ.

Concerning the inner struggle of Aeneas (in Books 1–6), Virgil is unique among epic writers to include the psychological dimension of Aeneas's passion and his *pietas*. Paul also describes the internal workings of passion but centers his gospel on "faith." In both Romans and the *Aeneid*, faithfulness is personified in a righteous servant for the purpose of a divinely elected people. Paul does not compete with these philosophical ideas; he reverses the inherent Roman value system with the truth of the Gospel.

Unlike any of his other letters, Paul, in Romans, introduces the body with a thematic statement emphasizing God's elective, salvific process in history: "to the Jew first and then to the Gentile." The intensity of this theme ("Jewish race!") cries out against an imperial context where the Roman race dominates. According to Paul, God reveals two configurations of δικαιοσύνη—God's righteousness through faith and God's righteousness through wrath. This religious-philosophical outline has parallels to Aristotelian and Platonic tracts, and in the case of Romans, the faithful Christ-king brings earthly disorder into conformity with the divine blueprint, with πίστις as the bond of the Christian community. Righteousness is to be lived out through the resurrection power

---

154. For intercession as well as the emphasis of the "right hand" in the *Aeneid*, see 7.235, 8.557–58, and 9.289. Venus often intercedes to Jupiter on behalf of her son Aeneas (Rome's destiny) against the hostility of Juno, who regularly intervenes to hinder and cause suffering to the Trojans. Early in the epic, Virgil makes it clear that grief exists in the heavens (*nostro doluisti saepe dolore*, 1.669) over Juno's hatred against Aeneas.

of Christ in the believer. Virgil follows a similar religious-philosophical pattern when he scripts Aeneas as the faithful king who experiences a reordering of his soul in obedience to divine will to bring about a divine plan, where *pietas* is the bond of the community. It seems that Paul is either supplanting the idea of justice in the *furor-pietas* configuration from the *Aeneid*, or both authors are structuring their writings with common philosophical ideas in mind.

Distinctly, the just wrath that Paul describes in Romans 1 does not parallel the irrational *furor* from the heavens in the mythical account of the *Aeneid*, but the topic of irrational passion is an important theme in both Romans and the *Aeneid*. In the second section of the body of Romans, Paul moves the discussion to the inner working of "passion." Paul uses the device of "speech-in-character" to depict the internal struggle that was first announced in Romans 1—the refusal to acknowledge God and his sentencing sinners to be handed over to their desires (ἐπιθυμίαις) and passions (πάθη). The Spirit of God in Christ reverses the sentence pronounced in Rom 1, with sinners appropriating faithful obedience figured forth in Jesus. It may be that Paul's rhetoric in 7:7–25 resembles a tragic soliloquy, which would strengthen the possibility that Paul countervails principles of Virgil's epic. As previously discussed, Aeneas overcomes desire (*furor*) with faithfulness (*pietas*) for the sake of his people and the future of Rome. In Romans, Christ overcomes desire in the people of God, a present event which brings about the future salvation for all of the elect.

This study does not challenge the fact that Paul's theology is rooted in the Old Testament. This is especially true concerning Paul's message of eternal reward for "good works" that can be traced to mercy, sacrifice, and judgment in a Levitical context. However, some of Paul's terminology in Romans 5–8 shares several characteristics with imperial propaganda—clemency to the nations (reconciliation), the language of "abundance," and an eschatological figure who represents the culmination of Providence in the universal history of humankind. Even so, it appears that Paul evokes the Old Testament portrayal of kingship. Augustus did not emphasize his position as "king." Virgil did (in reference to Aeneas and the royal prophecies concerning Augustus). It is rather striking, too, that the opening verses of Romans negate the main tenets presented in the *Aeneid*. In other words, in Romans 1–8, Paul reverses Roman values when he speaks to all Christian believers (not only persons of status), and his concepts of "conquering" and dominion refer to a personal, loving, and intimate relationship.

Other aspects in Romans show a more distant connection to Roman values. Throughout the letter, "faith" connotes a sense of "faithfulness" or "duty." Attention turns to God's faithfulness to his people (3:1–2), which reflects Paul's understanding of the Roman virtue of "*fides*" (keeping one's word, *Aen.* 6.346). He also emphasizes a grand, faithful patriarch who serves as a prototype of faithful behavior, from whom descends a royal savior (Abraham and his descendant Jesus Christ—a possible contrast to Aeneas and Augustus). And while there is no comparison to Paul's declaration of propitiation for sinners through Christ's blood, Virgil does implicitly script death as sacrifice. The wrath of the gods and moral justice combine when Aeneas sacrifices his enemy, Turnus, for the cause of Rome. Aeneas acts with moral justice, with *pietas* and *fides*, as the instrument of *deum ira*, rather than its object. Those listening to the reading of Paul's letter, who are familiar with Virgil's epic, might recognize Paul's implicit emphasis that the Son of God is both the instrument and object of God's wrath, a message of salvation to those in Rome.

5

God's Faithfulness to Save His People

The whole epistle stands under the banner of no person being justified by works and even the pious not entering the kingdom of God on the basis of their piety.[1]

AFTER DECLARING TO THE ROMAN BELIEVERS THE PERMANENT AND immeasurable love of Christ, and after revealing the intercessory nature of Christ and the Spirit, Paul is moved to considerable anguish as he grieves on behalf of his people, a nation entrusted with the very words of God. In the form of a lament and in midrashic style (9:1—11:32), Paul explains God's actions in history, revealing his faithful character to keep his promises to "Israel."[2] This section of the letter makes clear

---

1. Käsemann, *Romans*, 317.

2. For representative views that Romans 9-11 is the climax of the letter, see Wright, *Climax of the Covenant*, 234; Dunn, *Romans 9-16*, 519. For 9:6-29 as a midrash, see Stegner, "Romans 9:6-29," 37-52. Blumenfeld sees Romans 9-11 as a distinct mix of Jewish midrash and Greek allegory; *Political Paul*; 365-66. He argues that just as midrash is didactic and homiletic of a scriptural text, allegory is a transformation of the Homeric text intended to make poetry conform with reasoned argument (also popular among first-century Stoics). Blumenfeld draws the comparison of a philosopher (or scholar) providing "enlightened reading" to defend the failure of the gods in the Homeric "scripture" to Paul harmonizing God's actions with Scripture (e.g., children of Abraham) when he appeals to Old Testament *logia*; ibid. This "'story of Israel' touches

the meaning of Paul's theme, "to the Jew first and then to the Gentile," and it provides a foundation for Paul to admonish directly a church that he has not visited (12:1—15:13). Paul's words do not evidence a close relationship to the church, yet he candidly confronts their attitudes. In an honest, informal tone, he discusses his missionary plans with them (15:14-33) and gives a lengthy greeting to specific individuals who meet in house churches (16:1-24).[3] Based on these literary divisions in the second half of Paul's letter, chapter 5 of this study follows a sequential progression to find specific content and themes that might echo important aspects of Virgil's message in the *Aeneid*, with particular attention given to the tragic emotions Paul experiences on behalf of the elect (9:1-3), the unity expressed in the olive tree metaphor (11:15-24), and relevant Roman cultural values in the final sections of his letter (12:1—15:13 and 15:14—16:27).

The Salvation of All Israel (Rom 9:1—11:36)

Paul laments over Israel and describes their failure as a "stumbling" or "trip" (9:33; and 11:11). Now aware of their loss, ethnic Israel rejects the Messiah, and they become irrationally jealous and angry over God's inclusion of the Gentiles. Paul describes the grafting and engrafting of branches from an olive tree as a visual picture of God's mercy to the Jews and Gentiles, and in uncharacteristic language, Paul redefines the non-Christian Jews as "enemies" on account of the Gospel (11:28).

Tragic Israel

Paul uses an oath formula to confirm that the sorrow he experiences "in Christ" (9:1) is genuine. His grief is "great" and "unceasing" (9:2), which demonstrates an attitude of unselfish burden: "For I could pray to be cursed from Christ on behalf of my brothers, those who were born according to my own race" (9:3). His heart's expression echoes the

---

on all the basic points in an overarching drama of salvation history by means of 'covenant linearity' in which God is proving faithful to the chosen people throughout the surprising twists and turns of salvation history"; Longenecker, *Narrative Dynamics*, 64. Longenecker emphasizes that Paul is concerned about Israel's past, present, and future in Romans 9-11.

3. Paul knew of at least three house churches (16:5, 14-15), but wrote one letter to represent himself to all of the separate groups of believers in Rome, a unified body; Malherbe, *Social Aspects*, 70.

intercessory nature similar to the Old Testament prophets.[4] Paul does not explicitly mention Israel's unbelief in relation to the Gospel as the reason for his sorrow,[5] and will describe Israel's failure as a "trip."

Paul's historical and theological perspective in Romans shares similarities with the epic genre, even though tragedy involves mythological content and the epic plot centers around an unfortunate mistake (rather than a moral sin).[6] The concepts of reversal and recognition had become a natural part of first-century Greco-Roman thinking, partially due to centuries of Greek education and the curriculum of Homer's epics. So when Paul writes his theological and historical letter, his readers might readily cipher elements of reversal and recognition. For example, when Paul grieves for his race, ethnic Israel, his suffering occurs on behalf of his own people, an important element of tragedy. The centerpiece of Paul's gospel is the sacrificial death of God's Son, revealing the deep compassion of God for his people, and Paul himself is brought into grief (9:1–5).[7] What makes the story of Israel suspenseful is the fact that they are not aware of their loss at first, but soon become jealous (recognition). The Gentiles inherit God's blessing, and enmity exists between ethnic Israel and the Gospel (reversal).[8] Paul's practical aim in writing is to exhort his listeners to have this same mind of Christ, to show compassion. In a general sense, the preservation of a political relationship is involved—the future of God's children.

Thus, Paul discloses his grief to demonstrate that God's compassion is at work within him, which also motivates him to defend the veracity of God's promise. By doing so, Paul may be dismissing the mythologi-

---

4. It is necessary to view Paul's hermeneutic against the prophetic hermeneutic of the Old Testament; in this way Paul creates "prophetic agony" in 9:1–3, 10:1–2, and 11:1; Evans, "Paul," 570. "In short, the pathos of 9:1–5 subtly invites all the hearers to share Paul's agony over Israel"; Keck, "Pathos in Romans," 93.

5. Räisänen, "Paul, God, and Israel," 180.

6. For information on the epic genre, see the section "Literary Principles" in chapter 2 of this study.

7. Bruce Metzger discusses five possible meanings of Rom 9:5; Metzger, "Punctuation of Romans 9:5," 95–112. If the view is taken that Paul underscores the divinity of Christ here, then an argument can be made that Paul might be countering the false message of a divine Caesar. The discussion over these possible renderings is lengthy. For a comprehensive bibliography of 9:5, see Fitzmyer, *Romans*, 556–57.

8. In Romans 9–11, Paul aims to resolve the tension that the Jews are "enemies"; Moo, *Epistle to the Romans*, 549.

cal claims of Rome. In the opening scene of the *Aeneid*, Aeneas prays to heaven concerning the loss of life at Troy and says, "that I could not have fallen in the open fields of Troy, and pour out my spirit at your hand" (1.94-6), and he openly laments the fallen glory of Troy (1.372). When recounting the battle of Troy to Dido, he heaves a heavy sigh (*ingentem gemitum*, 1.485-86) from the depths of his heart concerning the casualties of war, and when he remembers his people and homeland, unspeakable grief and sorrow well up within him (*renovare dolorem . . . lamentabile regnum . . . luctuque*, 2.3-12).[9] This emotive personality creates a balance between two conflicting interests—Aeneas's own needs and that of Rome's destiny—and it also reveals his virtues of *religio* and *pietas*. However, in Rom 9:1-3, while Paul does grieve on behalf of his own race, the emphasis rests not on his own virtue but on his genuine sorrow "in Christ" and "in the Holy Spirit."

Divine Faithfulness

In Rom 9:6, Paul continues a discourse that he started earlier in his letter concerning God's faithfulness (3:3). The words of God had been entrusted to the Jews and now Paul asks, "Has the Word of God failed?" He answers in midrashic style (with three interrelated passages: 9:6-29, 9:30—10:21, and 11:1-32) by stating that not all of the descendants of Abraham are considered "Israel" and that the "children of the promise" are not the "children of the flesh" (9:8). To support this claim, Paul alludes to the patriarchs (Abraham, Gen 18:10; Isaac, Gen 25:21; and Jacob, Gen 25:23),[10] which leads to a central point that the "older" son (Esau) will serve the "younger" (ὁ μείζων δουλεύσει τῷ ἐλάσσονι, 9:12; Mal 1:2-3).[11] But Paul seems to be emphasizing that the son of

---

9. For other passages of sorrow, see *Aen.* 1.208-9, 2.726-9, 5.350, and 6.332. Aeneas's grief involves the aspect that some people cannot be saved, such as with Pallas (10.467-71). It might also be important to note that immortality means eternal grief in the *Aeneid* (e.g., 12.878-84) and both Homeric and Virgilian epics stress eternal sorrow (e.g., the Homeric Hercules suffers because he witnesses the deaths of his loved ones). For passages that accent the Roman race, see *Aen.* 1.7, 270-71, 565-66; 6.834; and 8.512-13.

10. The allusion to the patriarchs reveals God's action in history, unlike the parade of heroes in the *Aeneid* which exalts the Roman people.

11. Paul's use of ἐλάσσονι emphasizes the meaning of an "inferior" position, which would make sense in a Hebrew culture; see BDAG, s. v. ἐλάσσων. This distinction becomes significant in Paul's admonitions concerning the "weak" and the "strong" in

lower status (the younger/weaker) will be served by the one of "greater" status (the older/superior). In this Old Testament context, God judges the Edomites (Esau's descendants) as a way of magnifying the sentence that will follow against Israel's priests. God shows his love to Israel by disciplining the nation of Edom with his wrath, a sign to the priests of Israel, those benefiting from God's blessing, that God's just wrath would soon be carried out with intensity against Israel. Writing with great pathos, Paul uses the Malachi quotation to accent the deserved judgment of Israel; even more so, he reinforces the truth that the covenant privileges still continue for ethnic Israel.[12]

Paul defends the righteousness of God and his decisions in election by reminding the listeners that God is sovereign. God shows mercy to whom he desires, regardless of human effort (9:15–16; Exod 33:19).

Romans 14. Concerning Paul's use of Jacob and Esau, it is clear that these names refer to the countries of Israel and Edom in the Malachi quotation; Moo, *Epistle to the Romans*, 585–86. Warde Fowler comments on how moderns perceive Turnus as a hero in contrast to the way ancient Romans see Aeneas, which is as an agent of Jupiter in conquest and civilization: "So, too, it is in Jewish history; we feel with Esau more than with Jacob, and with David more than with Moses, who is nonetheless the grandest typical Israelite in the Old Testament. And, indeed, Virgil's theme here is less the development of a character or the portraiture of a hero than the idealization of the people of the Italy which he loved so well, who needed only a divinely guided leader and civilizer to enter upon the glorious career that was in store for them"; *Religious Experience*, 423.

12. According to his covenant with Israel, Yahweh both faithfully makes judgments and faithfully shows love. Andrew Hill finds this direct quotation of Mal 1:2–3 in Rom 9:13 as the author's use of antithesis, emphasizing an ironic "reversal of the future of two nations"; Hill, *Malachi*, 168. Hill understands Edom as a foil for Israel. Paul, who understands his own priestly role (Rom 15:16), makes a direct quotation from the opening passage of Malachi (the MT, LXX, and the New Testament agree with the exception of the word order of the Jacob clause of Rom 9:13). The book of Malachi reveals a coming day of judgment for priests of Yahweh because of their irreverence and unfaithful service (see Mal 1:7, 13–14; 2:6–10; and 3:5). Douglas Stuart asserts that Malachi, like no other single prophetic book, delineates all twenty-seven types of curses set forth in Leviticus and Deuteronomy; Stuart, "Malachi," 3:1259–60.

However, the major semantic significance rests on Yahweh's covenant love to Jacob over Esau (1:2–3). "Love" has a broad connotation, but refers here to Yahweh's divine love to his people Israel; Brown, Driver, and Briggs, *Hebrew and English Lexicon*, s.v. "אהב." The context seems to signify Yahweh's enduring, steadfast love—the "entire history of God's covenant relationship with Israel"; Huey, "An Exposition of Malachi," 12–21. Yahweh affirms his election to Israel by reminding them of his decision to demonstrate his wrath to the son he did not choose, Esau (representative of Edom, a synecdoche for Israel's enemies); Stuart, "Malachi," 1281. With Yahweh as the subject, אהב) connotes a "distinguishing, selective love," VanGemeren, *New International Dictionary*, 1:281–83. Also see Cranford, "Election and Ethnicity."

His manifest power against Pharaoh serves as a vehicle for proclamation, as God's name is sent throughout the earth (9:17; Exod 9:16). This execution of wrath establishes God's kingdom on earth, revealing his patience and plan for reaching the nations (9:22–23). With the *testimonia* of Old Testament Scripture, Paul supports his claim that both Jews and Gentiles comprise the true "Israel"—Gentiles are included in the remnant (Rom 9:25–26; Hos 1:10; 2:23) and God is faithful in preserving remnant Israel (Rom 9:27–28; Isa 10:22–23).[13]

Israel's "Trip"

In Rom 9:30—10:21, Paul returns to the themes of "righteousness" and "faith" and supports the axiom that Gentiles are included in the promise. He begins in 9:30—10:4 by showing how ethnic Israel relied on "works" of the Law rather than faith. Paul states that they "fell" on the stone of stumbling: "Behold, I place in Zion a stumbling stone and a rock of scandal, and the one believing upon him will not be put to shame" (9:33;

---

13. Rom 9:27b–28 is an amalgam of Hos 1:10 [LXX 2:1] and Isa 10:22–23. Paul quotes from the LXX—for synoptic parallel phrases of Isa 10:22–23 and 9:27b–28, see Dunn, *Romans 9–16*, 572. Paul's context seems to parallel the prophet's context—as a message of hope amidst disaster, and as a promise for Israel's future; Wagner, *Heralds of the Good News*, 107. Wagner notes that the function of Isa 10:22–23 does not paint a grim picture that "only" a remnant will be saved; rather, Paul includes himself in the calling of the Jews (using the plural pronoun "us" in Rom 9:24) to underscore God's faithfulness in preserving a remnant of Israel and bringing their chastisement to an end; ibid. Shum understands Paul's use of the remnant motif from Isaiah in Rom 9:27–29 to include negative overtones of punishment of a disobedient Israel, while on the other hand, it offers hope guaranteeing blessing of divine favor; Shum, "*Paul's Use of Isaiah*," 261. Childs remarks that Yahweh's anger against Assyria and Israel creates a "profound struggle" between the idea of a "people left over" and the "people of God delivered by faith"; Childs, *Isaiah*, 94. The contrast between the "remnant" and Yahweh's "promise" (to multiply the seed of Abraham as sand upon the seashore) creates tension; Young, *The Book of Isaiah*, 2:370–71. Young sees the purpose in Isa 10:22–23 as a message against false reliance upon the promise. Descent from Abraham is not a guarantee of promise, and eternal punishment is a manifestation of God's justice; ibid. Although the remnant language (τὸ ὑπόλειμμα) could be used negatively and threateningly, Paul has the positive sense in mind (e.g., Gen 45:7; 2 Kgs 19:31; Mic 4:7; and 5:7–8); Dunn, *Romans 9–16*, 572. John Heil offers an insightful perspective in that 9:27–29 is a "preliminary climax" to chapters 9–11; Heil, "From Remnant to Seed," 703–20.

Isa 28:16).[14] Moreover, Paul may have chosen the imagery of a "fall" (or "trip," προσέκοψαν)[15] to echo a well known Greco-Roman story.

Stowers believes that the Greeks would have heard the echoes of the footrace imagery of the funeral games for Patroclus in Book 23 of the *Iliad*.[16] In second place is Odysseus who prays to the goddess Athena for speed. She answers Odysseus's prayers and gives him speed, but she also trips the lead runner, Ajax, who slips and falls in the dung left from a cattle sacrifice. Odysseus, who was in second place, ends up winning unexpectedly, and Ajax finishes the race and shares in the prize. If Paul echoes the *Iliad*, he intentionally diverges from the footrace story; he shifts the direct address to the Gentile audience (11:13) by warning them not to be arrogant (11:18). Stowers argues that what would stand out in this parallel is that God does not play favorites, unlike the story in the *Iliad*.[17]

If an argument can be made for an intentional play on Iliadic imagery, it might make more sense to view Paul's selection of the word "trip" in light of the footrace in Book 5 of the *Aeneid*. Before the footrace, Aeneas enters the valley and sits on a raised throne among thousands of spectators and promises a reward for all participants, with special

---

14. The metaphor of the "stone" unifies Isaiah 28—"symbolizing a new community, a faithful remnant, a foretaste of the coming righteous reign of God which is ushered in by the promised messiah rule of Zion"; Childs, *Isaiah*, 209. The figurative language of a cornerstone in the Old Testament tends to be used in the context of the formation of community (e.g., Zech 10:4; and Ps 118:22); Blenkinsopp, *Isaiah 1–39*, 394. Blenkinsopp notes that Paul uses this in a new way when he combines Isa 28:16 with 8:14. It is possible that there was a "Stone *testimonium*," but it is likely that Paul is incorporating his own format, since he brings out the negative point about Israel's fall, the main point in this context (placing a phrase from Isa 8:14 in the middle of Isa 28:16); Moo, *Epistle to the Romans*, 630. Eldon Epp understands Paul's use of the "Stone" (10:4) for Christ as a way to demonstrate Israel's earliest relationship with God based on "faith" before the Law; "Jewish-Gentile Continuity," 90. In the Isaianic context, the stone refers to the "Immanuel whom God had promised to be the deliverer of his people"; Young, *Isaiah*, 1:288. While Paul does not explicitly identify the stone as Christ, his Christological convictions point to God's action in raising Christ from the dead and declaring him Lord; Wagner, *Heralds of the Good News*, 157.

15. The asyndeton (προσέκοψαν τῷ λίθῳ τοῦ προσκόμματος) at the beginning of 9:32b–33 gives a "special solemnity to the whole of the substance of what is being said"; Cranfield, *Romans*, 2:510.

16. Stowers, *Rereading of Romans*, 314–15.

17. Ibid. For the theme that God does not show favoritism, see Rom 2:6–11; 3:23, 29–30; 4:16; 10:11–13; and 11:32, 34–35.

prizes for first, second, and third place. The main contestants are Nisus (Trojan born), Euryalus, Diores, Salius (Greek-born), Patron, Helymus, and Panopes.[18] At the beginning of the race, Nisus takes the lead, with Salius running a distant second. Euryalus (a friend of Nisus) runs in third place behind Salius, followed by Helymus and Diores. Nisus keeps the lead right up until the finish when he suddenly slips on some mud, drenched with blood.[19] Before his fall, the youthful Nisus had already begun rejoicing at his win, but now in order to help his friend Euryalus, Nisus gets up and immediately trips Salius, who falls into the sand. Euryalus passes both of them and wins (Helymus finishes second and Diores in third).

The Grecian Salius demands that he be given his first place prize, which was taken from him by a trick. Aeneas does not alter the order of victory, but takes pity on the unfortunate outcome of his friend Salius and gives him a huge lion pelt. After Aeneas rewards Salius, the Trojan Nisus grieves and questions Aeneas about the reward for those who fell (*lapsorum*) but should have won, reminding him that compassion is deserved (5.353–56). Aeneas awards Nisus with a remarkable shield. In the *Aeneid*, "tripping" results in blessing for both Trojan and Greek.

In Rom 11:11–12, Paul again uses the imagery of Israel's fall, but punctuates the result of blessing for the Gentiles which causes Israel to become jealous, resulting in future blessing for repentant Israel too:

> Did they trip in order that they might fall? By no means.
> [μὴ ἔπταισαν ἵνα πέσωσιν; μὴ γένοιτο]
> But their transgression results in salvation to the Gentiles
>   in order that the Gentiles might make them jealous.
> But if their transgression means riches to the world
>   and their failure [τὸ ἥττημα] riches to the nations,
> how much more their fullness?

A few verses earlier, Paul introduces "jealousy" as a key to understanding the mystery of God's election by quoting the Torah: "I will make

---

18. The main competitors were Trojan, Greek Arcadian, and Sicilian.

19. As discussed in chapter 3 of this study, Virgil chooses the symbolism of blood from bull-sacrifice to cause Nisus's slip (5.327–33) rather than dung (from the parallel scene in Homer). In Book 5, the blood of slaughtered bulls causes the downfall, but in Book 9, it is the blood of slaughtered men (Euryalus and Nisus will be symbolically sacrificed). Dyson mentions that the blood-soaked ground occurs only once more in the *Aeneid* (immediately before Turnus summons Aeneas to the final combat); "*CAESI IUVENCI*," 280.

you jealous by those who are not a nation; I will make you angry by a nation without knowledge" (Rom 10:19; Deut 32:21).[20] The context is one of God's compassion in acting on behalf of Israel: "I continually extend my hands to a disobedient and stubborn people" (Rom 10:21; Isa 65:2). While it can be argued that Paul's recipients may have thought of the context of a compassionate reward given to Nisus and Salius,[21] this possible cultural play on words of the *Aeneid* footrace would be a "distant" echo at best, since the narratives do not share a close logical parallel.

From an overall perspective, God blesses the Gentiles, which stirs up anger and jealousy among his elect people. In other words, righteousness from heaven is revealed through Gentile faith, and divine wrath (a handing over to passion) facilitates the opportunity for jealousy and anger among ethnic Israel.[22] But in the end, God's decisions result in salvation for believing Jews and Gentiles. God's anger is just and perfect, without irrationality, and his righteous decisions reveal his compassion. This contrasts the *Aeneid*, where the source of jealousy comes from heaven through the goddess Juno, who acts out with impious jealousy and stirs unreasoned desire and internal fury among Dido and Turnus. It is this sense of injustice which provides Virgil with the motivation and material to write his tragic plot.

Christ's *Katabasis*

Paul reiterates his initial theme, "the just will live by faith" (1:17), when he alludes to Moses speaking about righteousness, "The man who does these things [the Law], will live in them" (Rom 10:5; Lev 18:5). Paul then personifies righteousness (Rom 10:6–8):[23]

---

20. Paul ends his second midrashic section (9:30—10:21) with another Old Testament *testimonium*—Ps 19:4, Deut 32:21, and Isa 65:1–2.

21. Israel's "trip" results in God's wrath. This could be considered an implicit sacrifice, since God's wrath against them brings about riches to the nations (10:12).

22. In Romans, pious "zeal" leads to the danger of missing the "righteousness of God"; Smiles, "The Concept of Zeal," 282–99.

23. Paul quotes the LXX; Dunn, *Romans 9–16*, 603. Dunn provides a synoptic parallel of phrases (Rom 10:6–8 and Deut 30:12–13). Paul personifies "Righteousness" in a similar manner that wisdom literature personifies "Wisdom"; Hays, *Echoes of Scripture*, 78. The Old Testament context is also positive—four negative parallels ("not too difficult, not too remote, not in heaven, not across the sea") accent the affirmation that Torah is near; Brueggemann, *Deuteronomy*, 268. For helpful background on Paul's use of the Old Testament in Rom 10:5–10, see Davies, *Faith and Obedience*, 189–203.

Do not say in your heart,
"Who might ascend into heaven?"
that is to bring Christ down, or
"Who will *descend into the abyss?*"
that is to bring Christ up from the dead.

Paul changes the "crossing of the sea" (Deut 30:13, LXX) to "will descend into the abyss" (Rom 10:7) to relate the Torah event more closely to the Christ event, for Christ has supplanted the "doing" of the Law with the word of faith.[24] But the phrase "will descend into the abyss" (καταβήσεται εἰς τὴν ἄβυσσον) is unique in that it departs in a marked way from any extant version of Deuteronomy.[25] "The pertinent question is not what is 'necessary' to provide 'a complete text' for understanding Paul's strange departures from the Deuteronomy text. It is more a question of which traditions were actually current in Paul's day, and how the ascent and descent motifs might have been heard at that time."[26] One of the well-known *katabasis* motifs in the first century was Aeneas's *katabasis*.

In Book 6, Virgil's description of Aeneas's descent to the underworld integrates material from a variety of sources. While there are similarities to Homer in Virgil's descriptions, much of the material has been assimilated from popular belief and folklore, organized by Orphic mystery religions and Pythagorean philosophy.[27] For example, well-known journeys to the underworld can be found in Dionysis's comical *katabasis* in Aristophines' *Frogs,* and the more serious myths of *Phaedo,*

---

24. Heil, "Christ," 497-98. The word of God (rbdh) which is exceedingly near you "in your mouth and in your heart" concludes the central section of Deuteronomy 30 and summarizes the content of the chapter; Christensen, *Deuteronomy,* 743-44. Christensen notes Paul's change of emphasis in Rom 10:7 to salvation by faith (the "word" is near you). Also see Ps 106:26 (LXX) and Jonah 2:4-7.

25. Humphrey, "The Rhetoric of Demonstration," 133. Dunn holds to the possibility that a text form had been lost; Dunn, *Romans 9-16,* 606. For an interpretation of these verses, according to oral principles and liturgical tradition, see Dewey, "Textuality in an Oral Culture," 116-18. The method of supplementing words from an Old Testament quotation is characteristic of an exegetical paraphrase; Bekken, "Paul's Use of Deut 30:12-14," 191. Paul employs a method similar to rabbinic form, but he does not use the type of pesher of Qumran; Seifrid, "Paul's Approach," 18.

26. Humphrey, "Rhetoric of Demonstration," 133; Humphrey reviews some of the imagery in later rabbinic times, particularly in relation to rabbinic and apocalyptic mysticism, see 133-34.

27. Williams, "Sixth Book," 192.

Gorgias, *Phaedrus*, and the story of Er in the *Republic* (which provided Virgil with creative story for his epic).[28] Thus, Virgil cannot be credited for an exclusive use of this accepted, imaginative *katabasis* imagery. What distinguishes Virgil's account is the complex connection of the Augustan present and the eschatology of the underworld, marking an end of one *saeculum* and the beginning of another; even so, a clear echo cannot be substantiated to Romans.

One Israel

By paralleling a self-description to that of the prophet Elijah (11:1–6),[29] Paul identifies himself as a prophet. This analogy strengthens his argument that God did not reject His people but foreknew a remnant called according to grace, not according to works (11:6).[30] In the Scriptural *testimonia*, Paul accents Israel's hardening.[31] But what appears to be a tragic situation is an opportunity for Paul to preach to the Gentiles, so that somehow he might move his own race to jealousy, resulting in salvation (11:13–14). Paul uses an olive tree metaphor to explain what he means (11:16–21).

Paul draws upon a traditional, well-known Jewish metaphor to signify Israel (Jer 11:16 and Hos 14:6), but his reference points are purposefully unique. Paul describes a cultivated olive tree (ἐλαία) where branches are cut out (Ethnic Israel) and a wild olive tree (ἀγριέλαιος) where branches (Gentiles) are "grafted" into them, to share in the nourishing sap of the olive tree root (which most likely refers to the patriarchs or Abraham).[32] This imagery is important to the ethnic context of chapters 9–11 and to the letter as a whole, but the wider context of

---

28. Ibid.

29. See 1 Kgs 19:10, 14, and 18.

30. Craig Evans discusses Paul's role as prophet in Romans 9–11 and in relation to the Elijah comparison; Evans, "Paul and the Prophets," 115–28.

31. See Deut 29:4; Isa 29:10; and Ps 69:22–23 (a lament psalm).

32. If the root (11:16) signifies the patriarchs, then the nourishment of the root refers to divine election "in which alone their special worth consists"; Cranfield, *Romans*, 2:567. The olive tree (ἐλαία, 11:17) belongs to the *Olea europaea L.* family from which there are sub-species: the *Olea europaea satira*, which includes the cultivated olive (καλλιέλαιος, 11:24), and the *Olea europaea oleaster*, which includes the wild olive (ἀγριέλαιος, 11:17); Esler, *Conflict and Identity*, 298–301.

Greco-Roman oleiculture also plays an important part in the meaning of this passage.[33]

The visual metaphor of 11:16b–24 falls into the categories of ancient rhetoric. First, the view that Paul erases the differences between the Israelite and non-Israelite subgroups does not make clear sense;[34] rather, Paul's use of the olive tree provides a "potent visual representation" of a "single entity that is nevertheless differentiated as to its parts."[35] It seems that Paul is familiar with the ancient practice of grafting, and diverges from the common cultural practice to make a particular didactic point. The theological concern here is "who" is portrayed in a bad light, the non-Israelites or the Israelites (commentaries generally follow the idea that non-Israelites, represented by the wild olive shoots, rejuvenate the cultivated olive tree).[36]

A closer look at some of the primary evidence reveals a different conclusion. Esler goes beyond the view of Baxter and Ziesler to include primary sources other than just Columella.[37] Theophrastus, an associate of Aristotle and an expert in botany, specifically discusses the use of grafting in propagating trees (including the olive tree).[38] His writings, in addition to archaeological evidence and current practices in Greece and Israel, point to the grafting of cultured olive trees on to the deeper rooted, stronger, and more fruitful wild olive tree, a process which eventually produces rich fruit for the grafted-in cultured olive shoot.[39]

33. Esler, "Ancient Oleiculture."

34. See Boyarin, *Radical Jew*, 22–25.

35. Esler, "Ancient Oleiculture," 109.

36. For representative views, see Dunn, *Romans 9–16*, 661; Stuhlmacher, *Paul's Letter*, 168; and Bryan, *Preface to Romans*, 181.

37. Baxter and Ziesler, "Paul and Arboriculture," 25–32. While Esler appreciates W. D. Davies's grasp of the point of the allegory, he believes that Davies does not consider the primary evidence. Davies, *Jewish and Pauline Studies*, 153–63. For the most part, the arguments of Esler contrast the statements of C. H. Dodd. See Dodd, *Epistle of Paul to the Romans*, 180.

38. See *De causis plantarum* 1.6.1–10 and *De historia plantarum* 2.1.1–4.

39. Esler, "Ancient Oleiculture," 114–15. The Romans preferred raising olives in nurseries rather than grafting olive trees. Esler reviews several Latin authors, antecedent to Paul, who wrote about grafting (116–17): Marcus Porcius Cato does not differentiate between cultivated and wild olive; see *On Agriculture* 28–29; 40.1–4; 45–46; Terentius Varro explicitly refers to Theophrastus in several places, but Varro does not explicitly mention grafting olive trees; see *On Agriculture* 1.39–41; and Lucius Junius Moderatus Columella writes to a Roman audience about the cultivation, variety, and ground types for the olive tree; *Res rustica* 3–5.

Only in some detail does Columella describe the cultivation of the olive tree.[40] The agriculturist trims the branches from the best olive trees, and plants them in a nursery. Five years later, the small plants are transplanted and appropriately pruned. Esler explains how Baxter and Ziesler (and others) refer to Columella's instructions concerning a tree that is thriving but not bearing fruit.[41] Such a tree is to be bored with a Gallic auger, and a green slip from a wild olive-tree is to be placed in the hole. The impregnated tree will become more productive. Columella describes a cultivated olive tree enhanced by a branch of a wild olive tree. But Columella is not discussing grafting in the proper sense, nor is he using the standard Latin word for "grafting" (*inserere*).[42] The idea here is not "rejuvenating" the tree but "kick-starting" a fairly young tree that is healthy but fruitless.[43] Columella's detailed coverage of grafting comes in a later section when discussing fruit-bearing trees (*pomiferae arbores*, 5.10–15); he echoes Theophrastus's general instructions that any kind of scion can be grafted into any tree, and he demonstrates this by describing how an olive tree can be grafted onto a *fig tree*.[44]

Esler concludes that Columella's instructions do not serve as a satisfactory explanation of the context for Paul's allegory (Rom 11.16b–24):[45] (1) Paul does not suggest any problem with the tree, but talks about the holiness of the root to the branches, and his imagery depicts the wild olive branch depending on the tree for fruitfulness (Rom 11:16–17), a contrast to Columella's description. (2) Paul seems to have the proper sense of "grafting" in mind, with the aim of obtaining fruit from the grafted branch.[46] Richness (πιότης) in 11:17 implies fruitfulness. (3) Paul regards the original insertion of the wild olive as "contrary to nature" (11:24), which does not coincide with Columella's categories; and (4) it is unlikely that Paul had ever come across Columella's instruc-

---

40. See *Res rustica* 5.9.1–17.

41. Esler, "Ancient Oleiculture," 118. See *Res rustica* 5.9.16

42. Ibid., 119.

43. Ibid.

44. Columella wrote another agricultural work called *De arboribus* in which he discusses some of this material in less detail.

45. Esler, "Ancient Oleiculture," 120–24.

46. This is suggested by Paul's six uses of ἐνεκεντρίζω, a word employed by Theophrastus for grafting, but not used by Columella in *Res rustica* 5.9.16; see Esler, "Ancient Oleiculture," 121.

tions. It makes more sense to understand Paul's choice of imagery in light of what was recognized by an eastern Mediterranean audience.

With this perspective, Paul reverses the traditional eastern Mediterranean process when he chooses the cultivated olive tree to represent Israel, and when he chooses the engrafted branches to represent the Gentiles as originating from the wild olive.[47] This language would be unflattering to the Gentiles. It is the stock that is the source of support and fertility, not the engrafted branches. Paul warns the graftings from the wild olive tree not to be arrogant and reminds them that they are dependent on the root which had given richness to the original cultivated branches (those that have been cut off—the Jews that rejected Christ). This literary divergence accents the unity between Gentile believers and ethnic Israel. Esler's interpretation makes sense of Paul's earlier use of jealousy (Rom 10:19; 11:11, and 14), and it does not erase the differences between social categories, nor does it demonstrate any superiority.[48] It is likely that the "root" refers to Abraham, which once again reaffirms God's impartiality.[49]

When Paul warns the Gentiles, the engrafted branches, not to boast, he reminds them that the root is what "bears" them; and the "unfaithfulness" of Israel allowed for their opportunity of "faith" (11:20).[50] He admonishes them not to be "high minded" but have fear for God's wrath, since he did not spare the natural branches (11:21–22) and since Israel has the opportunity to be grafted in again (11:23–24). In this context, Paul wants his listeners to know the mystery of God's election of the Jew first and then the Gentile (10:25), and he wants them to choose humility for the sake of unity (11:25).[51] Paul summarizes this

47. Ibid., 123. Also see Davies, *Jewish and Pauline Studies*, 163.

48. Esler, "Ancient Oleiculture," 124.

49. The kindness and severity of God is based on faith and unbelief respectively (11:23–24), which rephrases the argument concerning God's impartiality (Rom 2:6–11).

50. "Israel" is implied (11:20), not stated. Bourke asserts that the olive tree is a designation of the church in Christ, the children of Abraham; Bourke, *Study of the Metaphor of the Olive*, 111. The representation here of the body of Christ provides an important link to the practical admonitions that follow; particularly, see Rom 12:5.

51. Rom 11:25 is a summary of the olive tree metaphor, and "all Israel" in 11:26 refers back to 9:6 where not all of ethnic Israel is considered "Israel." The meaning of "all Israel" has been disputed for centuries, and the four general interpretations for this phrase include: (a) all the elect, Jews and Gentiles; (b) all the elect of the nation Israel; (c) every member of the nation of Israel; (d) the nation of Israel, but not each

mystery by stating that the Jews are enemies for the Gentiles' sake, but beloved on account of the fathers; for the deliverer who comes from "Zion" is Christ who brings salvation, the forgiveness of sins (11:27; Isa 59:20–21a).[52] Some of these themes, such as unity, humility, enemies, and deliverance are also key themes in the second half of the *Aeneid*.

In Book 7, the unity between the Latins and Trojans turns into discord, and Virgil purposefully evokes Roman feelings of revenge. The gods influence Turnus toward *furor*, and the suspense builds concerning whether Aeneas will respond with *pietas*. In Book 8, Aeneas sails up the Tiber river with two ships to meet with Evander, the king of a small Greek Arcadian community who lives on the future site of Rome. Approaching Evander with an attitude of humility and without fear, Aeneas extends an arranged branch (*ramos*, 8.128) as a sacred headband.[53] Aeneas acknowledges Evander's lineage (*stirpe*, 8.130) and reminds him of their shared origin.[54] Virgil uses the phrase "branch from

---

individual member; Cranfield, *Romans*, 2:576. For a helpful discussion of the two views of καί οὕτως with emphasis on the modal sense over the temporal sense in 11:26, see Horst, "Only Then Will All Israel be Saved," 521–25.

52. The reference to the salvation of "all Israel" in 11:26b–27 condemns the Jews and accents God's faithfulness; Shum, 262. A superiority issue threatened the church (14:10, 13; and 15:7), so Paul quotes Isaiah to ensure the success of his mission which includes Gentile offerings to the Jerusalem church (15:25–28); Allison, "Romans 11:11–15, 23–30. Allison sees the rejection of the Jewish Messiah and the success of the Gentile mission contrasting the Jewish eschatological expectations in Paul's day, and although the Jews did expect the "end" to hinge upon Israel's returning to Yahweh, they did not believe as Paul did that the "fullness of the Gentiles" would usher in the "end." See also Munck, *Paul*, 247–48. The rabbis interpreted Isa 59:20–21. messianically; see Michel, *Der Brief an die Römer*, 356. Morris concludes that Paul speaks of "all Israel" in a similar way that the Mishnah does—the whole nation with a few exceptions; Morris, *Epistle to the Romans*, 420–21.

53. Theodore Williams translates this line as "lifting this olive-branch with fillets bound"; *Aeneid of Virgil*, 262. The olive was a "rich emblem of peace" for the Romans, and they attributed Athena with its invention (*Georg.* 1.18); Sargeaunt, *Trees of Virgil*, 92. The uses of the olive tree play an important part in the *Aeneid*: the olive is the envoy's white flag (7.751, 8.116); when Aeneas leaves Sicily for Italy the second time, he crowns himself with olive leaves, hoping for peace (5.774); ambassadors are shaded with olive branches (11.100); olive oil is used to anoint Trojan athletes at Actium to celebrate their escape from their Greek foes (3.281); olive blossoms serve as crowns for victors (5.309); and olive oil facilitates the burning of sacrifice (6.254).

54. Evander and Aeneas are related through Dardinus (leader of Troy). Virgil reduces the tension between Greek and Roman pride. Historically speaking, when Augustus defeated Antony at Actium and conquered Alexandria, he ended any Hellenistic hope for the East to dominate the Roman West.

one blood" (*amborum scindit se sanguine ab uno*, 8.142). And while Virgil does not use the word *stirpe* (meaning the stock, stem, shoot, or root) in this particular passage, he does use the noun *stirpe* in other *Aeneid* passages to refer to "blood" in the sense of lineage (e.g., 7.98–9; and 11.394). Furthermore, in the final scenes, Virgil explicitly refers to the root (*stirpe*) of a sacred olive tree (*oleaster*, 12.766–80)[55] in which Aeneas's lance gets firmly stuck.

It is also interesting that Virgil accents the humble bond between the Trojans and the Greek Arcadians. Aeneas looks for a modest home for their country's gods (7.229) and finds this in Evander's Greek community. The poor immigrant, Evander, lives in a simple home on the Palatine (8.456). Virgil contrasts this humility with the enemy's "arrogant" power and "proud" race (8.483–84). And even though the Romans have supremacy over the Greeks (6.836–37), Virgil reveals an order for deliverance: the road to safety will come first through a Grecian city (6.96–97). By uniting the Greek Arcadians with the Trojans, Virgil brings together two traditional adversaries so that no people are excluded from Italy's origins. After Aeneas triumphs over Turnus, the nations experience peace and reconciliation.

Concerning Virgil's familiarity with the olive tree, this perennial plant was not native to Virgil's hometown of Mantua. The Italian olive tree (*Olea sativa*) probably originated from the Greek olive tree (ἐλαία), as it is distinguished from the *oleaster*.[56] Of the different varieties of olive, Virgil selects three in his *Georgics* (2.86).[57] Virgil objects to the *oleaster* used as a stock on which is grafted the olive, because if a fire occurred in the oliveyard, the fire would burn the trees below the grafting point (olives are not on their own roots, *non a stirpe valent*, *Georg.* 2.302–14).[58] Based on this information, Paul would not be borrowing or drawing a close parallel to a perspective like Virgil's, but this does not eliminate the idea that Paul countervails the message of the *Aeneid*.

---

55. Sailors who had been saved by the waves of the sea placed gifts on this tree.

56. Sargeaunt, *Trees of Virgil*, 91. Sargeaunt distinguishes the *olea* (also called the *oliva*; e.g., *felicis olivae*, 6.230) as having pointed leaves, and its leaf is not as heavy as is the *oleaster*.

57. Cato names ten varieties, and Columella names up to eleven; ibid., 90.

58. Other than grafting, methods of propagation include: (1) a small branch planted in the nursery and (2) roots can be produced from the old wood by cutting the trunk into small pieces; ibid.

Virgil prophesies that two people groups, the Romans and the Greeks, come from the same "root" (*stirpe*) and are unified in establishing an eternal, elect nation, the "Latins." Through story, Virgil narrates a pious Aeneas who approaches Evander with an attitude of humility to fulfill a divine plan. Paul, on the other hand, chooses a well-known Jewish metaphor of the olive tree, signifying Israel, and purposefully reverses the traditional eastern Mediterranean process to accent the unity between Gentile believers and ethnic Israel. These two people groups come from the same "root" (ῥίζα), and Paul makes it clear that God has a divine plan for an eternal, elect nation, "Israel." Building upon this olive tree metaphor, Paul instructs his listeners through loving imperatives to be humble and unified.

Purity and Devotion to God (Romans 12:1—15:13)

In the first section of the body of the letter (1:17—5:11), Paul explains how God's justice from heaven works through faith, and how God's justice works through wrath against those ruled by irrational passion (worshipping the creation rather than the creator). In the second section of the body (5:12—8:39), Paul discusses the past, present, and future of the believers in Christ Jesus, focusing on internal struggle and victory in Christ. In the third section (9:1—11:36), in midrashic style, Paul tells the "story of Israel" and reveals the truth about God's character in electing the Jew first, underscoring God's faithfulness. In the final section of the body of the letter (12:1—15:13), Paul speaks loving, practical imperatives for the believers in Rome to follow. Relevant to this discussion are the values that Paul teaches the Christians in Rome and the degree to which he might be reversing these prominent Roman values, particularly those modeled in the *Aeneid*.[59]

---

59. "On a social and political level he [Paul] urges the Roman Christians to submission and political quietism. On the other hand, Paul was not uncritical of the religious and moral pretensions of the imperial ideology as it was expressed under the rule of Augustus and propagated by the succeeding emperors. At the same time as he affirms the political rights of the authorities, he seems intentional in redefining and challenging central concepts and values in the imperial propaganda. Although Paul is silent about the threat of the imperial cult in Romans, he seems to be conscious of the inherent conflict between Roman ideology and Christian values"; Tellbe, *Paul*, 206.

Christian *Religio*

Paul continues his sacrificial theme from 3:21–26 when he exhorts believers to offer themselves (12:1): "Based on the mercies of God, present your bodies as a living sacrifice [θυσίαν], holy and pleasing to God, which is your spiritual service [λατρείαν]." It seems that Paul perceives his role as a "priest," performing sacrificial duties unto God in preparing the Roman church for their sacrifice unto God.[60] This sacrifice involves the "renewing of their minds . . . as to what is pleasing unto God" which is demonstrated by humble service in accordance with God's gifting to each person—a "distribution of measured faith" for the purpose of obedient action (12:2–3). The model of behavior for the believers is God's action through Christ's obedience (3:21–26), not esteemed Greek philosophical virtues.[61] In fact, Paul removes the need for "competition for honor . . . status . . . and power,"[62] and specifies seven gifts (12:4–8), followed by a long list of loving imperatives (12:9–21).[63]

---

60. Paul is a minister (λειτουργὸν) to Christ unto the nations carrying out his priestly duty (ἱερουργοῦντα) of the gospel of God in order that the offering of the Gentiles might be pleasing (εὐπρόσδεκτος) and sanctified (ἡγιασμένη, 15:16).

61. Paul understands the sin offering in relation to Christ, for Christ is the incarnate Son of God taking the place of sinners (the "place-taking cannot be *animal* place-taking"); Bell, "Sacrifice and Christology," 26. The *Aeneid* and Romans share a didactic aspect, but in Romans, Paul *directly* explains the religious devotion expected of God's elect people. Luke Timothy Johnson notes that Paul stresses attitude and not the differences in action, since actions accompany attitude; *Reading Romans*, 212. From a Greek philosophical perspective, Blumenfeld understands Paul's movement in 12:4–8 as Aristotelian (see *Nic. Eth.* 1.1094a28–29, 1.1094b7–12, and 10.1181b12–24), where a shift occurs from the individual to the πόλις and from ethics to politic, but Paul prefers the more simple body-state analogy over the analogy of πόλις and ψυχή; *Political Paul*, 382–83. Anthony Guerra explains how a significant emphasis of philosophical protreptic is an "urging toward virtue," which often arises out of crisis situation; Guerra, *Romans*, 176. He believes that Paul admonishes the congregation to pursue rational worship (12:1–2) with sobriety and virtue (12:3–8), which leads to harmony within the Christian community. Esler finds the terms "paranesis" and "ethical" to be too broad for this section of the letter; Esler, "Social Identity," 51–63. Esler concludes that Paul prescribes Aristotelian-like virtues on "how to live the good life"; ibid., 61.

62. Moxnes, "Honor," 217

63. The imperatives in Rom 12:9–21 may very well have a Palestinian origin; Kanjuparambil, "Imperatival Participles," 285–88. Kanjuparambil develops his arguments based on Daube's theory. See Daube, "Participle and Imperative," 467–88. Charles Talbert also bases his arguments on Daube's theory; see Talbert, "Tradition and Redaction," 83–93. Kent Yinger reinterprets the traditional view that the imperatives of 12:9–13 refer to those inside the congregation and sees 12:14–19 as referring to the

God's Wrath

Paul champions values that contrast Roman virtues, especially those of the *Aeneid*. He encourages the believers to bless those who persecute them, never to take revenge, and to practice a type of self-control that "leaves room for God's wrath," not one's own (12:14, 17, 19).[64] The phrase "δότε τόπον" means "giving place to another" or "making room for another," and τῇ ὀργῇ refers to God's wrath.[65] Paul bases his principles on Hebrew Scripture: "'Vengeance is mine,' says the Lord, 'I am the one who repays'"; "If your enemy is hungry, feed him; if he is thirsty, give him a drink, and by doing so you will heap burning coals on his head" (12:19-20; Lev 19:18; and Prov 25:21-22).[66] These attitudes are dissimilar to the violent, vengeful acts in the second half of the *Aeneid*; neither are they comparable to Aeneas's just wrath in killing Turnus.

Christian *Pietas*

Paul writes to the Christians in Rome: "Everyone must submit to those in authority over them, for there is no authority except that which has been given by God" (13:1). Because this section (13:1-7) stands out against its immediate context, and because of its unique content within the Pauline corpus, some scholars argue that this passage is an interpolation.[67] It might be that Paul seeks to bring about stability among the

---

"unbelievers" outside the Roman congregation; he maintains that the terms "persecuters" and "enemies" refer to those who are hostile within the Roman congregation; see Yinger, "Romans 12:14-21," 74-96.

64. Paul had access to the Jesus tradition; for the connection of Rom 12:17-20 to Matt 5:38-48, see Wenham, "Paul's Use of the Jesus Tradition," 17-24.

65. Smothers, "Give Place to the Wrath," 214.

66. Rom 12:19 agrees in part with the MT and in part with the LXX, but it is closest to the Targums; for a synoptic parallel of these see Dunn, *Romans 9-16*, 749. Dunn assumes that a different text from the LXX was current among the churches in the diaspora, and concludes that Christianity redefines the boundaries with a wider application of the Old Testament concept; ibid., 750. The LXX begins the verse with a conjunction (the MT does not), and changes the subject to σου ἡ χείρ; Wevers, *Greek Text of Leviticus*, 300. It may be that the Greek intends to convey the meaning, "you may not actively exact vengeance"; ibid. Furthermore, Tacitus records that the Jews were expelled at the instigation of "*Chrestus*" (*Ann.* 15.44) and that there was widespread frustration with taxation during the reign of Nero (*Ann.* 1.50-51). It could be that Gentile Christians were at risk for accepting the Jews; Dunn, *Romans 9-16*, 768. Concerning Paul's use of Prov 25:21-22, it is almost an exact quotation from the LXX.

67. For arguments on Rom 13:1-7 as an interpolation, see Keck, "What Makes

church to ensure a successful Spanish mission,[68] or something as simple as protecting the Christians "in the streets" of Rome.[69] However, it makes more sense to see Paul's commands as bringing about an attitude of religious "duty," a Roman value,[70] and philosophically speaking, Paul provides a visual representation of God's authority (13:1–7) through his "heavenly wrath" against those who rebel (1:18). The public servant, a servant of God, bears the sword of God to avenge and bring wrath upon the one who practices evil. Just as God works his righteousness through faith, he also works his justice through wrath.

Paul charges the Roman believers to be humble in their service to authority. This includes paying taxes which support the public servants who are devoted to carrying out God's authority (13:7).[71] Paul transitions from "debt" to "love and the Law" with the sentence—"do not owe anyone anything except to love one another" (13:8–10).[72] Paul concludes this section with interesting imagery (sleep, night, day, and light, 13:11–13), and parallels this with choosing Christ over sexual immorality (13:14): "Rather, clothe yourselves with the Lord Jesus Christ, and make up your mind beforehand not to give into your passions [ἐπιθυμίας]."

Romans Tick," 3–29; and Kallas, "Romans 13. 7," 365–74. For a careful construction of this text, see Stein, "The Argument of Romans 13:1–7," 334. For the suggestion that Paul's command in 13:4 refers to a benefactor, see Winter, "Public Honouring of Christian Benefactors," 94.

68. Towner, "Romans 13:1–7," 148.

69. Elliott, "Romans 13:1–7," 118.

70. This religious duty (*pietas*) is synonymous with Paul's use of obligation in 1:14.

71. In order to meet the demands of this text, a further shift of emphasis is needed, a more "holistic paradigm"; McDonald, "Romans 13:7," 540–49. McDonald discusses three general views of the situation in Rome—a charismatic community, Jewish nationalistic settlement, and agitation about taxes—and finds the issue of taxation to be the most logical motivation for this text. Based on Paul's use of key words (φόρος, τέλος, φόβος, τιμή) and the social context behind this passage, Thomas Coleman understands Paul's meaning of obligation as a "tangible" obligation; "Binding Obligations in Romans 13:7." 307–27; Coleman defends the view that Paul writes at a time of dissatisfaction in Rome over the burden of taxation in the Neronian Principate. See also Tac. *Ann.* 13.50; Suet. *Nero* 44.1. For a review of literature concerning Claudius's edict (whether A.D. 41 or A.D. 49), see Riesner, *Paul's Early Period*, 157–201. Also, it could be that Paul shares the Jewish values of responsibility toward authorities.

72. This love fulfills the Law (Rom 13:8–10 and Lev 19:18).

Mutual Acceptance[73]

After reviewing the general meaning of Paul's admonitions in the final section of the body of his letter (14:1—15:13), the Roman context of the terms "weak" and "strong" are discussed. These terms are significant to this study for several reasons: (1) Paul emphasizes God's election of Jacob, the son in the lesser (or weaker) status position (9:14); (2) the theme of humility and unity is a unique and central theme of the *Aeneid*; and (3) the Roman context behind these verses has only recently been investigated.[74]

Paul warns the believers that they should not judge each other; particularly those who eat meat should not judge those who do not eat meat (14:1-3). Jews in Rome of all social classes preserved their food laws (particularly abstention from pork), and those who violated these rules affronted the Jewish community (which includes the Gentiles who identified themselves with Jews by observing food laws).[75] Paul does not give a very clear description of this problem in Rome, which seems appropriate for a church he had not visited. Apparently, the judgments have come against a man's servant concerning a day when eating (or not eating) is important (14:4-6). At this point, Paul returns to imagery from chapters 1-8—he includes death and resurrection language ("whether we live or die, we are the Lord's," 14:8),[76] and reminds the listeners that each person will stand before the judgment seat of God and give an account of himself (14:12).[77] In other words, both the "strong" and the "weak" are responsible for the unity of the church and will be judged for their faith and actions in Christ.[78]

---

73. Stuhlmacher labels the section of 14:1—15:13 as "Mutual Acceptance within the Community"; see Stuhlmacher, *Paul's Letter*, 14. This is a fitting heading based on Paul's humble purpose to strengthen the church and "to be encouraged among you, by your faith and by mine" (Rom 1:12).

74. See Reasoner, *Strong and the Weak*, 1–10. For the view that Paul speaks to a general situation for "any" church, see Karris, "Rom 14:1—15:13," 155–78.

75. Barclay, "Study of Romans 14:1—15:6," 295.

76. Attempts to find evidence that supports Paul's soteriology tied to mysticism (based upon assimilation in initiation to the sufferings of deities) "crumbles away"; Wedderburn, "Soteriology," 71.

77. See Rom 2:6-11 and chapter 4 of this study.

78. Black, *Apostle of Weakness*," 199. For a succinct review of the arguments concerning the "strong" and "weak," see Gagnon, "Meaning of Romans 14:16," 675–89.

Paul repeats his admonition not to judge another person (14:13–18, a continuation of 14:1–12), since nothing is unclean, and adds that a believer should not cause a brother to stumble (most likely in reference to eating meat). Paul describes the kingdom of God as a kingdom of righteousness, peace, and joy in the Holy Spirit; it is not about food and drink (14:17).[79] Those who serve God are the ones who please God, and they gain the approval of men (14:18).

In Rom 14:19–23, Paul transitions to "peace" (14:17, 19) and repeats a similar charge in verse 20 as he did in verse 15c:

> Do not for the sake of food destroy the works of God (20).
> Do not let food destroy your brother for whom Christ died (15c).

Paul supplies his listeners with a "faith" principle—"if anyone waivers in what he eats, he has already been judged because he is not eating on the basis of faith; for everything done without faith is sin" (14:23).

Paul focuses on Jesus Christ (15:1–6) as a model for the believers to live unselfishly.[80] With endurance and by the encouragement of Scripture, the believers offer up one voice to glorify God, the Father of the Lord Jesus Christ (15:6). Here, Paul implicitly restates his theme "to the Jew first" when he writes that "Christ became a servant of the circumcised on behalf of the truth of God in order that he might confirm the promises of the fathers, so that the Gentiles on behalf of mercy will glorify God" (15:7–9).[81] He then supports this with Old Testament *testimonia* to prove that the nations have always been a part of God's salvific plan.[82]

---

79. For the possible Old Testament context of Daniel behind this text, see Shogren, "'Kingdom of God (Romans 14:17)'," 238–56.

80. For Paul as a "successful benefactor," see Joubert, *Paul as Benefactor*, 204–15.

81. For an interesting perspective on Christ at the center of the final praise, Christ serving the Jews and singing God's praises among the Gentiles; see Wagner, "The Christ," 473–85. Paul wants to show that God is merciful to the Jews and the Gentiles, but becoming a servant to the Jews and receiving the Gentiles are not the same thing; Lambrecht, "Syntactical and Logical Remarks," 259–61.

82. It could be that Paul uses his own anthology of Old Testament verses to accent hope (Ps 18:49, Deut 32:43, Ps 117:1, and Isa 11:10), a style which might reflect early synagogue proems; Hafemann, "Eschatology and Ethics," 161–92.

Reasoner investigates the Latin terms for "strong" and "weak" and discovers that these designations refer to social status in first-century Rome, particularly referring to a class lower than one's own.[83] "Weak" does not necessarily mean "poor," since the *collegia tenuirum* were voluntary associations of modest means (ones that could not support themselves), but the term often represented the lower class, or a cross section of the lower orders (slaves, freedpersons, and free born).[84] Plainly, the language of social power is present in the letter to the Romans. The terms "strong" and "weak" can best be interpreted along the lines of status, which links this discussion to the innate principles of honor and shame in Roman society, especially with respect to church social relations.[85] This does not refer to the idea of a formal honoring of a person, but the informal socio-dynamic that occurs within groups. Paul includes himself among the "strong," because he is not ashamed of the Gospel (15:1), so this issue does not involve the *gaining* of status;[86] rather, the commands are meant to discourage the "strong" from *emphasizing* their status. The "strong" (οἱ δυνατοί, 15:1) eat everything and place others below themselves. Reasoner sees the "strong" as Roman citizens or those residents who "display a proclivity to those things Roman," and the "weak" were *peregrini* without Romans citizenship, which included Jews.[87] In this case, the "weak" refer to Jewish and Gentile Christians.

The use of "all things pure" (πάντα μὲν καθαρά, 14:20) lends itself to a Jewish attitude, and it is clearly a term from Hellenistic Judaism.[88] Abstinence may accent reason, not desire, yet this does not seem to be

---

83. For the "strong," Reasoner surveyed the terms: *potens, firmus,* and *vis*; and for the "weak": *inferior, tenuis, invalidus,* and *infirmus*. The "weak" are interpreted (1) based on the Corinthian situation; (2) as Jewish believers; (3) as Gentile believers; (4) as both Jew and Gentile; (5) as practicing Jews outside the church; and (6) as agnosticism toward the historical situation in Rome; Reasoner, *Strong and the Weak*, 1–23. Reasoner cites a relevant comment from Cicero concerning the status of the plebs, "People are especially jealous of their equals, or those once beneath them [*inferioribus*]"; Cicero, *Pro Murena* 47.

84. Reasoner, *Strong and the Weak*, 50–51. Stowers defines the "weak" in Greek philosophical terms as "less mature"; *Rereading of Romans*, 321.

85. Reasoner, *Strong and the Weak*, 59. For honor as the "apex" of the pyramid of social values, see Peristiany, *Honour and Shame*," 1–15.

86. Reasoner, *Strong and the Weak*, 60–61.

87. Ibid., 63.

88. Ibid., 101.

tied to Stoicism, since Stoics were not known for vegetarian practices.[89] While Paul makes Jewish distinctions throughout his letter, there is no reference in the Torah to weak and strong, which means that this issue is a composite of Jewish and pagan values.[90] Furthermore, the phrase φρονῶν τὴν ἡμέραν κυρίῳ φρονεῖ (14:6) shows that the attitude is a Christian one.[91] What this means is that the observance of days by the "weak" emerges then as "a pious means" of asserting some level of political power within the church.[92]

In the *Aeneid*, Virgil uses the Latin terms *invalidus* for "weak" and *potens* for "strong" in a manner that might have a similar connotation to ἀσθενῶν and δυνατοὶ in Romans.[93] Concerning the "weak," Virgil uses an explicit reference (*invalidum*, 5.716-17) in which Nautes reminds Aeneas of his divine race and tells him to allow those who are weak, fearful, and wearied to settle in Sicily, rather than sail to Italy (5.709-10). Ships had been lost and some of the crew lacked the courage needed to travel—old men, fearful women, and the faint of heart. The "weak" were set apart on an Island called Acesta, while Aeneas led the brave to Italy (5.724-25). Virgil uses *potens* in different ways to signify power: Italy's power by arms (3.164), Rome's greatness (6.871), Turnus's great lineage (7.56), and powerful fury (11.340). But an important instance of *potens* refers to the Roman "strong" who inspire the courage of Italy (12.827). In this light, the strong and weak are part of the elect people, but the difference is in the level of courage.[94]

Paul reverses several traditional Roman values. He speaks of love, not revenge; he emphasizes humility, not dominance; and he finds that church unity under the Lordship of Christ is where power is generated, not in arms or diplomacy. Yet like the *Aeneid*, Paul advocates a dutiful tone and right behavior, and he shares the idea of humility between two peoples as a means to having victory. The "ultimate" foundation

---

89. For Roman culture and accepted practices of ascetism; ibid., 64-87.

90. Ibid., 136-37.

91. Ibid., 158.

92. Ibid., 144-45.

93. Virgil does not use *firmus* and *tenuis* in the *Aeneid* in the same way that Paul uses ἀσθενῶν and δυνατοὶ in Romans (for *inferior*, see 6.170; 12.630). Virgil most frequently uses *vis* for the meaning of "stength," often referring to rational and irrational powers in a negative sense (e.g., 1.529, 616; and 5.454).

94. In Romans, the "weak" lack faith (14:1-2, 23).

and motivating force which the Roman Christians would have heard is Paul's social ethic of obligation,[95] and for the "weak" and "strong," this force is the debt of love, based on God's faithfulness:

> Christ's not pleasing himself from 15:3 is interpreted in 15:8–9a by the fact that "Christ became a servant (διάκονον) of the circumcision on behalf of the truth of God in order that he might establish the promises of the fathers" (15:8) . . . this reference to Christ as a "servant" (διάκονον), unique in Paul's writing, refers not primarily to Christ's identity, but to his activity of mediation and role as a representative agent, with the connotation of the constraint and duty . . . Christ is entrusted with taking on a task for another, in this case that of confirming the promises on behalf of God as a mediator of God's glory.[96]

Paul ends the body of his letter to the Romans by celebrating the kingship of Christ over all of the nations (15:13).

Priestly Duty of Gospel Proclamation (Romans 15:14—16:27)

Paul speaks directly about his plans to evangelize Spain in the closing remarks of his letter. His unusually long list of greetings evidences his desire to strengthen both Jewish and Gentile Christians. In the final lines of his letter, Paul makes a sudden announcement, that the God of peace will soon bring about a crushing defeat to Satan.

Paul's Purpose

Paul perceives his role as a priest serving Jesus Christ unto the Gentiles by the power of the Holy Spirit (15:16). Therefore, Paul can only boast in Jesus Christ concerning what is accomplished by the Holy Spirit, the obedience of the Gentiles (15:17–18). Likewise, Paul has seen his priestly duty fulfilled from Illyricum all the way around to Jerusalem, and he "hopes to make a complete circuit of the nations."[97] Because of

---

95. Hafemann, "Eschatology and Ethics," 167.
96. Ibid., 168.
97. Knox, "Romans 15:14–33," 11; Knox understands that Paul speaks in circular terms (κύκλῳ, 15:19), and the territory that Paul has already evangelized (Palestine, Syria, Asia Minor, and Greece) forms a circle of nations around the Mediterranean Sea. There might be a distant allusion to Greek philosophy in that circles represented

this, Paul's long-term goal is to go to Spain, after he fulfills his immediate plans to go to Jerusalem for the service of the saints, to bring an offering of the Gentiles to help meet the physical needs of the Jews.[98]

Based on Paul's remarks, some aspects of the maturity level of the church in Rome can be ascertained. The Roman church is well-nourished: "But I am convinced, my brothers, that you are full of all goodness, full of all knowledge and able to instruct one another" (Rom 15:14). They are faithful and obedient; Paul "reminds" his listeners of God's truth rather than speaking to them with a tone of discipline (15:15).[99] While Paul considers the Roman church to be healthy, he does not seem to believe that the church has produced a "full" harvest. Consequently, he desires to evangelize Rome in cooperation with the Roman Christians (1:13–15).

Divine Justice

Before Paul concludes his letter, he makes a unique statement: "The God of peace will soon crush Satan underneath your feet."[100] Paul uses military symbolism to communicate a "true myth," a literal and artistic metaphor.[101] Here the contrast is between the spiritual and the physical—Satan is the ruler of the hierarchy of evil, and Paul informs the small Roman congregation that they will have their feet on Satan. Paul

---

completeness and perfection (e.g., see Aristotle *On the Heavens* 2.11, 14). In the *Aeneid*, Virgil also employs circles for sacred reasons; see 1.269, 395–96; 6.229; and 9.152–53.

98. With the exception of Rom 15:14-33, the rest of Romans (1:1—15:13 and 16:1–27) is written in a formal tone.

99. Paul speaks directly here about things he somewhat veiled in the opening sections of his letter; Weimma, "Preaching the Gospel," 356. In writing to Rome, Paul is not as blunt with the truth as he is in Galatians; he is more diplomatic in his approach to influence the community; Byrne, "Paul's Prophetic Bid," 94.

100. This is the only time Paul directly speaks of Satan's defeat in his letters, and it is the only mention of Satan in Romans; Macky, "Crushing Satan," 121.

101. Macky defines "myth" as a fantastic story written in symbolic form, and he defines "true myth" as a myth used to provide "real" insight into the mysterious realities of life, since myth cannot be translated into literal speech; Macky, "Crushing Satan," 133. Macky expresses his appreciation for Bultmann's desire to make the Gospel understandable and meaningful, particularly in relation to God's acts in history: Macky, *Bible in Dialogue*, 177–98. For Old Testament and intertestamental passages to "Crushing Enemies Underfoot," see Macky, *St. Paul's Cosmic War Myth*, 212–14. Macky believes the most important Old Testament passage behind this text is Daniel 7. Also see 1 Cor 15:24, Ps 110:1, and 2 Thess 2.

gives no hint of irony, and his emphasis on "soon" removes any possibility of hyperbole.[102] Rather, it seems that Paul communicates metaphorically. Paul does not use the verb συντρίβω elsewhere in his letters, and outside of the New Testament, the verb means to "annihilate/conquer" or "crush." Paul seems to use it in this sense of "standing victorious over the dead body of the enemy."[103] In this case, Paul means that God in Christ conquers Satan, but believers in Christ, members of his body, stand in victory over the conquered enemy.[104] Paul speaks in eschatological terms when he writes "soon," which probably draws upon his earlier imagery from Rom 13:11-12 ("Know that this is the time, the hour has already come for you to awake from sleep ... the day is near"). However, Macky's conclusions lack a fitting nexus, as Paul describes "the God of Peace" acting peacefully, while at the same time he uses military symbolism for conquering Satan.[105]

Paul may be countervailing the popular Roman ending of the mythological epic when Aeneas kills Turnus. The Trojan king personifies Rome and foreshadows the savior Augustus when he defeats Turnus in a climactic final battle, bringing peace to the nations. The enemy, Prince Turnus, comes to embody irrational passion and evil. Virgil introduces Turnus as appearing at midnight (7.414), and Allecto, who bears war and death in her hands, incites Turnus to a "frenzy of war" (7.462). Turnus is transformed into a beast, as depicted in the symbols on his armor (7.783-84)—an image of the metamorphosis of Io (an animal metamorphis by the work of the gods) and a fire-breathing

---

102. For the discussion of the use of ἐν τάχει in reference to the defeat of Satan and his final binding as part of a larger eschatological hope in Judaism, see Dunn, *Romans 9-16*, 905-6.

103. Macky, "Crushing Satan," 124.

104. Ibid., 125. This makes sense in light of Paul's description of the unity of the "body of Christ" in Rom 14:4. Interpreting this text as an allusion to Gen 3:15 also makes perfect sense. Macky offers two other possibilities that are less plausible: (a) believers act under God's power to crush, and (b) God in Christ conquers Satan and then leads the people of God to stand over the dead enemy; ibid., 126.

105. Macky lists some of the views for the subject of the metaphor: Paul may refer to (1) real, non-supernatural events within the church; (2) "driving Satan's agents in Rome" (which contradicts Rom 13:1-7); or (3) the final overcoming of evil; ibid., 131-32. He concludes that Paul speaks symbolically concerning the last battle, God's elimination of all evil. In looking for a referent he suggests imagining a great dragon with human features and Christ in fiery splendor descending to conquer with his mere appearance; ibid., 132. See also Macky, *St. Paul's Cosmic War*, 211-18.

Chimaera (a mythical demon, 6.288). He stands as the enemy of the future of the elect people.[106] Aeneas acts as an agent of divine vengeance, killing Turnus, a faithful and righteous act, bringing the enemy to his feet and peace to the world.

Whether Paul closes his gospel with this literary ending in mind or not, he wants his Christian recipients in Rome to know that Jesus Christ's death and resurrection are the decisive salvific key in history.[107] Paul makes a new claim about something that had never happened before—"God was active in history in and through a man in a way only foreshadowed but not previously realized."[108] This apocalyptic climax was based on an ancient promise from Hebrew Scripture, a way of "reaffirming the continuity of the past with the future . . . it is the tension of a single people (Israel) chosen for his own out of all the nations by the one God . . . the divine intention from the first."[109]

Summary

Paul expresses his unending grief on behalf of his race, echoing the intercessory nature of the Old Testament prophets; but he does not explicitly mention Israel's unbelief as the reason for his sorrow. Instead he describes Israel's failure as a "trip." In midrashic style, he narrates salvation history—God faithfully working through a promised remnant—but he does so with elements of reversal and recognition that would make sense to a first-century Greco-Roman audience. In other words, God's elect people, Israel, become jealous over Gentile inclusion, making the ethnic Jews enemies on account of the Gospel. Paul builds unity among the church through an olive-tree metaphor, where both Jew and Gentile are encouraged to remain humble. This teaching provides a basis for Paul's practical admonishments concerning the "strong" and the "weak."

The *Aeneid* and the letter to the Romans share some similar elements. Aeneas and Paul grieve with unceasing sorrow for their races.

---

106. Virgil describes him as a wolf tormented by the fury of famine, riding wildly with bloodless jaws and iron-hot resentment in his bones (9.59–60). He murders and terrorizes with a thirst for blood (9.731, 757).

107. Dunn, "Problem of Continuity," 387.

108. Ibid., 388.

109. Ibid., 383, 388.

Two people groups—Trojans and Greeks in the *Aeneid*; Jews and Gentiles in Romans—experience victory as they fulfill the promise to establish an elect nation. In the *Aeneid*, Virgil narrates an episode where the "weak" within the Trojan ranks lack courage, and the brave sail on to Italy to fight. In Romans, Paul admonishes the "strong" not to cause the "weak," who lack faith, to stumble. One of the most striking possible echoes is Paul's olive tree metaphor, where two nations stem from the same root, and in the *Aeneid*, two nations unite from one blood. Other distant similarities include blessing despite a trip, *katabasis* imagery, and jealousy as a relevant force. Both Paul and Virgil write to influence their listeners for political reasons, and obligation and duty are key themes, especially as modeled through a god-man representative.

Even so, Paul champions values contrary to the virtues of Rome, especially those of the *Aeneid*. He encourages the believers to bless those who persecute them, not to take revenge, and to leave room for God's wrath, not one's own. The main obligation for both the "weak" and the "strong" is love, and victory comes through a unified body of believers under the power and Lordship of Jesus Christ, not by arms or diplomacy. God is faithful to save his people.

Conclusion

WHEN PAUL WRITES TO ROME AND INTRODUCES HIS LETTER WITH the phrase "the appointed Son of God in power," it is important to try to understand why he would write such a phrase to a believing community at the center of the Roman Empire. In this socio-historical analysis, Paul's inverse response to his wider culture becomes a significant piece in the interpretation of key themes in Romans. In other words, in addition to his primary response to the influence of Judaism in the Roman church, he also interacts with another set of values—Roman imperial ideals. Since Paul writes to a church he has not visited, and since the organizational dynamic of the early church in Rome was at an incipient stage of development, he may have decided to choose a "contra-literary" rhetorical strategy to reject and countervail the significant themes of an already established false "gospel," the *Aeneid*.

In this case, Paul would reverse important values of the Greco-Roman culture and establish new principles for his recipients, particularly to influence the upwardly mobile Jewish and Gentile Christians, as well as a possible extended audience, since it seems that he expected his letter to have lasting theological impact. This study does not assume that Paul read the *Aeneid*, but suggests that during Paul's travel and imprisonments that he listened to the basic plot and episodes from those who retold Virgil's epic story (e.g., Roman citizens, soldiers, educated elite, or philosophers, etc.). As a missionary, Paul writes intelligently, with diplomacy, speaking the language of his hearers.

Summary of Findings

Augustus favored Virgil. After returning from Actium, the young emperor requested that Virgil read the *Georgics* to him for four days in succession, and when his resonant voice became tired, the *Princeps* had his close adviser, Maecenas (and patron of Virgil), took turns with Virgil in reading to him. It was Augustus who encouraged Virgil to write a nationalistic epic to surpass Homer's works, and while other Augustan poets wrote official praises to Caesar, only Virgil presented a lengthy epic about a god-man hero Aeneas, which linked Rome's past to the present and contained detailed prophecies about the divine son Augustus. His mythological-historical account proclaimed Roman dominion, renewal, and hope—a "gospel" to the nations. Enthused by Virgil's progress on the *Aeneid,* Augustus demanded, while away on a campaign, that Virgil send him any section right away. When three of the first six books were completed, the emperor and some of his family listened to Virgil's reading and were greatly moved by his inspiration.

Writing as a poet-prophet, Virgil speaks directly to his Roman audience; he acts as a guarantor of truth and the spokesman for Aeneas's mission—the foundation of Rome. Even though Virgil repeats the experience of the epic cycle (the chain of epic narratives that combine Homer's poetry), he first bases the direction and shape of his moral epic around Augustan symbolism and the themes for the Augustan hero—a θεός ἀνήρ and sacrificial servant of *pietas*. Divine external forces test Aeneas's faithfulness, which affects Rome's destiny. As the Trojan prince's character develops in the first half of the poem, it becomes evident that he personifies Rome and foreshadows the promised savior, Caesar Augustus. Virgil scripts the repetitious, singular action of Aeneas to model Roman virtues—such as *pietas, religio, disciplina, fides,* and *constantia*—and to influence his audience towards a moral aim. The unexpected, opposite changes of action in the plot cause suffering, which often involve death and enmity among Aeneas's people and his compatriots, and are intended to arouse the emotions of compassion and fear from the listeners. The pious, fatherly, and kingly characteristics of Aeneas are meant to parallel those of Augustus after Actium, who portrays himself as a *paterfamilias* to his empire. Virgil seeks to influence people to imitate Aeneas's religious devotion and submission, which means faithful obedience to Augustus and the State.

Virgil begins his epic with a philosophical question concerning why wrath from heaven comes against the son of a god. The conflicts between Dido and Aeneas (Books 1-4) and between Aeneas and Turnus (Books 9-12) are acted out as a representation of the contrast in heaven between Jupiter, who represents justice and order, and Juno, who represents fury and destruction. The plot centers around a *furor-pietas* theme, with the first half of the Aeneid narrating the development and inner struggle of Aeneas, and the second half narrating the external battles between Aeneas and his impious foes.

In the first six books, Aeneas endures considerable grief on behalf of his people and his mission, but also learns about the divine plan and eschatological purpose for himself, the remnant, and Rome. The destructive *furor* that Aeneas inwardly overcomes symbolizes the Roman-Augustan ideal accomplished by a divine hero. Through Aeneas's descent into the underworld (*katabasis*), the listeners learn that *pietas* is a moral action of a resurrected hero. In addition to Virgil's unique psychological emphasis in this section, the poet also highlights the fatherly attributes of Aeneas and the distinct prophecies which foretell the Golden Age of Augustus.

In the last six books, Aeneas defeats destructive *furor* on the battlefield. With his just and pious character, he fulfills the word of Jupiter, which prepares the way for the appointed savior Augustus. Aeneas's alliance with Evander, a humble Greek Arcadian, reveals a shared origin of the Trojans and the Greeks ("branch from one blood"), and it contrasts the arrogant enemy represented by the maniacal, enraged Turnus. Aeneas justly kills Turnus, a sacrifice for the future of Rome.

Paul's gospel follows a similar philosophical framework that the *Aeneid* employs. Paul's intricate argument in the first three sections of the body (1:17—11:32) resembles a "theological" philosophical tractate, as Paul frames the first section (1:17—5:13) with the revelation of two configurations of God's righteousness—God's righteousness through faith and God's righteousness through wrath. It is likely that Paul incorporates a religious-philosophical framework centering around a faithful Christ-king who brings earthly disorder into conformity with the divine blueprint, with πίστις as the bond of the Christian community. Virgil's epic poem follows a similar religious-philosophical pattern when he scripts Aeneas as the faithful king who experiences a reordering of his soul in obedience to divine will, bringing about a divine plan where *pietas* is the bond of the community. Either Paul is supplanting the idea of justice in the *furor-pietas* configuration from the *Aeneid*, or both authors are structuring their writings with common philosophical ideas in mind.

It is also interesting that the major themes of Paul's letter contradict the major tenets of Virgil's false gospel. The Augustan poet harnesses the current philosophical, religious, and historical issues of his time by uniquely depicting, in mythical and poetic detail, the sacred themes of Rome: (a) revealing the nature of wrath from heaven; (b) linking the past to the present through the inner struggle of a god-man, and (c) prophesying the future savior, Augustus Caesar, and his eschatological impact on the destiny of the Roman people. Paul's letter prescript (1:1–7) countervails these main elements, which also foreshadows the main sections of his letter. Christ is the "appointed Son of God in power" from the "seed of David" as prophesied by the Old Testament prophets and Hebrew Scripture. In the body of the letter, Paul reveals that heavenly wrath is just, without disorder (1:18—3:26); that Christ has overcome passion in the believers' lives, an internal process (5:12—8:39); and that God is faithful in his election of a remnant, an ordered plan which impacts all of God's people (9:1—11:36).

Paul may not only be countervailing Virgil's philosophical framework and major themes, but he may also be nullifying Virgil's purpose in writing an epic. Paul places priority on the "Jewish race" in the order of divine election, an intense claim against an imperial context where the Roman race dominates. In this way, Paul reverses Virgil's central theme in a manner similar to the way in which Virgil reversed Homer's epic. Virgil, a poet-prophet, tells of the gods having elected the Trojan Aeneas (and his Roman descendants) to establish a Latin nation, not a Greek nation, to rule the world. Paul, on the other hand, describes himself, using Levitical language, as "set apart into the gospel of God," and later identifies himself with the Old Testament prophet Elijah. Paul centers his message around the single action of Christ's redemptive work (3:21-26), which provides a model for believers as they live out their faith among each other and their communities. He absolutely rejects the imperial ideology concerning an elect Roman descendant who brings peace to the world; instead, God's order of election comes through the Jew first.

A similar philosophical framework and sharp contrasts in content, however, do not prove that Paul responds or interacts with the major themes and imagery of the *Aeneid*. In fact by the end of Augustus's reign, the themes of societal degeneration, the sinful age, and the wrath of the gods were popular ideas, particularly in relation to the return of the Golden Age. Commonplace, too, were the philosophical discussions of internal mastery over the passions, so much so that these beliefs were voiced in some circles of Hellenistic Judaism.

Furthermore, Virgil's twelve books of poetry do not read anything like Paul's letter. The prophecies in the *Aeneid* are deceitful, and the fantastic descriptions in many of the episodes contain dark material. Most of the story speaks to Roman tradition, for the purpose of ideological conquest, and written law is not a theme. Paul's arguments, on the other hand, are grounded, supported by Old Testament allusions and imagery, and logically written, addressed to small groups of Christians. No irrational *furor* exists in the heavens, and no physical battles are fought. Instead, Paul confronts the beliefs of Judaism, particularly concerning the Law, addressing an inner struggle (7:14–15) and socio-ethical conflict (Rom 14:1—15:7). He declares that peace and propitiation come through the blood of the Savior Jesus Christ, and that the main obligation for Christians is love, not revenge.

It might be reasonable to conclude that Paul confronts some Roman values, and that he does not specifically counter the *Aeneid*. Many of the themes discussed seem to be part of common first-century Roman culture and thought—such as vice lists, dramatic grief, religious duty, jealousy, *katabasis*, kingship, and blessing from a "trip." Additionally, the concepts in Romans of patriarchal faithfulness (4:1-25; 9:5; 11:28; 15:8), "obligation language" (1:14; 4:1; 8:12; 13:7–8; 15:1, 27), and the unique phrase ὑπακοὴν πίστεως (1:5; 16:26) make sense when interpreted against the background of a Roman culture where values such as duty and *pietas* are honored. But the fact that *all* of these ideas have some thematic overlap in both the *Aeneid* and Romans most likely suggests something more than a coincidence, and what seems relevant in this comparison, then, are the ideas and literary aspects that originated or were made significant by the *Aeneid*.

Several aspects set the *Aeneid* apart from its own culture, which leads to the conclusion that Paul "marginally" echoes the *Aeneid* when he writes the Gospel of God; nonetheless, this statement cannot be proved. First, the immediate success and acceptance of Virgil's epic poem in Roman society thrusts the concepts of the *Aeneid* into the philosophical arena of ideas. Second, the lengthy, cohesive nature of Virgil's epic narrative allows for "story" to become sacred, much like Homer's works. It would make sense that Paul supplants some of these themes, such as a significant passage describing Abraham's faithfulness, in contrast to the wider context of "father" Aeneas and his relationship to the savior Augustus. Third, Virgil introduces a unique psychological perspective in the epic genre when he scripts Aeneas's internal spiritual and emotional struggle. In this way, Virgil's Roman readers collectively experience Aeneas's emotions and identify with their national hero. Finally, Virgil's dramatic description of Romans uniting with Greeks and sharing a common origin ("branch from one blood") is unusual and most striking (especially in light of the parallels with *stirpe*). Paul's unique olive tree metaphor also accents humility and a shared origin (or "root"), but his exceptional claim concerning God's faithfulness to Jews and Gentiles is the true gospel.

Relevance for New Testament Studies

This work responds to the call of New Testament scholarship to integrate socio-historical research concerning the Roman empire with New Testament interpretation, and it participates in an area that has only recently enjoyed significant attention. Using the *Aeneid* as an interpretive "lens" to re-read the "gospel" of Romans has produced new and interesting perspectives concerning the major themes and imagery in Paul's letter. Most importantly, the value of any information that contributes to the meaning of the inspired Word of God cannot be measured, and understanding the wider, complex context of imperial values in first-century, polyethnic Rome allows for New Testament exegetes to make better interpretive decisions, particularly in light of the recipients' frame of reference. This means that first-century documents, inscriptions, coins, and visual art provide helpful insight into historical connotations, societal conversations, and social practices that determine the meaning of particular word symbols. Thus, in addition to directly supporting socio-historical goals, this study encourages other overlapping methodologies and disciplines, such as philosophy, anthropology, rhetoric, etc., to apply relevant research for the purpose of understanding God's Word.

Bibliography

Aageson, James W. "Typology, Correspondence, and the Application of Scripture in Romans 9–11." *JSNT* 31 (1987) 51–72.
Aalders, Gerhard. *Political Thought in Hellenistic Times.* Amsterdam: Hakkert, 1975.
Abbott, Frank F. *A History and Description of Roman Political Institutions.* London: Ginn, 1901.
Adamiak, Richard. *Justice and History in the Old Testament: The Evolution of Divine Retribution in the Historiographies of the Wilderness Generation.* Cleveland: Zubal, 1982.
Adams, Edward. "Abraham's Faith and Gentile Disobedience: Textual Links Between Romans 1 and 4." *JSNT* 65 (1997) 47–66.
Adcock, Frank E. *Roman Political Ideas and Practice.* Jerome Lectures. Ann Arbor: University of Michigan Press, 1959.
Adler, Eve. *Vergil's Empire: Political Thought in the Aeneid.* Lanham, MD: Rowman & Littlefield, 2003.
"Aeneas, Sicily and Italy." In *The Roman Antiquities of Dionysius of Halicarnassus*, translated by Earnest Cary, 343–44. LCL. Cambridge: Harvard University Press, 1961.
Agosto, Efrain. "Patronage and Commendation, Imperial and Anti-Imperial." In *Paul and the Roman Imperial Order*, edited by Richard A. Horsley, 103–23. Harrisburg, PA: Trinity, 2004.
Aland, Barbara, Kurt Aland, Johannes Karavidopoulos, Carlo M. Martini, and Bruce M. Metzger, eds. *Novum Testamentum Graece.* 27th rev. ed. Stuttgart: Deutsche Bibelgesellschaft, 1993.
Albrecht, Michael von. "Zur Tragik von Vergils Turnusgestalt: Aristotelisches in der Schlusszene der Aeneis." In *Silvae: Festschrift für Ernst Zinn zum 60. Geburtstag*, edited by Michael von Albrecht, 1–5. Tübingen: Niemayer, 1970.
Allison, Dale C. "Romans 11:11–15: A Suggestion." *Perspectives in Religious Studies* 12 (Spring 1985) 23–30.
Altheim, Franz, and Harold Mattingly. *A History of Roman Religion.* London: Methuen, 1938.
Alvis, John. *Divine Purpose and Heroic Response in Homer and Virgil: The Political Plan of Zeus.* Lanham, MD: Rowman & Littlefield, 1995.

Bibliography

Anderson, Bernhard W., editor. *The Old Testament and Christian Faith: A Theological Discussion*. New York: Harper & Row, 1963.
Anderson, William J., and Richard Phené Spiers. *The Architecture of Greece & Rome: A Sketch of Its Historic Development*. London: Batsford, 1903.
Anderson, William S. "Virgil's Second *Iliad*." *TAPA* 88 (1957) 17–30.
Andrews, E. A., William Freund, Charlton T. Lewis, and Charles Short. *A Latin Dictionary*. New York: Oxford University Press, 1998.
Appianus. *Appian's Roman History*. LCL. Cambridge: Harvard University Press, 1912.
Aristotle. *Art of Rhetoric*. LCL. Cambridge: Harvard University Press, 1967.
———. *Metaphysics*. LCL. Cambridge: Harvard University Press, 1936.
———. *Nichomachean Ethics*. LCL. Cambridge: Harvard University Press, 1926.
———. *On the Heavens*. LCL. Cambridge: Harvard University Press, 1939.
———. *On the Soul*. LCL. Cambridge: Harvard University Press, 1957.
———. *Poetics*. LCL. Cambridge: Harvard University Press, 1995.
———. *Politics*. LCL. Cambridge: Harvard University Press, 1944.
Armstrong, David. *Vergil, Philodemus, and the Augustans*. Austin: University of Texas Press, 2004.
Arnold, Edward V. *Roman Stoicism*. Cambridge: Cambridge University Press, 1911.
Atkinson, J. E. "Seneca's 'Consolatio ad Polybium.'" In *ANRW* II.32.2 (1985) 860–84.
Aune, David, editor. *Greco-Roman Literature and the New Testament: Selected Forms and Genres*. Sources for Biblical Study. Atlanta: Scholars, 1988.
———. *The New Testament in Its Literary Environment*. Library of Early Christianity. Philadelphia: Westminster, 1987.
Austin, R. G. *The Fourth Book of the Aeneid*. Oxford: Blackwell, 1951.
Bacon, Helen H. "The *Aeneid* as a Drama of Election." *TAPA* 116 (1986) 305–34
Bailey, Cyril. *Religion in Virgil*. New York: Barnes & Noble, 1969.
Baird, William. "Romans 1:1–17." *Int* 33 (1979) 398–403.
Bandara, C. "Sacrificial Levels in Virgil's *Aeneid*." *Arethusa* 14 (1981) 217–39.
Barchiesi, Alessandro. *La Traccia del Modello*. Biblioteca di "Materiali e Discussioni per l'Analisi Dei Testi Classici." Pisa: Giardini, 1984.
Barclay, John M. G. "'Do We Undermine the Law?': A Study of Romans 14:1—15:6." In *Paul and the Mosaic Law*, edited by James D. G. Dunn, 287–308. WUNT 89. Tübingen: Mohr, 1996.
———. *Jews in the Mediterranean Diaspora from Alexander to Trajan (323 BCE–117 CE)*. Edinburgh: T. & T. Clark, 1996.
Barnes, Jonathan, editor. *The Cambridge Companion to Aristotle*. Cambridge: Cambridge University Press, 1995.
———. "Rhetoric and Poetics." In *The Cambridge Companion to Aristotle*, edited by Jonathan Barnes, 259–86. Cambridge: Cambridge University Press, 1995.
Barrett, C. K. *A Commentary on the Epistle to the Romans*. Black's New Testament Commentaries. London: A. & C. Black, 1957.
Bassler, Jouette. "Divine Impartiality in Paul's Letter to the Romans." *NovT* 26 (1984) 43–58.
Basson, W. P. *Pivotal Catalogues in the Aeneid*. Amsterdam: Hakkert, 1975.
Bauer, Walter, Frederick W. Danker, and William Arndt. *A Greek-English Lexicon of the New Testament and Other Early Christian Literature*. 3rd ed. Revised and edited by Frederick W. Danker. Chicago: University of Chicago Press, 2000.

Baxter, A. G., and J. A. Ziesler. "Paul and Arboriculture: Romans 11:17-24." *JSNT* 24 (1985) 25-32.
Beard, Mary, John A. North, and S. R. F. Price. *Religions of Rome*. Cambridge: Cambridge University Press, 1998.
Beare, R. "Invidious Success: Some Thoughts on the End of the *Aeneid*." *Proceedings of the Virgilian Society* 4 (1964) 18-30.
Beker, Johan Christiaan. *Paul the Apostle: The Triumph of God in Life and Thought*. Philadelphia: Fortress, 1980.
Bekken, Per Jarle. "Paul's Use of Deut. 30:12-14 in Jewish Context." In *The New Testament and Hellenistic Judaism*, edited by Peder Borgen and Søen Giversen, 183-203. Aarhus: Aarhus University Press, 1995.
Belfiore, Elizabeth S. *Tragic Pleasures: Aristotle on Plot and Emotion*. Princeton: Princeton University Press, 1992.
Bell, Richard H. "Sacrifice and Christology in Paul." *Journal of Theological Studies* 53 (2002) 1-27.
Benario, Herbert W. "The Tenth Book of the *Aeneid*." *TAPA* 98 (1967) 23-36.
Bernard, John D, editor. *Vergil at 2000: Commemorative Essays on the Poet and His Influence*. New York: AMS, 1986.
Billows, Richard. "The Religious Procession of the *Ara Pacis Augustae*: Augustus' Supplication in 13 B.C." *Journal of Roman Archeology* 6 (1993) 80-92.
Black, C. Clifton. "Pauline Perspectives on Death in Romans 5-8." *JBL* 103 (1984) 413-33.
Black, David Alan. *Paul, Apostle of Weakness: Astheneia and Its Cognates in the Pauline Literature*. American University Studies. New York: Lang, 1984.
Black, Matthew. *Romans*. New Century Bible. London: Oliphants, 1973.
Bleicken, Jochen. *Augustus: eine Biographie*. Berlin: Fest, 1998.
———. *Geschichte der römischen Republik*. Oldenbourg Grundriss der Geschichte. München: R. Oldenbourg, 1999.
———. *Zwischen Republik und Prinzipat zum Charakter des Zweiten Triumvirats*. Abhandlungen der Akademie der Wissenschaften in Göttingen. Göttingen: Vandenhoeck & Ruprecht, 1990.
Blenkinsopp, Joseph. *Isaiah 1-39*. AB 19A. New York: Doubleday, 2000.
Blumenfeld, Bruno. *The Political Paul: Justice, Democracy and Kingship in a Hellenistic Framework*. JSNTSup 210. London: T. & T. Clark, 2003.
Bockmuehl, Markus. "1QS and Salvation at Qumran." In *Justification and Variegated Nomism*, edited by D. A. Carson, 1:381-414. WUNT 2/140. Grand Rapids: Baker Academic, 2001.
Bonz, Marianne P. *The Past as Legacy: Luke-Acts and Ancient Epic*. Minneapolis: Fortress, 2000.
Borg, Marcus. "A New Context for Romans 13." *NTS* 19 (1972) 205-18.
Bormann, Lukas, Kelly Del Tredici, and Angela Standhartinger, editors. *Religious Propaganda and Missionary Competition in the New Testament World: Essays Honoring Dieter Georgi*. NovTSup 74. Leiden: Brill, 1994.
Born, L. K. "The Perfect Prince According to the Latin Panegyrists." *AJP* 55 (1934) 20-35.

Botha, Pieter. "The Verbal Art of the Pauline Letters: Rhetoric, Performance and Presence." In *Rhetoric and the New Testament: Essays from the 1992 Heidelberg Conference*, edited by Stanley E. Porter and Thomas H. Olbricht, 409–28. JSNTSup 90. Sheffield: JSOT Press, 1993.

Bourke, Myles M. *A Study of the Metaphor of the Olive Tree in Romans 11*. Washington, DC: Catholic University of America, 1947.

Bovie, S. M. "The Imagery of Ascent-Descent." *AJP* 77 (1956) 337–58.

Bowersock, G. W. *Augustus and the Greek World*. Oxford: Clarendon, 1965.

Bowra, C. M. "Aeneas and the Stoic Ideal." In *Oxford Readings in Vergil's Aeneid*, edited by S. J. Harrison, 363–77. Oxford: Oxford University Press, 1933.

Boyancé, Pierre. *La Religion de Virgile*. Paris: Presses universitaires de France, 1963.

Boyarin, Daniel. *A Radical Jew: Paul and the Politics of Identity*. Berkeley: University of California Press, 1994.

Bradley, Keith R. *Slaves and Masters in the Roman Empire: A Study in Social Control*. New York: Oxford University Press, 1987.

Branick, Vincent P. "Apocalyptic Paul." *CBQ* 47 (1985) 664–75.

Branigan, Keith. "Images—Or Mirages—Of Empire? An Archeological Approach to the Problem." In *Images of Empire*, edited by Loveday Alexander, 91–105. JSOT Supplements 122. Sheffield: JSOT Press, 1991.

Brent, Allen. *The Imperial Cult and the Development of Church Order: Concepts and Images of Authority in Paganism and Early Christianity Before the Age of Cyprian*. Supplements to Vigiliae Christianae 45. Leiden: Brill, 1999.

Brindle, Wayne A. "'To the Jew First': Rhetoric, Strategy, History, or Theology?" *Bibliotheca Sacra* 159 (2002) 221–33.

Brown, Francis, Edward Robinson, S. R. Driver, and Charles A. Briggs. *The New Brown, Driver, Briggs, Gesenius Hebrew and English Lexicon*. Edited and translated by Edward Robinson. Peabody, MA: Hendrickson, 1979.

Brownlee, W. H. "Messianic Motifs and the New Testament." *NTS* 3 (1956–57) 12–30.

Bruce, F. F. *The Letter of Paul to the Romans: An Introduction and Commentary*. Tyndale New Testament Commentaries. Grand Rapids: Eerdmans, 1985.

———. "New Testament and Classical Studies." *NTS* 22 (1976) 229–42.

———. "A Reappraisal of Jewish Apocalyptic Literature." *Review and Expositor* 72 (1975) 305–15.

Brueggemann, Walter. *Deuteronomy*. Abingdon Old Testament Commentaries. Nashville: Abingdon, 2001.

Brunt, P. A. *Italian Manpower, 225 B.C.–A.D. 14*. London: Oxford University Press, 1971.

Bryan, Christopher. *A Preface to Romans: Notes on the Epistle in its Literary and Cultural Setting*. Oxford: Oxford University Press, 2000.

Burgess, Joseph A. "Rewards, but in a Very Different Sense." In *Justification by Faith*, edited by H. George Anderson et al., 94–110. Lutherans and Catholics in Dialogue 7. Minneapolis: Augsburg, 1985.

Burnett, Gary W. *Paul and the Salvation of the Individual*. Biblical Interpretation Series. Leiden: Brill, 2001.

Butcher, S. H. *Aristotle's Theory of Poetry and Fine Art*. New York: Dover, 1951.

Butler, Harold E. *The Sixth Book of the Aeneid*. Virgilian Studies. Oxford: Blackwell, 1920.

Byrne, Brendan. "Paul's Prophetic Bid to Win the Allegiance of the Christians in Rome." *Biblica* 74 (1993) 83-96.
Byrskog, Samuel. "Epistolography, Rhetoric and Letter Prescript: Romans 1.1-7 as a Test Case." *JSNT* 65 (1997) 27-46.
Caesar, Julius. *The Civil Wars*. LCL. Cambridge: Harvard University Press, 1914.
Cairns, Francis. *Virgil's Augustan Epic*. Cambridge: Cambridge University Press, 1989.
Callimachus. *Aetia, Iambi, Lyric Poems, Hecale, Minor Epic and Elegiac Poems*. LCL. Cambridge: Harvard University Press, 1958.
Cameron, Alan. *Callimachus and His Critics*. Princeton: Princeton University Press, 1995.
Campbell, Douglas A. "Romans 1:17—A Crux Interpretum for *Pistis Christou* Debate." *JBL* 113 (1994) 265-85.
Campbell, J. B. *The Emperor and the Roman Army, 31 BC—AD 235*. Oxford: Oxford University Press, 1984.
Campbell, William S. *Paul's Gospel in an Intercultural Context: Jew and Gentile in the Letter to the Romans*. Studies in the Intercultural History of Christianity 69. New York: Lang, 1991.
Camps, W. A. "A Note on the Structure of the *Aeneid*." *CQ* 4 (1954) 214-15.
Carey, Greg, and L. Gregory Bloomquist. *Vision and Persuasion: Rhetorical Dimensions of Apocalyptic Discourse*. St. Louis: Chalice, 1999.
Carson, D. A, editor. *Justification and Variegated Nomism*. 2 vols. WUNT 2/140, 181. Grand Rapids: Baker Academic, 2001, 2004.
Cato, Marcus Porcius, *De Agri cultura*. LCL. Cambridge: Harvard University Press, 1934.
Charlesworth, James H., editor. *Old Testament Pseudepigrapha*. 2 vols. Garden City, NY: Doubleday, 1983, 1985.
Childs, Brevard S. *Isaiah*. Old Testament Library. Louisville: Westminster John Knox, 2001.
Chilton, Bruce. "Aramaic and Targumic Antecedents of Pauline 'Justification.'" In *The Aramaic Bible: The Targums in Their Historical Context*, edited by D. R. G. Beattie and Martin McNamara, 379-97. JSOT Supplements 166. Sheffield: JSOT Press.
Chisholm, Kitty. *Rome, the Augustan Age: A Source Book*. London: Oxford University Press, 1981.
Christensen, Duane L. *Deuteronomy*. Word Biblical Commentary 5. Dallas: Word, 1991.
Christoffersson, Olle. *The Earnest Expectation of the Creature: The Flood-Tradition as Matrix of Romans 8:18-27*. Coniectanea Biblica. Stockholm: Almqvist & Wiksell, 1990.
Cicero, Marcus Tullius. *De Invention, De Optimo Genere Oratorum, Topica*. LCL. Cambridge: Harvard University Press, 1949.
———. *De Oratore*. LCL. Cambridge: Harvard University Press, 1976.
———. *Philippics*. LCL. Cambridge: Harvard University Press, 1969
———. *Pro Murena, Pro Sulla, Pro Flacco*. LCL. Cambridge: Harvard University Press, 1937.
———. *De Re Publica*. LCL. Cambridge: Harvard University Press, 1943.

Clark, Andrew D. "The Good and the Just in Romans 5:7." *TynBul* 41 (1990) 128–42.
Clausen, Wendell. "An Interpretation of the *Aeneid*." *HSCP* 68 (1964) 139–47.
———. "Theocritus and Virgil." In *Latin Literature*, edited by E. J. Kenney, 301–19. The Cambridge History of Classical Literature. Cambridge: Cambridge University Press, 1982.
———. *Virgil's Aeneid and the Tradition of Hellenistic Poetry*. Sather Classical Lectures. Berkeley: University of California Press, 1987.
Cohen, Albert K. *Delinquent Boys: The Culture of the Gang*. Glencoe, IL: Free Press, 1955.
———. "Sociological Research in Delinquent Subcultures." *American Journal of Orthopsychology* 27 (1957) 781–88.
Cohen, Anthony P. *Self Consciousness: An Alternative Anthropology of Identity*. New York: Routledge, 1994.
Cohen, Shaye J. D. "'Those Who Say They Are Jews and Are Not': How Do You Know a Jew in Antiquity When You See One?'" In *Diasporas in Antiquity*, edited by Shaye J. D. Cohen, 1–45. Brown Judaic Studies 288. Atlanta: Scholars, 1993.
Coleman, R. "The Gods in the *Aeneid*." *Greece and Rome* 29 (1982) 143–68.
Coleman, Thomas M. "Binding Obligations in Romans 13:7: A Semantic Field and Social Context." *TynBul* 48 (1997) 307–27.
Collins, Adela Y. *Cosmology and Eschatology in Jewish and Christian Apocalypticism*. Brill's Scholars' List. Leiden: Brill, 2000.
Collins, John J. "Towards the Morphology of a Genre." *Semeia* 14 (1979) 1–20.
Columella, *De Re Rustica, De Arboribus*. LCL. Cambridge: Harvard University Press, 1941.
Commager, Steele. *Virgil: A Collection of Critical Essays*. Englewood Cliffs, NJ: Prentice-Hall, 1966.
Conington, John. *The Works of Virgil*, 3 vols. Hildesheim: Olms, 1963.
Conte, Gian Biagio. *Virgilio, il genere e i suoi confini*. Milan: Garzanti, 1984.
———. *Latin Literature: A History*. Baltimore: Johns Hopkins University Press, 1994.
Conte, Gian Biagio, and Charles Segal. *The Rhetoric of Imitation: Genre and Poetic Memory in Virgil and Other Latin Poets*. Edited by Charles Segal. Ithaca, NY: Cornell University Press, 1986.
Conway, Robert S. *Harvard Lectures on the Vergilian Age*. Cambridge: Harvard University Press, 1928.
———. *Poetry and Government: A Study of the Power of Vergil*. London: Manchester University Press, 1928.
Cordier, A. *Études sur le Vocabulaire Épique dans l'Énéide*. Collection d'Études Latines. Paris: Les belles lettres, 1939.
———. *L'Allitération Latine. Le Procédé dans l'Énéide de Virgile*. Paris: Librairie philosophique J. Vrin, 1939.
Cranfield, C. E. B. *A Critical and Exegetical Commentary on the Epistle to the Romans*. 2 vols. International Critical Commentary. Edinburgh: T. & T. Clark, 1979.
———. "The Works of the Law in the Epistle to the Romans." *JSNT* 43 (1991) 89–101.

Cranford, Michael. "Election and Ethnicity: Paul's View of Israel in Romans 9:1–13." *JSNT* 50 (1993) 27–41.
Crawford, Michael H. *Coinage and Money Under the Roman Republic*. Library of Numismatics. Berkeley: University of California Press, 1985.
Crook, J. A. *Law and Life of Rome*. Aspects of Greek and Roman Life. London: Thames & Hudson, 1967.
Danker, Frederick W. *Benefactor: Epigraphic Study of a Graeco-Roman and New Testament Semantic Field*. St. Louis: Clayton, 1982.
Daube, David. "Participle and Imperative in 1 Peter." In *The First Epistle of St. Peter*, 467–88. London: Macmillan, 1947.
Davies, Glenn N. *Faith and Obedience in Romans: A Study in Romans 1–4*. JSNTSup 39. Sheffield: JSOT Press, 1990.
Davies, W. D. *Jewish and Pauline Studies*. Philadelphia: Fortress, 1984.
Deissmann, Gustav A. *Light from the Ancient East*. Translated by L. R. M. Strachan. Grand Rapids: Baker, 1978.
Dewey, Joanna. "Textuality in an Oral Culture: A Survey of the Pauline Traditions." *Semeia* 65 (1994) 37–65.
Di Cesare, Mario A. *The Altar and the City: A Reading of Vergil's Aeneid*. New York: Columbia University Press, 1974.
Dihle, Albrecht. *Greek and Latin Literature of the Roman Empire from Augustus to Justinian*. New York: Routledge, 1994.
Dio, Cassius Cocceianus. *Dio's Roman History*. LCL. Cambridge: Harvard University Press, 1969.
———. *The Augustan Settlement: Roman History 53–55.9*. Edited and translated by John Rich. Classical Texts. Warminster: Aris & Phillips, 1990.
Dion, Paul E. "The Aramaic 'Family Letter' and Related Epistolary Forms in Other Oriental Languages and in Hellenistic Greek." *Semeia* 22 (1981) 69–71.
Dionysius. *The Roman Antiquities of Dionysius of Halicarnassus*. LCL. Cambridge: Harvard University Press, 1961.
Dodd, C. H. *The Epistle of Paul to the Romans*. Moffatt New Testament Commentary. New York: R. Long & R. R. Smith, 1932.
———. *According to the Scriptures*. London: Nisbet, 1952.
Donfried, Karl P., editor. *The Romans Debate*. Peabody, MA: Hendrickson, 1991.
Doty, William, G. *Letters in Primitive Christianity*. Guides to Biblical Scholarship: New Testament Series. Philadelphia: Fortress, 1973.
Drew, D. L. *The Allegory of the Aeneid*. Oxford: Blackwell, 1927.
Duckworth, George E. "The *Aeneid* as a Trilogy." *TAPA* 88 (1957) 1–10.
———. "The Significance of Nisus and Euryalus for *Aeneid* 9–12." *AJP* 88 (1967) 129–55.
———. *Structural Patterns and Proportions in Vergil's Aeneid*. Ann Arbor: University of Michigan Press, 1962.
———. *Vergil and Classical Hexameter Poetry: A Study in Metrical Variety*. Ann Arbor: University of Michigan Press, 1969.
Dunn, James D. G. "'How New Was Paul's Gospel?': The Problem of Continuity and Discontinuity in Paul." In *Gospel in Paul: Studies on Corinthians, Galatians and Romans for Richard N. Longenecker*, edited by L. Ann Jervis and Peter Richardson, 367–88. JSNTSup 108. Sheffield: Sheffield Academic, 1994.

———. "The Origin and Character of the Christian Community in Rome." In *Romans 1-8*, xliv–xlvi. Word Biblical Commentary 38A. Dallas: Word, 1988.

———. *Romans 1-8*. Word Biblical Commentary 38A. Dallas: Word, 1988.

———. *Romans 9-16*. Word Biblical Commentary 38B. Dallas: Word Books, 1988.

———. "Romans 13:1-7: A Charter for Political Quietism?" *Ex Auditu* 2 (1986) 55–68.

Durry, Marcel. *Les Cohortes Prétoriennes*. Bibliothèque des Écoles Françaises d'Athènes et de Rome. Paris: E. de Boccard, 1938.

du Toit, A. B. "Persuasion in Romans 1:1–17." *Biblische Zeitschrift* 33 (1989) 192–209.

Dyson, Julia T. "*CAESI IUVENCI* and *PIETAS IMPIA* in Virgil." *CJ* 91 (1996) 277–86.

———. *King of the Wood: The Sacrificial Victor in Virgil's Aeneid*. Norman: University of Oklahoma Press, 2001.

Eastman, Susan. "Whose Apocalypse? The Identity of the Sons of God in Romans 8:19." *JBL* 121 (2002) 263–77.

Eden, Kathy. *Poetic and Legal Fiction in the Aristotelian Tradition*. Princeton: Princeton University Press, 1986.

Eden, P. T. *A Commentary on Virgil: Aeneid VIII*. Mnemosyne Supplements 35. Leiden: Brill, 1975.

Edwards, M. J., Martin Goodman, S. R. F. Price, and Christopher Rowland. *Apologetics in the Roman Empire: Pagans, Jews, and Christians*. Edited by M. J. Edwards. Oxford: Oxford University Press, 1999.

Ehrenberg, Victor. *Documents Illustrating the Reigns of Augustus and Tiberius*. Oxford: Clarendon, 1955.

Eidinow, J. S. C. "Dido, Aeneas, and Iulus: Heirship and Obligation in *Aeneid* 4." *CQ* 53 (2003) 260–67.

Eisenbaum, Pamela. "Paul as the New Abraham." In *Paul and Politics: Ekklesia, Israel, Imperium, Interpretation*, edited by Richard A. Horsley, 130–45. Harrisburg, PA: Trinity, 2000.

Ellinger, K. et al. *Biblia Hebraica Stuttgartensia*. 5th ed. Stuttgart: Deutsche Bibelgesellschaft, 1997.

Elliott, Neil. "Paul and the Politics of Empire." In *Paul and Politics: Ekklesia, Israel, Imperium, Interpretation*, edited by Richard A. Horsley, 17–39. Harrisburg, PA: Trinity, 2000.

———. *The Rhetoric of Romans: Argumentative Constraint and Strategy and Paul's Dialogue with Judaism*. JSNTSup 45. Sheffield: JSOT Press, 1990.

———. "Romans 13:1-7 in the Context of Imperial Propaganda." In *Paul and Empire: Religion and Power in Roman Imperial Society*, edited by Richard A. Horsley, 184–205. Harrisburg, PA: Trinity, 1997.

Ellis, E. Earle. *Paul's Use of the Old Testament*. 1981. Reprinted, Eugene, OR: Wipf & Stock, 2003.

Else, Gerald F. *Aristotle's Poetics: The Argument*. Cambridge: Harvard University Press, 1957.

Engberg-Pedersen, Troels. *Paul and the Stoics*. Louisville: Westminster John Knox, 2000.

———. "Paul, Virtues, and Vices." In *Paul in the Greco-Roman World*, edited by J. Paul Sampley, 608–33. Harrisburg, PA: Trinity, 2003.

Epp, Eldon J. "Jewish-Gentile Continuity in Paul: Torah and/or Faith (Romans 9:1–5)." *Harvard Theological Review* 9 (1986) 80–90.
Esler, Philip. "Ancient Oleiculture and Ethnic Differentiation: The Meaning of the Olive-Tree Image in Romans 11." *JSNT* 26 (2003) 103–24.

———. *Conflict and Identity in Romans: The Social Setting of Paul's Letter*. Minneapolis: Fortress, 2003.

———. "Social Identity, the Virtues, and the Good Life: A New Approach to Romans 12:1—15:3." *Biblical Theology Bulletin* 33 (2003) 51–63.

Evans, Craig. "Paul and the Hermeneutics of 'True Prophecy': A Study of Romans 9–11." *Biblica* 65 (1984) 560–70.

———. "Paul and the Prophets: Prophetic Criticism in the Epistle to the Romans (with special reference to Romans 9–11)." In *Romans and the People of God: Essays in Honor of Gordon D. Fee on the Occasion of His 65th Birthday*, edited by Sven Soderlund and N. T. Wright, 115–28. Grand Rapids: Eerdmans, 1999.

Exler, Francis Xavier J. *The Form of the Ancient Greek Letter: A Study in Greek Epistolography*. Washington, DC: Catholic University of America, 1923.

Fanthem, Elaine. "Fighting Words: Turnus at Bay in the Latin Council." *AJP* 120 (1999) 259–80.

Farrell, Joseph. *Vergil's Georgics and the Traditions of Ancient Epic: The Art of Allusion in Literary History*. New York: Oxford University Press, 1991.

Fears, J. R. "The Cult of Virtues and Roman Ideology." In *ANRW* II.17.2 (1981) 828–948.

———. "The Theology of Victory at Rome." In *ANRW* II.17.2 (1981) 737–827.

Feeney, D. C. "History and Revelation in Vergil's Underworld." In *Virgil*, edited by Philip R. Hardie, 4:221–43. Routledge Critical Assessments of Classical Authors. New York: Routledge, 1999.

———. *Literature and Religion at Rome: Cultures, Contexts, and Beliefs*. Roman Literature and Its Contexts. Cambridge: Cambridge University Press, 1998.

———. "The Taciturnity of Aeneas." In *Oxford Readings in Vergil's Aeneid*, edited by S. J. Harrison, 167–90. Oxford: Oxford University Press, 1990.

Fishwick, Duncan. *The Imperial Cult in the Latin West*. Études Préliminaires Aux Religions Orientales dans l'Empire Romain. Leiden: Brill, 1987.

Fitzmyer, Joseph A. "Aramaic Epistolography." *Semeia* 22 (1981) 25–57.

———. *Romans*. AB 33. New York: Doubleday, 1993.

Fowler, W. Warde. *The Religious Experience of the Roman People*. London: MacMillan, 1911.

Fraenkel, Eduard. "Some Aspects of the Structure of *Aeneid* 7." *JRS* 35 (1945) 1–14.

Friedrich, J., W. Pöhlmann, and P. Stuhlmacher. "Zur historichen Situation und Intention von Röm 13:1–7." *Zeitschrift für Theologie und Kirche* 73 (1976) 131–66.

Gagnon, Robert A. J. "The Meaning of *ymon to agathon* in Romans 14:16." *JBL* 117 (1998) 675–89.

Gaius. *The Institutes of Gaius*. Translated by William M. Gordon. London: Duckworth, 1988.

Gale, M. R. "The Shield of Turnus (*Aeneid* 7.783–92)." *Greece and Rome* 44 (1997) 176–221.

Galinsky, G. Karl. *Aeneas, Sicily, and Rome*. Princeton Monographs in Art and Archaeology. Princeton: Princeton University Press, 1969.
———. "*Aeneid* 5 and the *Aeneid*." *AJP* 89 (April 1968) 157–85.
———. "The Anger of Aeneas." *AJP* 109 (1988) 321–48.
———. *Augustan Culture: An Interpretive Introduction*. Princeton: Princeton University Press, 1996.
———. "Empirical and Theoretical Approaches to Literary Genre." In *The Interpretation of Roman Poetry*, edited by G. Karl Galinsky, 104–23. Studien zur klassischen Philologie. New York: Lang, 1992.
———. "The Hercules-Cacus Episode in *Aeneid* 8." *AJP* 87 (1966) 18–51.
———, editor. *The Interpretation of Roman Poetry*. Studien zur klassischen Philologie. New York: Lang, 1992.
Garlington, D. B. "The Obedience of Faith in the Letter to the Romans." *Westminster Theological Journal* 55 (1993) 281–97.
Garnsey, Peter, and Richard P. Saller. *The Roman Empire: Economy, Society, and Culture*. London: Duckworth, 1987.
Gaunt, David M. "The Creation-Theme in Epic Poetry." *Comparative Literature* 29 (1977) 213–20.
Gelzer, Matthias. "Nobility and the Principate." In *The Roman Nobility*, 141–61. Oxford: Blackwell, 1969.
George, E. *Aeneid 8 and the Aitia of Callimachus*. Mnemosyne Supplements 27. Leiden: Brill, 1974.
Georgi, Dieter. "God Turned Upside Down—Romans, Missionary Theology and Roman Political Theology." In *Paul and Empire: Religion and Power in Roman Imperial Society*, edited by Richard A. Horsley, 148–57. Harrisburg, PA: Trinity, 1997.
———. *Remembering the Poor: The History of Paul's Collection for Jerusalem*. Translated by Ingrid Racz. Nashville: Abingdon, 1992.
———. *Theocracy in Paul's Praxis and Theology*. Translated by David E. Green. Minneapolis: Fortress, 1991.
———. "Who Is the True Prophet?" In *Paul and Empire: Religion and Power in Roman Imperial Society*, edited by Richard A. Horsley, 36–46. Harrisburg, PA: Trinity, 1997.
Georgi, Heinrich. *Die politische Tendenz der Äneide Vergils*. Stuttgart: Grüninger, 1880.
Girard, René. *Violence and the Sacred*. Baltimore: Johns Hopkins University Press, 1977.
Golden, Leon. *Aristotle on Tragic and Comic Mimesis*. American Classical Studies. Atlanta: Scholars, 1992.
Goodenough, E. R. "The Political Philosophy of Hellenistic Kingship." *Yale Classical Studies* 1 (1928) 55–102.
Goodman, Martin. *Mission and Conversion: Proselytizing in the Religious History of the Roman Empire*. Oxford: Oxford University Press, 1994.
———, editor. *Jews in a Graeco-Roman World*. Oxford: Oxford University Press, 1998.

———, and Jane Sherwood. *The Roman World, 44 B.C.—A.D. 180*. Routledge History of the Ancient World. London: Routledge, 1997.
Gordon, Richard. "The Veil of Power." In *Paul and Empire: Religion and Power in Roman Imperial Society*, edited by Richard A. Horsley, 126–37. Harrisburg, PA: Trinity, 1997.
Gowan, Donald E. *Eschatology in the Old Testament*. Philadelphia: Fortress, 1986.
Gowing, Alain M. *The Triumviral Narratives of Appian and Cassius Dio*. Michigan Monographs in Classical Antiquity. Ann Arbor: University of Michigan Press, 1992.
Gransden, K. W. *Virgil's Iliad: An Essay on Epic Narrative*. Cambridge: Cambridge University Press, 1984.
Grant, Michael, editor. *Readings in the Classical Historians*. New York: Macmillan, 1992.
Grant, Robert M. "Early Christianity and Greek Comic Poetry." *CP* 60 (1965) 157–63.
Greene, William C. *Moira Fate, Good, and Evil in Greek Thought*. Cambridge: Harvard University Press, 1944.
Grenier, Albert. *The Roman Spirit in Religion, Thought, and Art*. The History of Civilization. New York: Knopf, 1926.
Grieb, A. K. *The Story of Romans: A Narrative Defense of God's Righteousness*. Louisville: Westminster John Knox, 2002.
Grimal, Pierre. *Essai sur l'Art Poétique d'Horace*. Paris: S.E.D.E.S., 1968.
———. *Roman Cities*. Edited and translated by G. Michael Woloch. Madison: University of Wisconsin Press, 1983.
Grimm, R. E. "Aeneas and Andromache in *Aeneid* 3." *AJP* 88 (1967) 151–62.
Grobel, Kendrick. "Chiastic Retribution-Formula in Romans 2." In *Zeit und Geschichte*, edited by Erich Dinkler, 255–61. Tübingen: Mohr/Siebeck, 1964.
Grube, G. M. A. *On Poetry and Style*. Library of Liberal Arts. New York: Liberal Arts Press, 1958.
Gruen, Erich S. *Imperialism in the Roman Republic*. European Problem Studies. New York: Holt, Rinehart, and Winston, 1970.
———. *Culture and National Identity in Republican Rome*. Ithaca, NY: Cornell University Press, 1992.
Guerra, Anthony J. *Romans and the Apologetic Tradition*. Cambridge: Cambridge University Press, 1995.
Hafemann, Scott J. "Eschatology and Ethics: The Future of Israel and the Nations in Romans." *TynBul* 51 (2000) 161–92.
Hahn, E. Adelaide. "Vergil's Linguistic Treatment of Divine Beings." *TAPA* 88 (1957) 56–67.
Halliwell, Stephen. "Introduction." In *Poetics*, edited and translated by Stephen Halliwell, 1–27. LCL. Cambridge: Harvard University Press, 1995.
Hannak, Emanuel. *Appianus und seine Quellen*. Vienna: Beck, 1869.
Hannestad, Niels. *Roman Art and Imperial Policy*. Aarhus: Aarhus University Press, 1986.
Hardie, Philip R. *The Epic Successors of Virgil: A Study in the Dynamics of a Tradition*. Roman Literature and Its Contexts. Cambridge: Cambridge University Press, 1993.

———. "Lucretius and the *Aeneid*." In *Virgil's Aeneid: Cosmos and Imperium*, 157–240. Oxford: Clarendon, 1986.
———, editor. *Virgil*. 4 vols. Routledge Critical Assessments of Classical Authors. New York: Routledge, 1999.
———. *Virgil's Aeneid: Cosmos and Imperium*. Oxford: Clarendon, 1986.
———. "Virgil's Epic Techniques: Heinze Ninety Years On." *CP* 90 (1995) 267–76.
Hardison, O. B. *Aristotle's Poetics: A Translation and Commentary for Students of Literature*. Englewood Cliffs, NJ: Prentice-Hall, 1968.
Harris, William V. *Ancient Literacy*. Cambridge: Harvard University Press, 1989.
Harrison, E. L. "Cleverness in Virgilian Imitation." *CP* (1970) 241–43.
Harrison, J. R. "Paul, Eschatology and the Augustan Age of Grace." *TynBul* 50 (1999) 79–91.
———. "Paul and the Imperial Gospel at Thessaloniki." *JSNT* 25 (2002) 71–96.
Harrison, S. J. "Divine Action in *Aeneid* Book 2." In *Oxford Readings in Vergil's Aeneid*, edited by S. J. Harrison, 46–59. Oxford: Oxford University Press, 1990.
———, editor. *Oxford Readings in Vergil's Aeneid*. Oxford: Oxford University Press, 1990.
———. "The Survival and Supremacy of Rome: The Unity of the Shield of Aeneas." *JRS* 87 (1997) 70–76.
Hawthorne, Gerald F., Ralph P. Martin, and Daniel G. Reid, editors. *Dictionary of Paul and His Letters*. Downers Grove, IL: InterVarsity, 1993.
Hays, Richard B. *Echoes of Scripture in the Letters of Paul*. New Haven: Yale University Press, 1989.
———. *The Faith of Jesus Christ: An Investigation of the Narrative Substructure of Galatians 3:1—4:11*. SBLDS 56. Chico, CA: Scholars, 1983.
———. "'Have We Found Abraham to be Our Forefather According to the Flesh': A Reconsideration of Rom 4:1." *NovT* 27 (1985) 76–98.
Heil, John P. "Christ, the Termination of the Law (Romans 9:30–10:8)." *CBQ* 63 (2001) 484–98.
———. "From Remnant to Seed of Hope for Israel: Romans 9:27–29." *CBQ* 64 (2002) 703–20.
Heinze, Richard. *Virgil's Epic Technique*. Translated by Hazel Harvey, David Harvey, and Fred Robertson. Berkeley: University of California Press, 1993.
Henry, Elisabeth. *The Vigour of Prophecy: A Study of Virgil's Aeneid*. Carbondale: Southern Illinois University Press, 1989.
Highet, Gilbert. *The Speeches in Vergil's Aeneid*. Princeton: Princeton University Press, 1972.
Hill, Andrew E. *Malachi*. AB 25D. New York: Doubleday, 1998.
Hinds, Stephen. *Allusion and Intertext: Dynamics of Appropriation in Roman Poetry*. Roman Literature and Its Contexts. Cambridge: Cambridge University Press, 1998.
Hollingshead, James R. *The Household of Caesar and the Body of Christ: A Political Interpretation of the Letters from Paul*. Lanham, MD: University Press of America, 1998.
Hollis, S. A. "Hellenistic Colouring in Vergil's *Aeneid*." *HSCP* 94 (1992) 269–85.
Homer. *The Odyssey*. LCL. Cambridge: Harvard University Press, 1919.
———. *The Iliad*. LCL. Cambridge: Harvard University Press, 1925.

Hooker, M. D. *From Adam to Christ: Essays on Paul.* Cambridge: Cambridge University Press, 1990.

———. "Paul and Covenantal Nomism." In *Paul and Paulinism: Essays in Honour of C. K. Barrett*, edited by S. G. Wilson, 47–56. London: SPCK, 1982.

Horsfall, N. M. "Dido in the Light of History." In *Oxford Readings in Vergil's Aeneid*, edited by S. J. Harrison, 127–44. Oxford: Oxford University Press, 1990.

———. "Numanus Remulus: Ethnography and Propaganda in *Aeneid* 9.598ff." In *Oxford Readings in Vergil's Aeneid*, edited by S. J. Harrison, 305–15. Oxford: Oxford University Press, 1990.

———. "Style, Language, and Meter." In *A Companion to the Study of Virgil*, edited by Nicholas Horsfall, 217–48. Mnemosyne Supplement 151. Leiden: Brill, 1995.

———. "Virgil and the Conquest of Chaos." In *Oxford Readings in Vergil's Aeneid*, edited by S. J. Harrison, 466–77. Oxford: Oxford University Press, 1990.

Horsley, Richard A. "Introduction." In *Paul and Empire: Religion and Power in Roman Imperial Society*, edited by Richard A. Horsley, 1–15. Harrisburg, PA: Trinity, 1997.

———, editor. *Paul and Empire: Religion and Power in Roman Imperial Society*. Harrisburg, PA: Trinity, 1997.

———, editor. *Paul and Politics: Ekklesia, Israel, Imperium, Interpretation*. Harrisburg, PA: Trinity, 2000.

———, editor. *Paul and the Roman Imperial Order*. Harrisburg, PA: Trinity, 2004.

———. "Paul's Counter-Imperial Gospel." In *Paul and Empire: Religion and Power in Roman Imperial Society*, edited by Richard A. Horsley, 140–47. Harrisburg, PA: Trinity, 1997.

Horst, Pieter W. van der. "'Only Then Will All Israel be Saved': A Short Note on the Meaning of *Kai Outos* in Romans 11:26." *JBL* 119 (2000) 521–25.

Huey, F. B. "An Exposition of Malachi." *Southwestern Journal of Theology Studies* 30 (1987) 12–21.

Hügi, Markus. *Vergils Aeneis und die hellenistische Dichtung.* Noctes Romanae 4. Bern: Haupt, 1952.

Humphrey, Edith M. "Why Bring the Word Down? The Rhetoric of Demonstration and Disclosure in Romans 9:30—10:21." In *Romans and the People of God: Essays in Honor of Gordon D. Fee on the Occasion of His 65th Birthday*, edited by Sven Soderlund and N. T. Wright, 129–48. Grand Rapids: Eerdmans, 1999.

Hurtado, L. "The Doxology at the End of Romans." In *New Testament Textual Criticism: Its Significance for Exegesis: Essays in Honour of Bruce M. Metzger*, edited by Eldon J. Epp, 185–99. New York: Clarendon, 1981.

Husain, Martha. *Ontology and the Art of Tragedy: An Approach to Aristotle's Poetics.* SUNY Series in Ancient Greek Philosophy. Albany: State University of New York Press, 2002.

Hutton, James. "Introduction." In *Aristotle's Poetics*, translated by James Hutton, 1–23. New York: Norton, 1982.

Jebb, Richard. *The Growth and Influence of Classical Greek Poetry.* Port Washington, NY: Kennikat, 1969.

Jenkyns, Richard. *Virgil's Experience: Nature and History, Times, Names, and Places.* New York: Clarendon, 1998.

Jewett, Robert. "The Corruption and Redemption of Creation." In *Paul and the Roman Imperial Order*, edited by Richard A. Horsley, 25-46. Harrisburg, PA: Trinity, 2004.

———. "Honor and Shame in the Argument of Romans." In *Putting Body and Soul Together: Essays in Honor of Robin Scroggs*, edited by Virginia Wiles, 258-73. Valley Forge, PA: Trinity, 1997.

———. "Response: Exegetical Support from Romans and Other Letters." In *Paul and Politics: Ekklesia, Israel, Imperium, Interpretation*, edited by Richard A. Horsley, 58-71. Harrisburg, PA: Trinity, 2000.

———. *Romans*. Hermeneia. Minneapolis: Fortress, 2007.

———. "Romans as an Ambassadorial Letter." *Int* 36 (1982) 5-30.

Jocelyn, H. D. "Ancient Scholarship and Virgil's Use of Republican Latin Poetry." *CQ* 14 (1964) 280-95.

Johnson, Luke Timothy. *Reading Romans: A Literary and Theological Commentary*. Reading the New Testament. Macon, GA: Smyth & Helwys, 2001.

Johnson, W. R. *Darkness Visible: A Study of Vergil's Aeneid*. Berkeley: University of California Press, 1976.

Jones, A. H. M. *Augustus*. New York: Norton, 1971.

———. "Elections Under Augustus." *JRS* 41 (1955) 112-19.

Jones, Henry S. "Senatus Populusque Romanus." In *The Augustan Empire 44 B.C.— A.D. 70*, edited by Stanley A. Cook, 159-81. Cambridge Ancient History 10. Cambridge: Cambridge University Press, 1934.

Jones, John. *On Aristotle and Greek Tragedy*. New York: Oxford University Press, 1962.

Josephus, Flavius. *Jewish Antiquities*. LCL. Cambridge: Harvard University Press, 1979.

Joubert, Stephan. *Paul as Benefactor: Reciprocity, Strategy and Theological Reflection in Paul's Collection*. WUNT 2/124. Tübingen: Mohr/Siebeck, 2000.

Judge, E. A. *The Social Pattern of the Christian Groups in the First Century: Some Prolegomena to the Study of New Testament Ideas of Social Obligation*. London: Tyndale, 1960.

———. *Rank and Status in the World of the Caesars and St. Paul*. University of Canterbury Publications. Christchurch, NZ: University of Canterbury, 1982.

Kallas, James. "Romans 13:1-7: An Interpolation." *NTS* 11 (1964-65) 365-74.

Kanjuparambil, Philip. "Imperatival Participles in Rom 12:9-21." *JBL* 102 (1983) 285-88.

Karris, Robert J. "Rom 14:1—15:13 and the Occasion of Romans." *CBQ* 35 (1973) 155-78.

Käsemann, Ernst. *An die Römer*. Handbuch zum Neuen Testament. Tübingen: Mohr/Siebeck, 1973.

———. *Commentary on Romans*. Translated and edited by Geoffrey W. Bromiley. Grand Rapids: Eerdmans, 1980.

Keck, Leander. "'Jesus' in Romans." *JBL* 108 (1989) 443-60.

———. "Pathos in Romans?" In *Paul and Pathos*, edited by Thomas H. Olbricht and Jerry L. Sumney, 71-96. SBL Symposium Series 16. Atlanta: Society of Biblical Literature, 2001.

———. "Paul as Thinker." *Int* 47 (1993) 27-38.

———. "What Makes Romans Tick." In *Pauline Theology III: Romans*, edited by David M. Hay and E. Elizabeth Johnson, 3–29. Minneapolis: Fortress, 1995.
Keesmaat, Sylvia C. "Exodus and the Intertextual Transformation of Tradition in Romans 8:14–30." *JSNT* 54 (1994) 29–56.
———. *Paul and His Story: (Re)Interpreting the Exodus Tradition*. JSNTSup 181. Sheffield: Sheffield Academic, 1999.
Kirk, G. S. *Homer and the Oral Tradition*. Cambridge: Cambridge University Press, 1976.
Klein, George L. "An Introduction to Malachi." *Criswell Theological Review* 2 (1987) 221–33.
Knauer, G. N. "Vergil's *Aeneid* and Homer." *Greek, Roman, and Byzantine Studies* 5 (1964) 61–84.
Knox, John. "Romans 15:14–33 and Paul's Conception of His Apostolic Mission." *JBL* 83 (1964) 1–11.
Kühn, Werner. *Götterszenen bei Vergil*. Bibliothek der klassischen Altertumswissenschaften 2/41. Heidelberg: Winter, 1971.
Kümmel, Werner G. *Introduction to the New Testament*. Translated by Howard Clark Kee. Nashville: Abingdon, 1975.
Kuss, Otto. *Der Römerbrief*. Regensburg: Pustet, 1957.
Kyrtatas, Dimitris J. *The Social Structure of the Early Christian Communities*. New York: Verso, 1987.
Lacey, W. K. "Pater Potestas." In *The Family in Ancient Rome: New Perspectives*, edited by Beryl Rawson, 121–40. Ithaca, NY: Cornell University Press, 1986.
Lamberton, Robert, editor. *Homer's Ancient Readers: The Hermeneutics of Greek Epic's Earliest Exegetes*. Princeton: Princeton University Press, 1992.
Lambrecht, Jan. "The Confirmation of the Promises: A Critical Note on Romans 15:8." *Ephemerides Theologicae Lovanienses* 78 (2002) 156–60.
———. "Syntactical and Logical Remarks on Romans 15:8–9a." *NovT* 42 (2000) 257–61.
———. "Why is Boasting Excluded: A Note on Rom 3:27 and 4:2." *Ephemerides Theologicae Lovanienses* 61 (1885) 365–69.
———. *The Wretched "I" and Its Liberation: Paul in Romans 7 and 8*. Grand Rapids: Eerdmans, 1992.
Lange, Johann Peter. *The Epistle of Paul to the Romans*. Edited by Philip Schaff. Translated by J. F. Hurst. New York: Scribner, 1986.
Lee, M. Owen. *Fathers and Sons in Virgil's Aeneid: Tum Genitor Natum*. Albany: State University of New York Press, 1980.
Levick, Barbara. *The Government of the Roman Empire*. Totowa, NJ: Barnes & Noble, 1985.
Lewis, Martha W. *The Official Priests of Rome under the Julio-Claudians: A Study of the Nobility from 44 B.C. to 68 A.D.* Papers and Monographs of the American Academy in Rome. Rome: American Academy in Rome, 1955.
Liddell, Henry George, and Robert Scott, eds. *Greek-English Lexicon*. Revised by Henry Stuart Jones and Roderick McKenzie. Oxford: Clarendon, 1968.
Livy. *The History of Rome*. Translated by W. Roberts. New York: Dutton, 1921.
Lloyd, Robert B. "The Character of Anchises in the *Aeneid*." *TAPA* 88 (1957) 44–55.

Lloyd-Jones, David Martyn. *Romans: An Exposition of Chapter 8:5–17: The Sons of God*. Grand Rapids: Zondervan, 1975.

Lloyd-Jones, H. "Curses and Divine Anger in Early Greek Epic." *CQ* 52 (July 2002) 1–14.

Lock, Walter. "The Use of *Peripeteia* in Aristotle's Poetics." *Classical Review* 9 (1895) 251–53.

Longenecker, Bruce W. *Eschatology and the Covenant: A Comparison of 4 Ezra and Romans 1–11*. JSNTSup 57. Sheffield: JSOT Press, 1991.

———. *Narrative Dynamics in Paul: a Critical Assessment*. Louisville: Westminster John Knox, 2002.

Longenecker, R. N. "The Focus of Romans: 5.1—8.39 in the Argument of the Letter." In *Romans and the People of God: Essays in Honor of Gordon D. Fee on the Occasion of His 65th Birthday*, edited by Sven Soderlund and N. T. Wright, 49-69. Grand Rapids: Eerdmans, 1999.

Lorimer, H. L. *Homer and the Monuments*. London: Macmillan, 1950.

Lucas, F. L. *Tragedy in Relation to Aristotle's Poetics*. London: Woolf, 1927.

Luck, Georg, and G. Karl Galinsky, editor. *Perspectives of Roman Poetry: A Classics Symposium*. Symposia in the Arts and the Humanities. Austin: University of Texas Press, 1974.

Lyne, R. O. A. M. *Further Voices in Vergil's Aeneid*. Oxford: Oxford University Press, 1987.

———. "Vergil and the Politics of War." *CQ* 33 (1983) 188–203.

———. *Words and the Poet: Characteristic Techniques of Style in Vergil's Aeneid*. Oxford: Oxford University Press, 1989.

MacDonald, William L. *The Architecture of the Roman Empire*. Yale Publications in the History of Art. New Haven: Yale University Press, 1982.

Mack, Sara. *Patterns of Time in Vergil*. Hamden, CT: Archon, 1978.

MacKay, L. A. "Hero and Theme in the *Aeneid*." *TAPA* 94 (1963) 157–66.

Macky, Peter W. *The Bible in Dialogue with Modern Man*. Waco, TX: Word, 1970.

———. "Crushing Satan Underfoot (Romans 16:20) Paul's Last Battle Story as True Myth." *Proceedings, Eastern Great Lakes and Midwest Biblical Societies* 13 (1993) 121–33.

———. *St. Paul's Cosmic War Myth: A Military Version of the Gospel*. New York: Lang, 1998.

MacMullen, Ramsay. *Romanization in the Time of Augustus*. New Haven: Yale University Press, 2000.

Malherbe, Abraham J. *Social Aspects of Early Christianity*. Philadelphia: Fortress, 1983.

———. *Ancient Epistolary Theorists*. Sources for Biblical Study. Atlanta: Scholars, 1988.

Maltby, Robert. *A Lexicon of Ancient Latin Etymologies*. Leeds: Cairns, 1991.

Marshall, I. Howard. "Salvation, Grace and Works in the Later Writings in the Pauline Corpus." *NTS* 42 (1996) 339–58.

———. "Romans 16:25–27—An Apt Conclusion." In *Romans and the People of God: Essays in Honor of Gordon D. Fee on the Occasion of His 65th Birthday*, edited by Sven Soderlund and N. T. Wright, 170-84. Grand Rapids: Eerdmans, 1999.

Martin, Ralph P. "Reconciliation: Romans 5:1–11." In *Romans and the People of God: Essays in Honor of Gordon D. Fee on the Occasion of His 65th Birthday*, edited by Sven Soderlund and N. T. Wright, 36–48. Grand Rapids: Eerdmans, 1999.

Martindale, Charles, editor. *The Cambridge Companion to Virgil*. Cambridge Companions to Literature. Cambridge: Cambridge University Press, 1997.

Martyn, J. Louis. *Theological Issues in the Letters of Paul*. Nashville: Abingdon, 1997.

Matthaei, Louise E. "The Fates, the Gods, and the Freedom of Man's Will in the *Aeneid*." *CQ* 11 (January 1917) 11–26.

McComiskey, Thomas E., editor. *The Minor Prophets*, 3 vols. Grand Rapids: Baker, 1992.

McDonald, James. "Romans 13:7: A Test Case for New Testament Interpretation." *NTS* 35 (1989) 540–49.

McDonald, Patricia M. "Romans 5:1–11 as a Rhetorical Bridge." *JSNT* 40 (1990) 81–96.

McGushin, P. "Virgil and the Spirit of Endurance." In *Virgil*, edited by Philip R. Hardie, 3:218–43. Routledge Critical Assessments of Classical Authors. New York: Routledge, 1999.

McNamara, Martin, translator. *Targum Neofiti 1: Deuteronomy*. The Aramaic Bible 5A. Collegeville, MN: Liturgical, 1997.

Meeks, Wayne A. *The First Urban Christians: The Social World of the Apostle Paul*. 2d ed. New Haven: Yale University Press, 2003.

———. "Social Functions of Apocalyptic Language in Pauline Christianity." In *Apocalypticism in the Mediterranean World and the Near East: Proceedings of the International Colloquium on Apocalypticism, Uppsala, August 12–17, 1979*, edited by David Hellholm, 687–705. Tübingen: Mohr/Siebeck, 1983.

Melanchthon, Philipp. *Melanchthon on Christian Doctrine: Loci Communes, 1555*. Edited and translated by Clyde L. Manschreck. New York: Oxford University Press, 1965.

Mellor, Ronald. *Tacitus*. New York: Routledge, 1993.

Mendell, C. W. "The Influence of the Epyllion on the *Aeneid*." *Yale Classical Studies* 12 (1951) 216–19.

Mette-Dittmann, Angelika. *Die Ehegesetze des Augustus: eine Untersuchung im Rahmen der Gesellschaftspolitik des Princeps*. Stuttgart: F. Steiner, 1991.

Metzger, Bruce M. "The Punctuation of Romans 9:5." In *Christ and Spirit in the New Testament*, edited by Barnabas Lindars, 95–112. Cambridge: Cambridge University Press, 1973.

———. *A Textual Commentary on the Greek New Testament*. New York: United Bible Societies, 1971.

Michel, Otto. *Der Brief an die Römer*. Göttingen: Vandenhoeck & Ruprecht, 1966.

Miles, Gary B. *Livy: Reconstructing Early Rome*. Ithaca, NY: Cornell University Press, 1995.

Millar, Fergus. *The Emperor in the Roman World, 31 BC–AD 337*. Ithaca, NY: Cornell University Press, 1977.

———. "State and Subject: The Impact of Monarchy." In *Caesar Augustus: Seven Aspects*, edited by Fergus Millar and Erich Segal, 37–60. Oxford: Clarendon, 1984.

———. *A Study of Cassius Dio*. Oxford: Clarendon, 1964.

Monti, Richard C. *The Dido Episode and the Aeneid: Roman Social and Political Values in the Epic*. Mnemosyne Supplements 66. Leiden: Brill, 1981.

Moo, Douglas J. *Romans 1–8*. Wycliffe Exegetical Commentary. Chicago: Moody, 1991.

———. *The Epistle to the Romans*. New International Commentary on the New Testament. Grand Rapids: Eerdmans, 1996.

Moore, Clifford H. "Prophecy in Ancient Epic." *HSCP* 32 (1921) 99–175.

———. "Latin Exercises from a Greek Schoolroom." *CP* 19 (1924) 475–85.

Morgan, Llewelyn. *Patterns of Redemption in Virgil's Georgics*. Cambridge Classical Studies. Cambridge: Cambridge University Press, 1999.

Morris, Leon. *The Epistle to the Romans*. Grand Rapids: Eerdmans, 1988.

Morrison, Robert B., and Hugh P. O'Neill. *Vocabulary of Vergil's Aeneid*. Chicago: Loyola University Press, 1926.

Moskalew, Walter. *Formular Language and Poetic Design in the Aeneid*. Mnemosyne Supplements 77. Leiden: Brill, 1982.

Moule, H. C. G. *Epistle of St. Paul to the Romans*. New York: Armstrong, 1985.

Mounce, Robert H. *Romans*. New American Commentary. Nashville: Broadman & Holman, 1995.

Moxnes, Halvor. "Honor, Shame, and the Outside World in Romans." In *The Social World of Formative Christianity and Judaism*, edited by Jacob Neusner, 207–18. Philadelphia: Fortress, 1988.

Mullens, H. G. "Tragic Optimism in the *Aeneid*." *Greece & Rome* 11 (1942) 137–38.

Munck, Johannes. *Christ & Israel: An Interpretation of Romans 9–11*. Translated by Ingeborg Nixon. Philadelphia: Fortress, 1967.

———. *Paul and the Salvation of Mankind*. Translated by Frank Clarke. Richmond: John Knox, 1959.

Murray, John. *The Epistle to the Romans*. New London Commentary on the New Testament. London: Marshall, Morgan & Scott, 1967.

Murray, O. "The Attitude of the Augustan Poets Toward *Rex* and Related Words." *CJ* 60 (1964–65) 241–46.

Nagy, Gregory. *Pindar's Homer: The Lyric Possession of an Epic Past*. Baltimore: Johns Hopkins University Press, 1990.

Nanos, Mark D. "The Jewish Context of the Gentile Audience Addressed in Paul's Letter to the Romans." *CBQ* 61 (1999) 283–304.

———. *The Mystery of Romans: The Jewish Context of Paul's Letter*. Minneapolis: Fortress, 1996.

Nelis, Damien. *Vergil's Aeneid and the Argonautica of Apollonius Rhodius*. Classical and Medieval Texts, Papers, and Monographs. Leeds: Francis Cairns, 2001.

Neusner, Jacob, editor. *The Social World of Formative Christianity and Judaism*. Philadelphia: Fortress, 1988.

Newman, John K. *The Concept of Vates in Augustan Poetry*. Collection Latomus. Brussels: Latomus, revue d'études latines, 1967.

Newton, Francis. "Recurrent Imagery in *Aeneid* 4." *TAPA* 88 (1957) 31–43.

Nickelsburg, George W. E. *Resurrection, Immortality, and Eternal Life in Intertestamental Judaism*. Harvard Theological Studies. Cambridge: Harvard University Press, 1972.

Nickle, Keith F. *The Collection: A Study in Paul's Strategy*. Studies in Biblical Theology. Naperville, IL: Allenson, 1966.
Nicolaus. *Nicolaus of Damascus' Life of Augustus: A Historical Commentary Embodying a Translation*. Smith College Classical Studies. Translated by Clayton Morris Hall. Menasha, WI: Banta, 1923.
Nicoll, W. S. M. "The Sacrifice of Palinurus." *CQ* 38 (1988) 459–72.
Nisbet, R. G. M. "Aeneas Imperator: Roman Generalship in an Epic Context." *Proceedings of the Virgilian Society* 17 (1978–80) 50–61.
Norden, Eduard. *Aeneis Buch VI*. Leipzig: Teubner, 1926.
———. *Ennius und Vergilius*. Stuttgart: Teubner, 1966.
———. *Kleine Schriften zum klassischen Altertum*. Berlin: de Gruyter, 1966.
Nortwick, Thomas van. "Aeneas, Turnus, and Achilles." *TAPA* 110 (1980) 303–14.
Norwood, Francis. "The Tripartite Eschatology of *Aeneid* 6." *CP* 49 (1954) 15–26.
Nygren, Anders. *Commentary on Romans*. Translated by Carl C. Rasmussen. Philadelphia: Muhlenberg, 1949.
O'Brien, Peter. *Introductory Thanksgivings in the Letters of Paul*. NovTSup 49. Leiden: Brill, 1977.
O'Hara, James J. *Death and the Optimistic Prophecy in Vergil's Aeneid*. Princeton: Princeton University Press, 1990.
———. *True Names: Vergil and the Alexandrian Tradition of Etymological Wordplay*. Ann Arbor: University of Michigan Press, 1996.
O'Hara, James. "Virgil's Style." In *The Cambridge Companion to Virgil*, edited by Charles Martindale, 241–58. Cambridge: Cambridge University Press, 1997.
Olson, Stanley N. "Epistolary Uses of Expressions of Self-Confidence." *JBL* 103 (1984) 585–97.
Origen. *Commentary on the Epistle to the Romans: Book 6–10*. Translated by Thomas P. Scheck. Fathers of the Church. Washington, DC: Catholic University of America Press, 2002.
Oster, Richard E. "'Congregations of the Gentiles' (Rom 16:4) A Culture-Based Ecclesiology in the Letters of Paul." *Restoration Quarterly* 40 (1998) 39–52.
O'Sullivan, Neil. "Aristotle on Dramatic Probability." *CJ* 91 (1995) 49–63.
Otis, Brooks. *Virgil: A Study in Civilized Poetry*. Oklahoma Series in Classical Culture. Norman: University of Oklahoma Press, 1995.
Ovid. *Fasti*. LCL. Cambridge: Harvard University Press, 1989.
Patterson, Annabel M. *Roman Images*. Edited by Annabel M. Patterson. Baltimore: Johns Hopkins University Press, 1984.
Paschalis, Michael. *Virgil's Aeneid: Semantic Relations and Proper Names*. Oxford: Oxford University Press, 1997.
Peristiany, John G. *Honour and Shame: The Values of Mediterranean Society*. Chicago: University of Chicago Press, 1966.
Philo. *On the Creation, Allegorical Interpretation*. LCL. Cambridge: Harvard University Press, 1929.
Plato. *Republic*. LCL. Cambridge: Harvard University Press, 1937.
———. *Laws*. LCL. Cambridge: Harvard University Press, 1943.
Plutarch. *Plutarch's Lives*. LCL. Cambridge: Harvard University Press, 1959.
Porter, Stanley. "The Argument of Romans 5: Can a Rhetorical Question Make a Difference?" *JBL* 110 (1991) 655–77.

Pöschl, Viktor. *The Art of Vergil: Image and Symbol in the Aeneid.* Translated by Gerda Seligson. Ann Arbor: University of Michigan Press, 1962.

———. "The Poetic Achievement of Vergil." *CJ* 56 (1961) 290–99.

Powell, Anton. *The Greek World.* London: Routledge, 1995.

Preminger, Alex, editor. *The New Princeton Encyclopedia of Poetry and Poetics.* New York: MJF Books, 1996.

Price, S. R. F. "Response." In *Paul and the Roman Imperial Order*, edited by Richard A. Horsley, 175–83. Harrisburg, PA: Trinity, 2004.

———. *Rituals and Power: The Roman Imperial Cult in Asia Minor.* Cambridge: Cambridge University Press, 1984.

Propertius, Sextus. *Elegies.* LCL. Cambridge: Harvard University Press, 1990.

Putnam, Michael C. J. "*Aeneid* 7 and the *Aeneid.*" *AJP* 91 (1970) 408–30.

———. *The Poetry of the Aeneid.* Cambridge: Harvard University Press, 1965.

Quinn, Kenneth. *Latin Explorations: Critical Studies in Roman Literature.* New York: Humanities Press, 1963.

———. *Virgil's Aeneid: A Critical Description.* Ann Arbor: University of Michigan Press, 1968.

Quint, D. "Repetition and Ideology in the *Aeneid.*" In *Virgil*, edited by Philip R. Hardie, 4:117–52. Routledge Critical Assessments of Classical Authors. New York: Routledge, 1999.

Raaflaub, Kurt A., Mark Toher, and G. W. Bowersock. *Between Republic and Empire: Interpretations of Augustus and His Principate.* Edited by Kurt A. Raaflaub. Berkeley: University of California Press, 1990.

Rahlfs, Alfred. *Septuaginta.* Stuttgart: Deutsche Bibelgesellschaft, 1979.

Räisänen, Heikki. "Paul, God, and Israel: Romans 9–11 in Recent Research." In *The Social World of Formative Christianity and Judaism*, edited by Jacob Neusner, 178–206. Philadelphia: Fortress, 1988.

Rankin, Oliver S. "Theories of Reward and Retribution in the Old Testament and in Later Judaism." In *Israel's Wisdom Literature: Its Bearing on Theology and the History of Religion*, 77–97. Edinburgh: T. & T. Clark, 1964.

Rawson, Beryl. "Caesar's Heritage: Hellenistic Kings and their Roman Equals." *JRS* 63 (1975) 161–74.

Reasoner, Mark. *The Strong and the Weak: Romans 14:1—15:13 in Context.* New York: Cambridge University Press, 1999.

Reid, J. S. "Human Sacrifices at Rome." *JRS* 2 (1912) 34–52.

Rhyne, C. Thomas. *Faith Establishes the Law.* SBLDS 55. Chico, CA: Scholars, 1981.

Riesner, Rainer. *Paul's Early Period: Chronology, Mission Strategy, Theology.* Grand Rapids: Eerdmans, 1998.

Robinson, James M. "The Historicality of Biblical Language." In *The Old Testament and Christian Faith: A Theological Discussion*, edited by Bernhard W. Anderson, 140–48. New York: Harper & Row, 1963.

Robinson, O. F. *Ancient Rome: City Planning and Administration.* London: Routledge, 1992.

Roetzel, Calvin, J. "No 'Race of Israel' in Paul." In *Putting Body & Soul Together: Essays in Honor of Robin Scroggs*, edited by Virginia Wiles, 230–44. Valley Forge, PA: Trinity, 1997.

---. "Paul as Organic Intellectual: The Shaper of Apocalyptic Myths." In *Common Life in the Early Church: Essays Honoring Graydon F. Snyder*, edited by Julian V. Hills, 221-43. Harrisburg, PA: Trinity, 1998.
Rudd, N. "Dido's Culpa." In *Oxford Readings in Vergil's Aeneid*, edited by S. J. Harrison, 145-66. Oxford: Oxford University Press, 1990.
Rushforth, G. *Latin Historical Inscriptions Illustrating the History of the Early Empire*. London: Oxford University Press, 1930.
Russell, D. S. *The Method and Message of Jewish Apocalyptic, 200 B.C.-A.D. 100*. Old Testament Library. Philadelphia: Westminster, 1964.
Salmon, E. T. "The Evolution of Augustus' Principate." *Historia* 5 (1956) 456-78.
---. *Roman Colonization Under the Republic. Aspects of Greek and Roman Life*. Ithaca, NY: Cornell University Press, 1970.
Sanday, W., and Arthur C. Headlam. *A Critical and Exegetical Commentary on the Epistle to the Romans*. International Critical Commentary. Edinburgh: T. & T. Clark, 1911.
Sanders, E. P. *Paul and Palestinian Judaism: A Comparison of Patterns of Religion*. Philadelphia: Fortress, 1977.
Sanders, J. A. "Habakkuk in Qumran, Paul, and the Old Testament." *Journal of Religion* 39 (1959) 232-244.
Sargeaunt, John. *The Trees, Shrubs, and Plants of Virgil*. Freeport, NY: Books for Libraries Press, 1969.
Saunders, Catharine. "Sources of the Names of Trojans and Latins in Vergil's *Aeneid*." *TAPA* 71 (1940) 537-55.
Schlunk, Robin R. *The Homeric Scholia and the Aeneid*. Ann Arbor: University of Michigan Press, 1974.
Schmithals, Walter. *Der Römerbrief ein Kommentar*. Gütersloh: Mohn, 1988.
Schnider, Franz, and Werner Stenger. *Studien zum neutestamentlichen Briefformular*. Leiden: Brill, 1987.
Schubert, Paul. *Form and Function of the Pauline Thanksgivings*. Berlin: A. Töpelmann, 1939.
Scullard, H. H. *Roman Politics*. Oxford: Clarendon, 1973.
Seaford, Richard. "Homeric and Tragic Sacrifice." *TAPA* 119 (1989) 87-95.
Sear, Frank. *Roman Architecture*. Ithaca, NY: Cornell University Press, 1983.
Seifrid, Mark A. "Paul's Approach to the Old Testament in Romans 10:6-8." *Trinity Journal* 6 (1985) 3-37.
Seneca, Lucius Annaeus. *Minor Dialogues Together with the Dialogue on Clemency*. Translated by Aubrey Stewart. Bohn's Classical Library. London: Bell, 1912.
---. *Moral Essays*. LCL. Cambridge: Harvard University Press, 1935.
Shogren, Gary S. "'Is the Kingdom of God About Eating and Drinking or Isn't It?' (Romans 14:17)." *NovT* 42 (2000) 238-56.
Shuchburgh, Evelyn. *Augustus: The Life and Times of the Founder of the Roman Empire (B.C. 63-A.D. 14)*. London: Unwin, 1903.
Shum, Shiu-Lun. *Paul's Use of Isaiah in Romans: A Comparative Study of Paul's Letter to the Romans and the Sibylline Oracles and the Qumran Sectarian Texts*. WUNT 2/156. Tübingen: Mohr/Siebeck, 2002.
Smallwood, E. Mary. *The Jews under Roman Rule: From Pompey to Diocletian*. Studies in Judaism in Late Antiquity 20. Leiden: Brill, 1976.

Smiles, Vincent M. "The Concept of 'Zeal' in Second-Temple Judaism and Paul's Critique of It in Romans 10:2." *CBQ* 64 (2002) 282-99.
Smith, E. Baldwin. *Architectural Symbolism of Imperial Rome and the Middle Ages.* Princeton: Princeton University Press, 1956.
Smith, Rebekah M. "Deception and Sacrifice in *Aeneid* 2.1249." *AJP* 120 (1999) 50323.
Smothers, Edgar. "Give Place to the Wrath (Rom. 12:19) An Essay in Verbal Exegesis." *CBQ* 6 (1944) 205-15.
Solmsen, Friedrich. "The World of the Dead in *Aeneid* Book 6." In *Oxford Readings in Vergil's Aeneid*, edited by S. J. Harrison, 208-23. Oxford: Oxford University Press, 1990.
Sparrow, J. H. A. *Half-Lines and Repetitions in Virgil.* New York: Garland Publishing, 1977.
Stadler, Theodor W. *Vergils Aeneis: eine poetische Betrachtung.* Einsiedeln: Benziger, 1942.
Stambaugh, John E. *The Ancient Roman City.* Ancient Society and History. Baltimore: Johns Hopkins University Press, 1988.
Starks, John H. "*Fides Anneia*: The Transference of Punic Stereotypes in the *Aeneid*." *CJ* 94 (1999) 255-83.
Stegner, William R. "Romans 9:6-29—a Midrash." *JSNT* 22 (1984) 37-52.
Stein, Robert H. "The Argument of Romans 13:1-7." *NovT* 31 (1989) 325-34.
Stendahl, Krister. *Paul Among Jews and Gentiles, and Other Essays.* Philadelphia: Fortress, 1976.
―――. *Final Account: Paul's Letter to the Romans.* Minneapolis: Fortress, 1995.
Stockton, David. "The Founding of the Empire." In *The Roman World*, edited by John Boardman, 121-49. Oxford History of the Classical World. Oxford: Oxford University Press, 1991.
Stone, Michael E., editor. *Jewish Writings of the Second Temple Period: Apocrypha, Pseudepigrapha, Qumran, Sectarian Writings, Philo, Josephus.* Compendia Rerum Iudaicarum ad Novum Testamentum. Philadelphia: Fortress, 1984.
Stowers, Stanley K. *The Diatribe and Paul's Letter to the Romans.* SBLDS 57. Chico, CA: Scholars, 1981.
―――. *Letter Writing in Greco-Roman Antiquity.* Library of Early Christianity. Philadelphia: Westminster, 1986.
―――. *A Rereading of Romans: Justice, Jews, and Gentiles.* New Haven: Yale University Press, 1994.
Stuart, Douglas. "Malachi." In *The Minor Prophets*, edited by Thomas E. McComiskey, 3:1245-396. Grand Rapids: Baker, 1992.
Stuhlmacher, Peter. *Paul's Letter to the Romans.* Translated by Scott J. Hafemann. Louisville: Westminster John Knox, 1994.
Suetonius. *Suetonius.* LCL. Cambridge: Harvard University Press, 1964.
Sutherland, C. H. V. *Roman History and Coinage, 44 B.C.-A.D. 69.* Oxford: Oxford University Press, 1987.
Syme, Ronald. *The Roman Revolution.* Oxford: Clarendon, 1939.
Tacitus, Cornelius. *Dialogus, Agricola, Germania.* LCL. Cambridge: Harvard University Press, 1914.
―――. *The Annals and Histories.* LCL. Cambridge: Harvard University Press, 1925.

———. *The Annals and the Histories*. Translated by A. Church and W. Brodribb. Chicago: Encyclopædia Britannica, 1955.
Talbert, Charles H. *Romans*. Smyth & Helwys Bible Commentary. Macon, GA: Smyth & Helwys, 2002.
———. "Tradition and Redaction in Romans 12:9–21." *NTS* 16 (1969) 83–93.
Tarrant, R. J. "Aeneas and the Gates of Sleep." *CP* 77 (1982) 51–55.
Taylor, Lily R. *Divinity of the Roman Emperor*. Roman History. New York: Arno, 1975.
Tellbe, Mikael. *Paul Between Synagogue and State: Christians, Jews, and Civic Authorities in 1 Thessalonians, Romans, and Philippians*. Coniectanea Biblica. Stockholm: Almqvist & Wiksell, 2001.
Theophrastus. *Enquiry into Plants and Minor Works*. LCL. Cambridge: Harvard University Press, 1916.
———. *De causis plantarum*. LCL. Cambridge: Harvard University Press, 1976.
Thomas, Richard. "*Furor* and *Furiae* in Virgil." *AJP* 112 (1991) 261–62.
———. "Callimachus Back in Rome." In *Callimachus*, edited by Annette Harder, 1:197–225. Hellenistica Groningana. Groningen: Forsten, 1993.
Thomas, Rosalind. "The Place of the Poet in Archaic Society." In *The Greek World*, edited by Anton Powell, 102–34. London: Routledge, 1995.
Thornton, Agathe. *The Living Universe Gods and Men in Virgil's Aeneid*. Mnemosyne Supplements 46. Leiden: Brill, 1976.
Townend, Gavin. "Literature and Society." In *The Cambridge Ancient History: The Augustan Empire, 43 B.C.–A.D. 69*, edited by Alan K. Bowman, Edward Champlin, and Andrew Lintott, 905–29. Cambridge: Cambridge University Press, 1996.
Towner, Philip H. "Romans 13:1–7 and Paul's Missiological Perspective: A Call to Political Quietism or Transformation?" In *Romans and the People of God: Essays in Honor of Gordon D. Fee on the Occasion of His 65th Birthday*, edited by Sven Soderlund and N. T. Wright, 149–69. Grand Rapids: Eerdmans, 1999.
VanGemeren, Willem A., editor. *New International Dictionary of Old Testament Theology and Exegesis*. 5 vols. Grand Rapids: Zondervan, 1997.
Varro, Marcus Terentius. *Res Rusticae*. LCL. Cambridge: Harvard University Press, 1934.
Virgil. *Eclogues, Georgics, and Aeneid*. LCL. Cambridge: Harvard University Press, 1999.
Voelz, James W. "Multiple Signs, Levels of Meaning and Self as Text: Elements of Intertextuality." *Semeia* 69–70 (1995) 149–64.
Vos, Geerhardus. *The Pauline Eschatology*. Grand Rapids: Eerdmans, 1952.
Wagner, J. Ross. "The Christ, Servant of Jew and Gentile: A Fresh Approach to Romans 15:8–9." *JBL* 116 (1997) 473–85.
———. *Heralds of the Good News: Isaiah and Paul "in Concert" in the Letter to the Romans*. NovTSup 101. Leiden: Brill, 2002.
Wallace, Richard. *The Three Worlds of Paul of Tarsus*. New York: Routledge, 1998.
Wallace-Hadrill, Andrew. "The Golden Age and Sin in Augustan Ideology." *Past and Present* 95 (1982) 19–36.
———. "Image and Authority in the Coinage of Augustus." *JRS* 76 (1986) 66–87.
———, editor. *Patronage in Ancient Society*. London: Routledge, 1990.

———. *Suetonius: The Scholar and His Caesars*. New Haven: Yale University Press, 1984.
Wan, Sze-kar. "Collection for the Saints as Anticolonial Act." In *Paul and the Roman Imperial Order*, edited by Richard A. Horsley, 203–10. Harrisburg, PA: Trinity, 2004.
Ward, Richard. "Pauline Voice and Presence as Strategic Communication." *Semeia* 65 (1994) 95–107.
Wardman, Alan. *Religion and Statecraft Among the Romans*. Baltimore: Johns Hopkins University Press, 1982.
Ward-Perkins, J. B. *Roman Imperial Architecture*. New Haven: Yale University Press, 1981.
Watts, Rikki E. "'For I Am Not Ashamed of the Gospel': Romans 1:16–17 and Habakkuk 2:4." In *Romans and the People of God: Essays in Honor of Gordon D. Fee on the Occasion of His 65th Birthday*, edited by Sven Soderlund and N. T. Wright, 3–25. Grand Rapids: Eerdmans, 1999.
Wedderburn, A. J. M. *The Reasons for Romans*. Minneapolis: Fortress, 1991.
———. "The Soteriology of the Mysteries and Pauline Baptismal Theology." *NovT* 29 (1987) 53–72.
Weimma, Jeffrey A. D. "Preaching the Gospel in Rome: A Study of the Epistolary Framework of Romans." In *Gospel in Paul: Studies on Corinthians, Galatians and Romans for Richard N. Longenecker*, edited by L. Ann Jervis and Peter Richardson, 337–66. JSNTSup 108. Sheffield: Sheffield Academic Press, 1994.
Wenham, David. "Paul's Use of the Jesus Tradition." In *The Jesus Tradition Outside the Gospels*, edited by David Wenham, 7–38. Gospel Perspectives 5. Sheffield: JSOT Press, 1985.
West, D. A. "The Bough and the Gate." In *Oxford Readings in Vergil's Aeneid*, edited by S. J. Harrison, 224–38. Oxford: Oxford University Press, 1990.
———. "*Cernere Erat*: The Shield of Aeneas." In *Oxford Readings in Vergil's Aeneid*, edited by S. J. Harrison, 295–304. Oxford: Oxford University Press, 1990.
———. "Multiple-Correspondence Similes in the *Aeneid*." *JRS* 59 (1969) 40–49.
Wevers, John W. *Notes on the Greek Text of Leviticus*. Septuagint and Cognate Studies Series 44. Atlanta: Scholars Press, 1997.
White, John L. "Ancient Greek Letters." In *Greco-Roman Literature and the New Testament: Selected Forms and Genres*, edited by David Aune, 85–105. Sources for Biblical Study 21. Atlanta: Scholars, 1988.
———. *The Apostle of God: Paul and the Promise of Abraham*. Peabody, MA: Hendrickson, 1999.
———. *The Form and Function of the Body of the Greek Letter: A Study of the Letter-Body in the Non-Literary Papyri and in Paul the Apostle*. SBLDS 2. Missoula, MT: Scholars Press for the Society of Biblical Literature, 1972.
White, Peter. *Promised Verse: Poets in the Society of Augustan Rome*. Cambridge: Harvard University Press, 1993.
Wigodsky, Michael. *Vergil and Early Latin Poetry*. Wiesbaden: Steiner, 1972.
Wiles, Gordon P. *Paul's Intercessory Prayers: The Significance of the Intercessory Prayer Passages in the Letters of St. Paul*. Society for New Testament Studies Monograph Series 24. Cambridge: Cambridge University Press, 1974.
Wilkenson, L. P. "The Language of Virgil and Horace." *CJ* 9 (1959) 181–92.

Willett, Tom W. *Eschatology in the Theodicies of 2 Baruch and 4 Ezra*. Journal for the Study of the Pseudepigrapha Supplements 4. Sheffield: JSOT Press, 1989.
Williams, Deryck. "The *Aeneid*." In *Latin Literature*, edited by E. J. Kenney, 333-69. Cambridge History of Classical Literature. Cambridge: Cambridge University Press, 1982.
Williams, George. "Did Maecenas 'Fall from Favor'? Augustan Literary Patronage." In *Between Republic and Empire: Interpretations of Augustus and His Principate*, edited by Kurt A. Raaflaub, 258-75. Berkeley: University of California Press, 1990.
Williams, Gordon W. *Figures of Thought in Roman Poetry*. New Haven: Yale University Press, 1980.
———. *Technique and Ideas in the Aeneid*. New Haven: Yale University Press, 1983.
———. *Tradition and Originality in Roman Poetry*. Oxford: Clarendon, 1968.
Williams, R. D. *The Aeneid*. Unwin Critical Library. Boston: Allen & Unwin, 1987.
———. "The Pictures on Dido's Temple." In *Oxford Readings in Vergil's Aeneid*, edited by S. J. Harrison, 37-45. Oxford: Oxford University Press, 1990.
———. "The Purpose of the *Aeneid*." In *Oxford Readings in Vergil's Aeneid*, edited by S. J. Harrison, 21-36. Oxford: Oxford University Press, 1990.
———. "The Sixth Book of the *Aeneid*." In *Oxford Readings in Vergil's Aeneid*, edited by S. J. Harrison, 191-207. Oxford: Oxford University Press, 1990.
Williams, Theodore C. *The Aeneid of Virgil*. Boston: Houghton Mifflin, 1908.
Wilson, C. H. "Jupiter and the Fates in the *Aeneid*." *CQ* 29 (1979) 361-71.
Wiltshire, Susan Ford. *Public and Private in Vergil's Aeneid*. Amherst: University of Massachusetts Press, 1989.
Winkler, Martin M. "'Tuque Optime Vates': Musaeus in Book Six of the *Aeneid*." *AJP* 108 (1987) 655-60.
Winter, Bruce W. "The Public Honouring of Christian Benefactors : Romans 13:3-4 and 1 Peter 2:14-15." *JSNT* 34 (1988) 87-103.
Witherington, Ben, and Darlene Hyatt. *Paul's Letter to the Romans: A Socio-Rhetorical Commentary*. Grand Rapids: Eerdmans, 2004.
Wlosok, A. "The Dido Tragedy in Virgil." In *Virgil*, edited by Philip R. Hardie, 4:158-81. Routledge Critical Assessments of Classical Authors. New York: Routledge, 1999.
Woodman, Tony, and David A. West. *Creative Imitation and Latin Literature*. Cambridge: Cambridge University Press, 1979.
———. *Poetry and Politics in the Age of Augustus*. Cambridge: Cambridge University Press, 1984.
Wright, N. T. *The Climax of the Covenant: Christ and the Law in Pauline Theology*. Minneapolis: Fortress, 1992.
———. "New Exodus, New Inheritance: The Narrative Structure of Romans 3-8." In *Romans and the People of God: Essays in Honor of Gordon D. Fee on the Occasion of His 65th Birthday*, edited by Sven Soderlund and N. T. Wright, 26-35. Grand Rapids: Eerdmans, 1999.
———. "Paul's Gospel and Caesar's Empire." In *Paul and Politics: Ekklesia, Israel, Imperium, Interpretation*, edited by Richard A. Horsley, 160-83. Harrisburg, PA: Trinity, 2000.

———. "Romans and the Theology of Paul." In *Society of Biblical Literature 1992 Seminar Papers*, edited by Eugene H. Lovering, 184–213. Atlanta: Scholars, 1992.

Yinger, Kent L. *Paul, Judaism, and Judgment according to Deeds*. Society for New Testament Studies Monograph Series 105. Cambridge: Cambridge University Press, 1999.

———. "Romans 12:14–21 and Nonretaliation in Second Temple Judaism: Addressing Persecution within the Community." *CBQ* 60 (1998) 74–96.

Young, Edward J. *The Book of Isaiah*. New International Commentary on the Old Testament. Grand Rapids: Eerdmans, 1972.

Zanker, Paul. *The Power of Images in the Age of Augustus*. Jerome Lectures. Ann Arbor: University of Michigan Press, 1988.

Zetzel, James E. G. "*Romane Memento*: Justice and Judgment in *Aeneid* 6." *TAPA* 119 (1989) 263–84.

www.ingramcontent.com/pod-product-compliance
Lightning Source LLC
Chambersburg PA
CBHW051637230426
43669CB00013B/2343